About the volume:

Capital cities accounted for more than a third of all European city growth during the sixteenth and seventeenth centuries. Almost all shared rapid population growth, high levels of mortality and heavy immigration. They became powerful transmitters of international cultural values and fashions, whether in dress, speech, architecture, material goods or leisure. They played a vital role in the transformation of early modern society, and their impact on regional, national and overseas hinterlands was immense, influencing demographic, economic and social structures and development.

This book comprises 11 chapters written by leading European and American urban historians, and combines a general consideration of the role of these great cities with a series of case studies. The main focus is central and western Europe, but the collection also examines the growth of state capitals in European empires outside Europe, including Latin America.

About the editors:

Peter Clark is director of the Centre for Urban History and Professor of Economic and Social History at the University of Leicester. Bernard Lepetit was joint-director of the Centre de Recherches Historiques at the Ecole des Hautes Etudes en Sciences Sociales, Paris. He died accidentally in the Spring of 1996.

D1391871

Historical Urban Studies

Series editors: Richard Rodger and Jean-Luc Pinol

Titles in this series include:

*Power, Profit and Urban Land: Landownership in Medieval
and Early Modern Northern European Towns*
edited by Finn-Einar Eliassen and Geir Atle Ersland

The Artisan and the European Town, 1500–1900
edited by Geoffrey Crossick

*Water and European Cities from the Middle Ages to the
Nineteenth Century*
edited by Jean-Luc Pinol and Dennis Menjeot

The Built Form of Colonial Cities
Manuel Texeira

Capital Cities and their Hinterlands in Early Modern Europe

For Herman Diederiks

Capital Cities and their Hinterlands in Early Modern Europe

Edited by

PETER CLARK and BERNARD LEPETIT

Published by
SCOLAR PRESS
Gower House
Croft Road
Aldershot
Hants GU11 3HR
England

Ashgate Publishing Company
Old Post Road
Brookfield
Vermont 05036-9704
USA

British Library Cataloging in Publication Data

Capital Cities and their Hinterlands in Early Modern Europe.
(Historical Urban Studies)
    1. Cities and towns — Europe — History. 2. Capitals (Cities) — Europe — History.
    3. Europe — History — 1492-.
    I. Clark, Peter, 1944-. II. Lepetit, Bernard, 1948-96.
    940.2'091732

    ISBN 1-85928-224-5

Library of Congress Cataloging-in-Publication Data

Capital cities and their hinterlands in early modern Europe/edited
    by Peter Clark and Bernard Lepetit.
        p.   cm.
    Revision of papers originally presented at a session on Metropolitan cities and their hinterlands, held Leuven, Belgium, summer 1990, during the International Economic History Congress; earlier versions of some of the papers were published in Metropolitan cities and their hinterlands in early modern Europe (1990).
    Includes bibliographical references and index.
    ISBN 1-85928-224-5
    1. Capitals (Cities) — Europe — History — Congresses. 2. Europe — History — 1492 — Congresses. 3. Metropolitan areas — Europe — Congresses. I. Clark, Peter, 1944- .
II. Lepetit, Bernard. III. Metropolitan cities and their hinterlands in early modern Europe.
D210.C26   1996
940.2-dc20

    ISBN 1-85928-224-5

95–50649
CIP

Typeset in Sabon by Express Typesetters Ltd, Farnham, Surrey
and printed in Great Britain by Ipswich Book Co. Ltd, Ipswich, Suffolk

Contents

Historical Urban Studies
General Editors' Preface

Density and proximity of buildings and people are two of the defining characteristics of the urban dimension. It is these which identify a place as uniquely urban, though the threshold for such pressure points varies from place to place. What is considered an important cluster in one context - a few hundred inhabitants or buildings on the margins of Europe - may not be considered as urban elsewhere. A third defining characteristic is functionality - the commercial or strategic position of a town or city which conveys an advantage. Over time, these functional advantages may diminish, or the balace of advantage may change within a hierarchy of towns. To understand how the relative importance of towns shifts over time and space is to grasp a set of relationships which is fundamental to the study of urban history.

Towns and cities are products of history, yet have themselves helped to shape history. As the proportion of urban dwellers has increased, so the urban dimension has proved a legitimate unit of analysis through which to understand the spectrum of human experience and to explore the cumulative memory of past generations. Though obscured by layers of economic, social and political change, the study of the urban milieu provides insights into the functioning of human relationships and, if urban historians themselves are not directly concerned with current policy issues, few contemporary concerns can be understood without reference to the historical development of towns and cities.

This longer historical perspective is essential to an understanding of social processes. Crime, housing conditions and property values, health and education, discrimination and deviance, and the formulation of regulations and social policies to deal with them were, and remain, amongst the perennial preoccupations of towns and cities - no historical period has a monopoly of these concerns. They recur in successive generations, albeit in varying mixtures and strengths; the details may differ but the central forces of class, power and authority in the city remain. If this was the case for different periods, so it was for different geographical entities and cultures. Both scientific knowledge and technical information were available across Europe and showed little respect for frontiers. Yet despite common concerns and access to broadly similar knowledge, different solutions to urban problems were proposed and adopted by towns and cities in different parts of Europe. This comparative dimension informs urban historians as to which were systemic factors and which were of a purely local nature: general and particular forces can be distinguished.

These analytical frameworks, considered in a comparative context, inform the books in this series.

Jean-Luc Pinol
Richard Rodger
1996

Université de sciences humaines de Strasbourg
University of Leicester

List of Tables and Figures

Tables

Figures

Notes on Contributors

Vera Bácskai is Professor in the Department of Economic and Social History at Eotvos Lorand University, Budapest. She is President of the Association of Hungarian Social Historians and has undertaken extensive research on early modern and modern urban social history. Her publications include *Towns and Urban Society in Early 19th Century Hungary* (editor, Budapest, 1989), *Bürgertum und Bürgerliche Entwicklung in Mittel- und Osteuropa* (Budapest, 1986), and numerous works in Hungarian.

Maria Bogucka has been Professor and Head of the Department for Early Modern History attached to the Institute of History, Polish Academy of Sciences since 1970. Her principal publications have included studies of Gdańsk as a centre of production in the fourteenth to seventeenth centuries (1964), Gdańsk's overseas trade in the first half of the seventeenth century (1970), and the history of towns and townspeople in Poland before partition (with H. Samsonowicz) (1986). She has also written many articles in European journals.

Peter Clark is Professor of Economic and Social History and Director of the Centre for Urban History, University of Leicester. He has written or edited a number of books on urban history including *The Transformation of English Provincial Towns 1600-1800* (1984), and *Small Towns in Early Modern Europe* (1995). He is general editor of the forthcoming *Cambridge Urban History of Britain*.

José Miguel López García is Associate Professor in the Department of Early Modern History, Autonomous University of Madrid, and Co-Director, Centre for Documentation and History of Madrid. He is author of various works on the social and economic history of the sixteenth to nineteenth centuries, especially city-country relations during the transition to capitalism in Castile.

Raymond Gillespie teaches at Maynooth College, Ireland. He has done research on many aspects of sixteenth and seventeenth century Irish society. Among his publications are *Colonial Ulster: the Settlement of East Ulster 1600-41* (Cork, 1985), and with Ciaran Brady, *Natives and Newcomers* (editors, Dublin, 1986).

Paul M. Hohenberg is Professor of Economics at Rensselaer Polytechnic Institute, New York State. With Lynn Hollen Lees he has written *The Making of Urban Europe 1000-1950* (1985) and he has edited (with H. Diederiks and M. Wagenaar) *Economic Policy in Europe since the Middle Ages* (1992).

Jean Jacquart is Professor Emeritus at the University of Panthéon-Sorbonne (Paris I). He is a specialist on rural history and the history of Paris and the Ile-de-France. His works include *La crise rurale en Ile-de-France (1550-1670)* (Paris, 1974); *François I* (Paris, 1981, 1994); *Paris et l'Ile-de-France au temps des paysans* (Paris, 1990).

Lynn Hollen Lees is Professor of History and current Chair of the Department of History at the University of Pennsylvania. Her publications include *Exiles of Erin: Irish Migrants in Victorian London* and *The Making of Urban Europe, 1000-1950*, co-authored with Paul Hohenberg. She has recently finished a study of the English poor laws.

Bernard Lepetit was a researcher and teacher at the Ecole des Hautes Etudes en Sciences Sociales, Paris, where he directed the Centre de Recherches Historiques. His last research was on the history of economic space. His publications include (with J. Hoock) *La ville et l'innovation en Europe 14e-19e siècles* (Paris, 1987); *Les villes dans la France moderne 1740-1840* (Paris, 1988) published in translation as *The Pre-industrial Urban System: France 1740-1840* (Cambridge, 1994); and (with D. Pumain) *Temporalités urbaines* (Paris, 1993). He was one of the co-directors of *Annales ESC*.

Santos Madrazo Madrazo is Associate Professor, Department of Early Modern History, Autonomous University of Madrid, and Co-Director, Centre for Documentation and History of Madrid. He has written various studies of the Spanish transport system 1750-1850 and the social history of pre-industrial Madrid.

Brigitte Marin is a former student of the Ecole Normale Supérieure de St Cloud, a former member of the Ecole Française at Rome, and a *maître de conférences* in early modern history at the University of Provence. Her research has been concentrated on the urban history of Southern Italy. She has published several articles on Naples in the early modern period in *Mélanges de l'Ecole française de Rome. Italie et Méditerrannée* (since 1989). Her work on *Reformes et espace urbain à Naples à l'époque des Lumières (1784-1799)* is forthcoming.

Michael Reed was until recently Professor of Topography at Loughborough University. His research interests include English small towns, especially their social and cultural history, and he is also working on a study of the pictorial representation of English towns before 1830. Among his publications are *The Buckinghamshire Landscape* (1979) and *The Landscape of Britain* (1990). He has also recently edited a special issue of *Storia Urbana* devoted to the English town.

David R. Ringrose has been Professor of History at the University of

California, San Diego since 1974. Major publications include *Madrid and the Spanish Economy, 1561-1850* (1983), *Imperio y Peninsula. Ensayor sobre historia economica de España* (1987), *Madrid, Historia de una capital* (1994), and *Spain, Europe, and the Spanish Miracles, 1700-1900* (Cambridge, forthcoming 1996/97).

Helga Schultz holds the chair of Economic and Social History at the University Viadrina Frankfurt (Oder) in Germany. She has undertaken extensive research on the economic and social history of Germany in early modern times and her publications include *Berlin 1650-1800. Sozialgeschichte einer Residenz* (Berlin, 1992) and (with Brigitte Meier) *Die Wiederkehr des Stadtbürgers. Städtereformen im europäischen Vergleich* (Berlin, 1994).

Preface

Despite their scale and dynamic impact on European society in the early modern period, the dozen and a half capital cities in early modern Europe have received relatively little systematic or comparative attention from historians. Perhaps, paradoxically, they are too well known: they suffer from intellectual tourism. Almost every scholar writing about European society, politics and cultural life in this era makes certain assumptions, more or less explicit, about their role, but in practice he or she usually ends up circumnavigating the subject rather than addressing it in detail. This is hardly surprising. As we shall see in this book, difficulties of definition, together with problems of documentation - the enormous mountain of records, the lack of comparability - beset the historian. But the study of the European capital city, with all its variegated impacts on regional, national, continental and global societies, continues to rank high on the historical agenda.

This present volume originated in a session on Metropolitan Cities and their Hinterlands, which Peter Clark organized at the International Economic History Congress held at Leuven in Belgium during the balmy late summer of 1990. Early versions of some of the papers published here were initially printed in the conference proceedings (E. Aerts and P. Clark, eds, *Metropolitan Cities and their Hinterlands in Early Modern Europe*, Leuven, 1990). However, for the purposes of this volume, all the earlier papers have been substantially revised. Moreover, in order to make a coherent collection, a number of new papers have been added, including some based on verbal presentations at the session; for the same reason it has not been possible to include all the original papers given at the conference.

There has been no attempt by the editors to establish a party line on metropolitan developments and impacts: the authors put forward a diversity of views and ideas. Because of the precarious nature of demographic calculations for big cities in this period, we have also made no effort to standardize population estimates for our capital cities.

The volume has been structured in broad geographical sections. After the editorial introduction and a general discussion of the demographic aspect of metropolitan relations with their hinterlands (by Paul Hohenberg and Lynn Lees), the book examines first of all the capital cities in North West Europe (London, Dublin, Paris), then looks at Mediterranean cities (Madrid and Naples), with a further section considering central Europe (Berlin, Budapest and Warsaw). Finally, David Ringrose in a wide-ranging paper examines links between European capitals and their American empires. The survey is far from exhaustive but it is hoped that this book with all its limitations will encourage and facilitate more extensive and systematic national and above all comparative research.

This volume has taken an above average time in gestation and we are grateful to the contributors for their patience and cooperation. Research for Chapters Three and Six has been supported by the European Union through the Human Capital Mobility programme. Two of the chapters (by Drs Jacquart and Marin) have been translated by Godfrey Rogers and we are indebted to the Centre de Recherches Historiques of the Ecole des Hautes Etudes en Sciences Sociales for their financial support for this work; Dr Rogers also prepared the index. Mrs Kate Crispin at the Centre for Urban History at Leicester kindly retyped a number of sections of the typescript. We are also grateful to our respective families for tolerating our absences to discuss or resolve editorial minutiae. Ever optimistic we hope that they feel our work justifies their forbearance.

P.A.C.
B.L.

Postscript

Just as this book went to the publisher in the summer of 1995, Herman Diederiks, a leading figure in European urban history and a close friend of Bernard Lepetit and I, died in an accident. Bernard at once suggested we dedicate this volume to him. It is therefore a tragic irony that Bernard himself died in another pointless accident in March 1996. He was one of the most brilliant of French historians, and a kind and charming man, especially supportive to young people. His death is a loss to us all.

P.A.C.

CHAPTER ONE

Introduction

Peter Clark and Bernard Lepetit

Metropolitan cities were among the economic, social and cultural marvels of early modern Europe: to use the phrase of Paul Hohenberg and Lynn Lees they were 'urban supernovas'. Thus Paris in the 1760s was said to be 'one of the most beautiful, the richest, the most populated, the most flourishing, cities of Europe', renowned for 'the prodigious number of superb buildings, the wisdom of its government and prodigious commerce'. In England, Dr Johnson declared that a man who was tired of London was tired of life, 'for there is in London all that life can afford'. Madame de Staël exclaimed that Berlin was 'the true capital of new Germany, of enlightened Germany'. A chorus of writers and commentators lauded the European great cities, often rating them against each other.[1] Certainly the metropolitan cities were in an urban class of their own during the early modern period, the capital cities in particular enjoying striking demographic growth. Thus Paul Bairoch notes that the growth of nine capital cities accounted for a third of the increase in the total urban population in Europe in the sixteenth and seventeenth centuries.[2] London's advance was of course spectacular: from 200,000 inhabitants in 1600 (50,000 in 1500), the population had risen to nearly a million by 1800. Paris more than doubled its population over the same period (to 660,000). The growth rate of new state capitals was no less dramatic: Vienna's population rose from 20-25,000 in about 1500 to 247,000 in 1800; Madrid grew from 65,000 in 1600 to 168,000 two centuries later; for Berlin the comparable figures were 10,000 and 172,000. Even the smaller centres such as Stockholm, Copenhagen, Lisbon, Brussels, Dublin, Warsaw and later Budapest achieved demographic growth well above the national average.[3]

The great metropolitan port cities, often city-states, of the Renaissance period - such as Venice, Genoa, Antwerp - have been the subject of scrutiny by numerous historians, plotting their rise and general decline by the seventeenth century.[4] By contrast, the state capitals which increasingly inherited the metropolitan mantle have only recently started to receive the attention they deserve. Even so there has been little attempt to examine them from a comparative perspective, while the central question of their impact on European society has been largely neglected.

There are obvious difficulties in studying these great cities in early modern Europe. One is their overwhelming scale – in the case of London in about 1700 nearly twenty times that of the biggest provincial city; the same was also true of late eighteenth century Naples; even in France with its cluster of great provincial centres, Paris was over five times greater than the nearest French city (Lyon).[5] As we shall see, in many cases capital cities were not only large and extensive, but subsumed a polyphony of communities marked by the complexity of their economic, social and political structures. Again there are problems of documentation, massive in archival abundance in some areas, but in other respects, particularly quantifiable data, more limited and selective. Thirdly, there are problems of definition. In terms of the metropolitan effect, we find no regularity or homogeneity in the area of influence – there are many different hinterlands, some spatially extensive, others more lateral; some local or regional, others national or international. As for the capital city itself, there was no single genus, rather a lexicon of metropolitan types.

In this short introduction we can only hope to sketch some of the problems and possibilities for the study of capital cities in the early modern period while attempting to put the following chapters into context. Most of these are case studies of a range of great European cities and their differential effects – there is no attempt here at universality. But the case studies are prefaced and concluded by wide-ranging comparative surveys of groups of capital cities and their hinterlands.

Capital cities

The essential mechanisms for the growth of capital cities are clear. One contemporary, Richard Cantillon in his *Essai sur la Nature du Commerce en Géneral* (1735), furnishes the best model. 'If a prince or lord ... fixes his residence in some pleasant spot and several other noblemen come to live there to be within reach of seeing each other frequently and enjoying agreeable society, this place will become a city. ... For the service of these noblemen, bakers, butchers, brewers, wine merchants, manufacturers of all kinds will be needed. ... There is no great nobleman whose expense upon his house, his retinue and servants does not maintain merchants and artisans of all kinds. ... A capital is formed in the same way as a provincial town, with this difference: that the largest landowners in all the state reside in the capital; that the king or supreme government is fixed in it and spends there the government revenues; that the supreme courts of justice are fixed there; that it is the centre of the fashions which all the provinces take as a model; that the landowners who reside in the provinces do not fail to come occasionally to pass some time in the capital and to send their children thither to be polished. That all the lands in the state contribute more or less to

maintain those who dwell in the capital.'[6] Everything is evident in these
lines written soon after 1730: the role of the state, fiscal levies,
administrative employment, the clustering for social reasons of the
landed classes, the importance of domestic servants, the capital's
function in the diffusion of information. Many of our ideas about
capital cities appear today as variations on the propositions of Cantillon
or as illustrations of them via detailed case studies.

The rapid rise of the new-style metropolitan cities of early modern
Europe was inextricably linked with the growth of European national
and princely states from the close of the Middle Ages. The increasingly
sedentary function of Courts (instead of the perpetual royal
peregrinations of the medieval period) and the expansive centralization
and bureaucratization of states, concentrated in old and new
governmental centres, was the necessary precondition for the
metropolitan take-off. Both Madrid and St Petersburg were the
inventions of powerful rulers: the former elevated from a small market
town by Philip II during the 1560s; the second converted from a marshy
waste by Peter the Great after 1703. In contrast, where central authority
was weak, capital cities faced more difficulties in asserting their primacy.
As Maria Bogucka shows in Chapter Ten, Warsaw had to compete hard
with other Polish cities such as Gdańsk and Cracow for metropolitan
ascendancy and only achieved it briefly in the late eighteenth century. In
the United Provinces The Hague, which reached only 38,000 people at
the end of the eighteenth century, had to contend for urban prominence
against Amsterdam and other big cities of the Randstad as well as facing
competition from the wealthy villages of its immediate countryside
which hobbled expansion.[7]

Governments invested their capitals with growing numbers of well
paid officials. By 1725 there were perhaps 2700 career officials in
London; this compares with about 3000 in the smaller city of Madrid in
the mid-eighteenth century. In sixteenth-century Paris, as Jean Jacquart
describes in Chapter Five, a third of all royal officials were based in the
city and, though this proportion subsequently declined, data from Paris
marriage contracts made in 1749 indicate military and civil officers,
nobles and commoners associated with the work of government,
comprised more than 10 per cent of the total sample; almost all belonged
to the wealthiest categories of the urban population. The
smaller capitals often had the largest official contingents: Stockholm in
about 1650 had as many as 2500 crown servants (as against 1500
burghers), all in a population totalling under 35,000. Alongside their
governmental functions capital cities often served as important military
centres, both to protect the state and to overawe the civic population. A
tenth of Stockholm's population in the eighteenth century belonged to

the military; a quarter of St Petersburg's inhabitants in 1789 were military families and the same proportion was found in Berlin for much of the eighteenth century. The Hague likewise was the main military centre in the Dutch Republic.[8] Capital cities also housed an array of royal courts and other agencies, and hosted the more or less erratic meetings of a country's representative institutions. To fund these activities capital cities were, as we shall see, deeply involved in the fiscal function of the state and, by the eighteenth century, often served as the dynamic interface between the law, administration and growing capital markets necessary for public finance.

Yet more important than the state itself were the great (and lesser) landowners who flocked like preening starlings to the capital, jostling to pick up the profits of royal patronage, civil and military office, financial contracts, titles and honours, as well as to attend parliamentary or governmental meetings. The presence of a contingent of landowners and nobility in town determined the pattern of most urbanization in pre-industrial Europe. The old metropolitan city-states declined in part due to the exodus of the civic nobility to their country estates. In contrast the European capitals blossomed because of a tidal influx of provincial landowners. In the seventeenth and eighteenth centuries, as Herman van der Wee has noted, 'the land rent in all its forms came to be very clearly concentrated in the towns'; nowhere more so than in the capital cities.[9] The smaller cities often had the largest proportions of landowners. In Vienna during the early eighteenth century it has been estimated that members of the Court nobility, together with the state bureaucracy, comprised 60 per cent of the active population. In the second half of the century over 17 per cent of the active population of Madrid comprised *hidalgos*, while London may have had more than two thousand great and lesser landowners living there under George II, congregating mainly in the West End. At Paris the *Almanach Royal*, which indicates the title, function and addresses of the élite (almost all nobles of the realm), recorded 350 aristocratic families tied to the Court who were resident in Paris in 1720; by 1750 the number had risen to 450, and by 1780 to 630. From the start of the eighteenth century the former aristocratic area in the centre of Paris, in the Marais *quartier*, became unfashionable. The *faubourg* of St Germain, to the west of the capital, took over the role initially, but after 1760 changes in the aristocratic life-style led to the development of new *quartiers*: the *faubourgs* of Rule, Chaussée d'Antin, and Porchrons to the north west of the city enabled the great nobility to combine an urban residence with a semi-rustic environment. As we will see in Chapter Seven, Naples during the seventeenth and eighteenth centuries was boosted by the enormous transfer of rent from the countryside to sustain the host of secular and ecclesiastical lords living there.[10]

The arrival of the magnate classes, often living in capitals for a large part of the year, provided a massive stimulus for luxury industries. In Madrid over half the manufacturing sector comprised workers in the luxury trades, while England's capital maintained a near monopoly in high quality trades such as musical instrument makers, jewellers and goldsmiths into the nineteenth century. Other sectors to benefit were the retailing and building industries. In the 1790s London shopkeepers, big and small, comprised up to 14 per cent of the total population, with substantial numbers ranked among the highest tax payers. Retailing was somewhat less developed in Madrid, but Paris had an army of successful shopkeepers supplying the fashionable requirements of the European ruling classes: from St Petersburg to London, there was hardly any princely court which it did not provision with furniture, paintings and harness and saddles. In the single year 1752, for instance, the royal house of Parma spent over 200,000 livres on the purchase of luxury goods at Paris. Thus in some measure all the courts of Europe belonged to Paris' hinterland.[11] There were other beneficiaries as well. With the spate of grand public works in capital cities, along with the construction or renovation of hotels and residences for the aristocracy and housing for the lesser orders, the building sector enjoyed great surges of growth, with the tentacles of urban construction sprawling out into the countryside (thus the built-up area of Paris and its suburbs expanded over thirty-fold during the eighteenth century).[12]

The professions, crucial brokers between governments, landowners and the mercantile classes, were also increasingly numerous. London had at least a quarter of English attorneys in 1729 and a third by 1800. In Madrid the number of lawyers more than trebled in the late eighteenth century, while the number of medical men doubled.[13] In terms of sheer size, however, the sector which expanded most as a result of the gentrification of capital cities was domestic service, particularly of women. At the end of the seventeenth century female servants comprised up to 13 per cent of London's total population, two or three times the level in provincial towns. Would-be servants dominated the flows of migrants to town and helped give the capital its high female sex ratio throughout the eighteenth century. Overall immigration to European capitals in the eighteenth century was heavily dominated by women, flooding not only into service but prostitution and commercial employment as well (notable exceptions to this rule were Rome and St Petersburg).[14]

Yet the Court function of capital cities, though powerful and dynamic, with its penumbra of related activities, never completely dominated metropolitan economies. In many instances it complemented rather than eclipsed important commercial functions. In London at the start of the eighteenth century the port with its complex of river, coastal, European and colonial trades continued to employ up to a quarter of the population. Other capitals like Dublin, Lisbon and Stockholm remained significant overseas ports. In the case of Budapest, as Vera Bácskai shows in Chapter Nine, the commercial city of Pest actually enjoyed more rapid growth than the offical city of Buda. Paris likewise maintained an important regional role as a trading entrepôt on the Seine, but it had a national significance too, at the end of the eighteenth century playing a key role in wholesale distribution, particularly for luxury wares. Thus the silk merchants of Lyon had direct access to the regional market as well as to international markets (especially in Germany and Spain), yet they used Parisian intermediaries to distribute their products across a large part of France.[15]

Buda and Pest, divided by the Danube, presented the most striking spatial representation of the multi-centred format of many capital cities in the early modern era. In London the old commercial and financial City was increasingly matched by the offical and aristocratic cantonment in Westminster and the West End, while the East End steadily developed as the port town. The links with the hinterland were frequently between particular metropolitan areas or communities and districts of the region. Thus migrants from the West of England predominated in those newcomers found in the western suburbs of London, while the Buckinghamshire gentry tended to reside in particular districts such as Covent Garden or Chelsea.[16]

Not only must we be wary of talking about the metropolis as an urban unit, but as we have said there was no single metropolitan genus. A number of these great cities had, of course, been national capitals since the Middle Ages: thus Paris, London, Edinburgh, Copenhagen, Stockholm, Lisbon. They had acquired a collage of functions, structures and hinterlands over time. Others had fulfilled this role less continuously or were new creations: thus Brussels (the seat of the Burgundian Court but not really a major capital until Austrian rule), The Hague, Madrid, Vienna, Berlin, Warsaw, Dublin, Budapest. Here in numerous instances there were strong rivalries with other established cities: Brussels against Antwerp, The Hague and the Randstad, Madrid and Toledo, Vienna and Prague. Not all were national capitals as such. Berlin and Vienna eventually metamorphosed from princely capitals into national centres; Edinburgh after 1707 declined from a national to a kind of colonial capital, as did Budapest; Naples had a reverse experience after 1734. Dublin was essentially created as a colonial capital and that was also true, as David Ringrose shows in Chapter Eleven, of Mexico City and Lima in Spanish America. Finally, with the tremendous colonial and commercial growth of the seventeenth and eighteenth centuries, a number of European capitals became imperial metropolises, with Madrid exercising some measure of political and cultural ascendancy over the Italian and Latin American capitals under Spanish rule, while Georgian London at the accession of George III presided over a network of 'colonial' or secondary capitals including Edinburgh and Dublin, as well as Boston, Philadelphia and New York in North America. In the pluralistic British world of the eighteenth century, however, London's role was increasingly that of *primus inter pares*, at least in the realm of ideas: Edinburgh and Dublin, and even some of the American cities, began to have an increasingly influential impact on London society.[17]

At this point it may be useful to recall some words of Fernand Braudel: great cities 'are what society, the economy and politics allow or oblige them to be. They are a yardstick, a means of measurement'.[18] The same ideas must shape our investigation of their relationship with their hinterlands.

Metropolitan hinterlands

In the eighteenth century the smoke and pollution generated by the multitudinous industrial firms and domestic hearths of London could be smelt many miles distant from the capital. Metereological data would suggest that, by the end of the eighteenth century, high energy consumption in the capital had created a heat-island effect in the Thames valley, with above average temperatures (and possible temperature inversion) compared to adjoining shires. The need for stone for the construction of London's bridges, streets and public buildings led to widespread quarrying in the south east of England, particularly mid-Kent, disfiguring the landscape with large pits. Paris drew its supplies of wood for heating and carpentry from the Morvan, transported thence by river in large rafts of floating logs.[19]

If the environmental hinterland of capitals remains largely unexplored, we know more about the demographic relationship. Even to maintain demographic equilibrium the great cities, with their high levels of mortality, had to suck in great masses of people. Their size explains the extent of the main zone of recruitment, their function explains the existence of more specialist flows of migrants which were often from greater distances. As Paul Hohenberg and Lynn Lees argue in Chapter Two, immigration to capital cities was predominantly local and regional in its character, though with specialist groups coming from further afield. London attracted up to 12,000 immigrants a year by the start of the eighteenth century, mostly recruited from the immediate and regional hinterland, though with substantial numbers of Scottish and, increasingly, Irish immigrants (by 1780 the capital had over 23,000). In the late eighteenth century Paris's gross immigration was running at 7-14,000 a year, the majority of the newcomers recruited from northern and eastern France, but masons came on a seasonal basis from the Limousin and the best stablemen from the Pays de Léon in Brittany.[20] No less striking was the distinctively international character of metropolitan immigration. Exceptionally, one fifth of Berlin's population were Huguenots at the start of the eighteenth century and, even in the much larger city of 1750, foreigners comprised an eighth of the population: more typically up to 6 per cent of eighteenth-century Parisians were foreigners and even insular London had, in addition to Scots and Irish, sizeable communities of Germans, Huguenots, Jews and blacks.[21] This ethnicity helped to promote the growth of international trade and manufactures (particularly in the luxury sector) and also to underpin the role of capitals as gateway cities, with more open, cosmopolitan and pluralistic societies.

Metropolitan cities depended not only on a constant infusion of human resources from the provinces but on material supplies. From the high Middle Ages, London was being supplied with basic foods from a wide arc of southern England and this supply area was steadily extended by the late seventeenth century so that meat travelled on the hoof from Scotland and Wales, cheese by ship from Suffolk and Cheshire and specialist beers and cider by a variety of means from the Midlands and the South West. By 1700 an increasingly important element in metropolitan consumption – sugars, spirits and spices – was imported from the colonies. As we will find in Chapter Five, thousands of tons of foodstuffs of all kinds were absorbed by Paris. Grain provisioning involved three great zones, the first extending just beyond the boundaries of the generality and including the Valois, the Brie and the Beauce; the second, more contested zone encompassed Picardy to the north west and Champagne to the east; a third extended across much of the country, though this was exploited heavily only during emergencies. Berlin's population was also supplied from a wide area – by the late eighteenth century embracing the Neumark, East and West Prussia and the area around Magdeburg. In turn, capital cities increasingly sold into an expanding arc of provincial society luxury goods and consumer durables; in England, as Michael Reed shows in Chapter Three, reaching across southern regions and particularly affecting towns.[22]

The institutional hinterlands of capitals varied greatly. In England the royal courts and agencies based in London had increasingly a national role, with the decline of ecclesiastical, seigneurial and civic courts and the disappearance in the seventeenth century of provincial bodies like the Council of the North and the Council in the Marches of Wales. No less important here was the expanded national authority of the Westminster Parliament, meeting annually after 1688 and with its jurisdiction extended to Scotland after 1707. In France the *parlement* of Paris had a more regional judicial remit although in certain matters it had a national jurisdiction, while in the case of Spain, Chapter Six by José López García and Santos Madrazo Madrazo, suggests an increasingly fractured institutional region around Madrid.[23]

Culturally, capital cities had a growing national influence, aided by their importance as printing and publishing centres. For France, Paris was the capital of the printing industry. State regulation of publishing, and in particular the tax on permits to publish, assured the capital's publishers a monopoly of the most numerous, important and best known works. Daniel Roche has estimated that up to 100,000 titles were printed or reprinted there in the course of the eighteenth century. In the later part of that century Berlin increased its publication of books eight-fold. By the eighteenth century many capital cities had become powerful transmitters of enlightenment values and fashions – in manners, dress, public sociability and leisure entertainment (theatre, opera, music) – across national societies. The proliferation of learned academies in towns across France, from the middle of the seventeenth century to the end of the eighteenth, with 40 functioning at one time or another, marked the growing conformity of provincial norms to the social and cultural values and ideas of Paris. The foundation itself of such an institution, with its assumption of royal approval, signals a kind of symbolic allegiance to the capital.[24] In England Peter Borsay has seen metropolitan cultural influences pervading much of the country by the mid-eighteenth century, though as we shall see recent work has also emphasized the way that such influences were reconfigured by provincial élites to furbish their own civic image and sense of identity.[25]

Two points need to be made about the extent of metropolitan hinterlands. Firstly, the definition of such areas frequently had a class dimension. The provincial consumers of metropolitan-style music or drama, the members of local academies or learned societies away from the capital, tended to belong to the upper classes, while litigants at the royal courts in the metropolis came from the better-off ranks of society. In the same fashion, production for the metropolitan food market usually involved commercially-oriented substantial farmers, not small tenant farmers or share-croppers. The more extensive the hinterland the greater the likelihood that participation involved only higher social groups. Secondly, many hinterlands were lateral rather than territorial. The transmission of new cultural fashions and ideas affected principally the biggest cities and towns with good communications and commercial ties with the capital; the countryside was often bypassed. Trade, likewise, followed the best transport links, usually river and coastal rather than overland routes.

The metropolitan hinterland was no metaphysical onion whose layers might be easily removed and dissected. Rather, to change the metaphor drastically, it was more like a ball of wool after a cat has played with it. One can, of course, identify an immediate *Um-land*, or constellation of villages and small towns close to the capital. From the late seventeenth century London, likewise, had a cluster of villages and other settlements to which the fashionable classes resorted at weekends or holidays for entertainment and where they increasingly took up residence, aided by improved communications to London. From the late eighteenth century the Viennese, likewise, showed a growing predeliction for the surrounding countryside, particularly the villages along the foothills of the Vienna Woods. By the end of the period, as Helga Schultz suggests in Chapter Eight, Berlin was surrounded by a growing industrial belt, reaching from Rummelsburg to Moabit and Spandau.[26] Beyond this immediate area the relative balance of regional, national and international hinterlands varied greatly according to the country (as Braudel noted), but also as we have suggested according to the precise function of the capital city itself.

Relationships

From the seventeenth century, if not before, commentators were anxious at what they described, using the increasingly common medical language of the period, as the parasitical effect of these great cities on society. James I of England complained that London would soon devour all England. In the early eighteenth century, the London *Craftsman* newspaper protested that the 'poverty of the country proceeds in a very great measure from the residence of the chief nobility and gentry in the town [the capital] where they live in the utmost extravagance and but rarely go into the country with any other design than to squeeze as much money as they can out of their tenants'. At Naples, according to Brigitte Marin, there was a recurrent debate about the negative effects of the city during the eighteenth century.[27]

Historians have tended to recycle the concepts of early commentators in discussing whether capital cities were parasites or engines of growth. *Prima facie* we can differentiate those cities which were more parasitical and those more favourable to economic development.[28] However it is not certain that such an approach makes much sense. Certainly, in the absence of a major improvement in agricultural production, a metropolitan centre could not grow without increasing its demands for food and other supplies from rural communities far and wide. Certainly the capital city is a major consumer – and killer – of population. Certainly, as we have noted, a great deal of the non-productive expenditure which occurred there was sustained from rents levied in the countryside. At the same time, it is a consumer market, communication hub and centre of innovations which enables or compels regions towards agricultural specialization or intensive production. This is as true for capitals as for other towns: the countryside pays dearly for its development but it is not necessarily the loser.

In considerable measure towns and countryside, capitals and their hinterlands, are subject to a reciprocity of activities and resources. If there is a question of parasitism it may depend on the dimension of a town. Paul Bairoch has demonstrated that it is important to distinguish between the economic and social optimum of an urban centre. According to Bairoch, 'it is probable that the technical and economic evolution which enabled the creation of very large cities led to an augmentation of their population beyond the optimal level. It is likely that the urbanization rate exceeded the optimal size and the urban ceiling had been pushed up. This was accompanied by the growing disenchantment of the population with the urban phenomenon.' Such tension helps to illuminate the public discourse on the metropolis during the eighteenth century. In 1733 l'Abbé de St Pierre published a memoir, 'Avantages que doit produire l'agrandissement continuel de la ville capitale d'un Etat', which is founded entirely on a distinction between the optimality of power and an optimal level based not on the living conditions of the townsfolk but on the effectiveness of urban control. 'Neither Paris, nor any other capital may ever be too big or too populous for the interests of the state, as long as all those bodies entrusted to maintain public order are augmented and enhanced in proportion to the number of inhabitants.'[29]

The complexities of the relationship between capital cities and their hinterlands are compounded by the fact that rates of metropolitan growth, though generally high, were far from constant. Thus London enjoyed a rapid take-off in the late sixteenth and early seventeenth centuries, followed by a more modest advance and even stagnation during the 1730s and 1740s. Paris experienced a roller-coaster of growth in the sixteenth century, with the population falling by a third to 200,000 in the early 1590s before rising strongly to about 300,000 in 1600 and 450,000 in 1650, but after this came a period of more modest increase into the eighteenth century. In some cases this volatility was due to external factors. The decline of Paris in the 1590s was caused by the siege of the city during the French Religious Wars, just as Vienna's population growth was severely disrupted by Turkish attacks in the 1520s and 1680s.[30] In other instances, however, the causation was probably endogenous, as with London in the early eighteenth century when stagnation stemmed from high levels of epidemic disease in the city, though it may also have had some link with economic depression in the agricultural region of the south east.[31]

It is clear, then, that any discussion of the consequences of metropolitan expansion must recognize a wide variety of experiences, depending on time, type of capital and hinterland, and area of activity. To start, it may be useful to look at the relationship between capital and hinterland in terms of specific areas. We have already noted the way that migration forged an umbilical link between capital and hinterland. In Denmark the growth of Copenhagen absorbed up to a quarter of the national surplus of population in that period, while London took up about half the natural increase in provincial England. In a world where the growth of resources was slow, rapid urban development was paid for by the decline or stabilization in the general population. As Hohenberg and Lees suggest, metropolitan immigration seems to have had a significant depressant effect on demographic growth in regional hinterlands, though this was not invariably the case: for instance, the area within 50 kilometres of Lisbon enjoyed substantially higher rates of increase than the country as a whole.[32] Where the population was held down it was not just the result of emigration to capitals. Disease mortality was high throughout our period and was almost certainly exported or reinforced by capital cities. In southern England there are indications of rising mortality in small towns by 1700 as a result of growing economic and disease contact with the capital. In late eighteenth-century Sweden, the main recruitment area for Stockholm suffered high levels of tuberculosis mortality just like the capital, as the circular flow of migrants maintained the disease. No less important, the changing composition of the migrational influx into capitals had an impact on the demographic structure of the hinterland. By the eighteenth century metropolitan immigration was heavily dominated by women. High outflows of female migrants from hinterlands may have skewed the demographic balance and thereby exacerbated demographic stagnation. On the plus side workers and traders, who had learned or enhanced skills and expertise in the capital, frequently moved out of capital cities into the provinces, disseminating metropolitan expertise and attitudes and stimulating economic growth.[33]

The following chapters emphasize the important impact of capital cities on the key economic areas of agriculture, industry and transportation. As far as the first is concerned, the English scenario in which high London demand, particularly from the late seventeenth century, promoted agrarian specialization and greater productivity in a ripple effect across the lowland region and then more selectively across the national hinterland, seems to have been towards one end of the spectrum. It was not alone. The local hinterland of Lisbon, likewise, seems to have profited strongly from metropolitan demand, with sharply rising grain output in the late eighteenth century despite national stagnation, and with wine and fruit production increasingly oriented towards the capital. Agricultural production in the Prague region evidently experienced a similar stimulus.[34] At the opposite end of the spectrum, however, we find cities such as Rome and Naples, at least before the end of the eighteenth century, which provisioned themselves by plundering the local and regional territory, with catastrophic consequences for the stability of rural society.[35]

Paris represents without question an intermediate type, as the prosperity of the great farmers of the Ile-de-France illustrates. The proximity of the capital enabled the best organized farmers to create, without any technical progress, innovative and profitable systems of production. François Chartier, active between 1730 and the 1760s, offers a good example. Like his father before him, he sold wheat at Paris. But he added to it another activity, feeding the horses of the king and aristocracy. He supplied them with fresh straw, deriving from this a third of the profits of his farm, and buying at a low price the dung from the royal stables with which to manure his lands. The inflow of money allowed him to store his wheat for a longer time, in order to sell it at the best time for the highest price. He was able to develop on a grand scale the fattening of sheep purchased in regions further and further away and sold after several months to Parisian butchers. This system required high investment but clearly advanced his income even more. The prosperity of the business stemmed from the way in which he joined together and profited from multiple markets, all of them tied to the capital.[36]

However, it is not sufficient to talk of capitals and agriculture simply in terms of market forces. In numerous countries governments, obsessed with metropolitan order, intervened to remove local restrictions within the regional hinterland on agricultural production and trade with the capital, thereby stimulating output. In the case of Paris during the seventeenth and eighteenth centuries, there were three markets for grain and meal: upstream the Port de Grève, where boats tied up from the Brie region having come via the Seine; downstream the Port de l'Ecole, to which boats made their way by the Oise and the Seine with corn from the Soissonais and Picardy; and finally Les Halles, which gathered in all the produce from a circuit of ten leagues (40 kilometres) around Paris, where urban purchasers were not allowed to purchase and where peasants and rural wholesalers were compelled by official decrees to carry their wheat directly to the Paris market.[37]

As already noted, industrial expansion in the metropolis was often heavily directed towards luxury manufactures. Luxury goods formed an increasingly important component in national and international trade, the result of the fashioning of a new consumer-conscious European élite linked by a network of metropolitan centres. However, more down-market trades suffered from the high labour costs of the metropolis as well as the competition of cheaper rural products. In some sectors, metropolitan trades responded to these challenges through large-scale centralized production (thus the rise of the great London breweries with their enormous factory-type complexes which dominated the metropolitan drink trade in the eighteenth century) or through a reversion to domestic putting out and sweated labour. In other cases industries were forced to emigrate from the capital, sometimes to the immediate region (as in the case of the London silk trade which moved to North Essex at the start of the nineteenth century, or the hat industry which moved to Bedfordshire), but more often outside the region altogether, as with the hosiery trades which migrated to the East Midlands (particularly Leicester and Nottingham) in the late seventeenth century. In a similar fashion, the linen industry in Ireland developed away from Dublin in Ulster.[38] Crucial here was the fact that high metropolitan wage rates also inflated industrial costs in the regional hinterland, making manufacturing there uncompetitive. Thus the iron and textile industries in the Weald to the south of London and the cloth trades in North Essex and East Anglia suffered accelerating decline in the late eighteenth century. As one might expect, however, this scenario was not universal. In the Budapest region and the areas close to Berlin, Lisbon and Prague, we find industries developing near the capital, and even in the London region, as Michael Reed shows in Chapter Three, specialist industries could prosper and thrive catering for metropolitan demand.[39]

Where the metropolis apparently had more general dynamic repercussions was in promoting transport improvement. The development of St Petersburg brought major advances in overland and canal routes. In the Austrian Netherlands, Brussels took the lead in the growth of paved inter-city routes across the country. London became the hub of expanding river, coastal and turnpike communications in England, especially in the early eighteenth century. All this was in part linked with the central role of metropolitan cities in the growth of postal networks and in the processes and politics of road construction, which always favoured the best placed centres in the urban hierarchy. The outcome, alongside advances in the technical performance of road vehicles, was a massive shrinkage in the temporal hinterlands of capitals. Thus in 1754 the journey time between London and York was said to be four days, in 1761 three and in the 1770s thirty-six hours, while the journey from Edinburgh to London took ten days in 1754 but only two days at the end of the century.[40]

The presence of great cities generally had deleterious consequences for the major urban centres in their regional hinterland, regarding numbers and size. The London region (the Home Counties) was notable for the virtual absence of urban centres with more than 8000 inhabitants in 1700; the exception was the textile town of Colchester and this, to prove the rule, was in demographic decline during the early eighteenth century. Vienna had very few towns of any significance in the extended hinterland. Of the 152 urban centres in the Paris basin in 1725, only five had more than 20,000 people and these were mainly on the regional periphery. But these demographic indicators have to be treated with caution: we must not confuse quantitative trends with qualitative ones. The paucity of large urban rivals in the hinterland did not necessarily signify urban atrophy; in some cases the opposite was the case. In England, London's demand for provisions and manufactured goods gave a powerful boost to the prosperity of the large number of smaller towns (with as few as one or two thousand inhabitants) in the south east, as one can see from the impressive array of public buildings and private houses built in them during the late seventeenth and early eighteenth centuries, though this regional halo effect was probably less pronounced and more patchy by 1800.[41] In France, it was around Paris that we find clustered small and middle-rank towns distinguished by their wealth (particularly of *rentiers*) and commercial activity.[42] In the eighteenth century, a town of 5000 inhabitants 30 kilometres from Paris was by definition more prosperous and dynamic than its counterparts in Lorraine or in the Massif Central, even if its population did not grow. Nationally there are indications that metropolitan primacy may have encouraged the evolution of a more integrated, rank-size hierarchy in the main countries of early modern Europe, though this was less evident in more peripheral countries such as Portugal, Ireland and Hungary.

Finally, two more aspects of the metropolitan impact are referred to in the following chapters: political and cultural influence. Paradoxically, perhaps, state capitals were quite often, if sporadically, centres of political dissent and opposition. Paris during the Ligue and Frondes as well as the Revolution, London during the 1640s, 1760s and 1790s, Dublin and Warsaw in the late eighteenth century are obvious examples. In part this stemmed from the presence there of large numbers of the political élite, the prosperity and literacy of the middling classes, and the escalating problems of political surveillance in gargantuan cities, often as we have said congeries of distinct communities. Increasingly there are indications that metropolitan radicalism spread to provincial cities – as for instance with the upsurge of Wilkesites clubs in the 1760s, not just in English towns but in the main American cities – though it is less certain that such influences had any long-term impact on provincial radicalism; by the close of the period, provincial cities in England and France were making their own autonomous running as anti-government centres.[43]

The growing political role of metropolitan cities was linked to their position as cultural command centres with a dominant position in education and printing. With their close association with the Court, metropolitan cities became, as we noted earlier, engines of cultural change. Throughout France the manners and literary tastes of the urban élite came to be shaped by those of the Parisian *beau monde*. In the British world, London-style coffee-houses, clubs, musical enter-tainments, clothes, language and fashions were exported not only to the region but to the national and imperial hinterlands, via the mediating agency of the colonial capitals. The hypertrophy of Naples, damaging in other respects, enabled the Italian Mezzogiorno to maintain its position in the cultural networks of progressive Europe and to participate fully in the Enlightenment. The physical transmutation of the European metropolis into a baroque and classical amphitheatre for the élite classes, with a repertoire of palaces and public buildings, improved streets and select *quartiers*, left a powerful imprint on provincial society as regional centres sought to remodel their image and identity in the metropolitan style.[44]

At the same time, we should be wary of assuming any universality of this metropolitan cultural impact. Most of the influence was socially selective, directed primarily towards the better-off classes, and this was more the case the greater the distance from the capital. In a way one can see this contributing to the conventional picture of the growing dichotomy of popular and élite cultures, but in provincial towns at least we can also see a partial delayed diffusion of élite values among the middling sector of society interacting with traditional class concerns. No less important, while provincial cities often accepted and welcomed metropolitan ideas and styles, there was no passive reception: local leaders usually sought to deploy and transform metropolitan values in a way that established their city's modernity and fashionability but also its distinctive identity. Far from there being a proliferation of metropolitan clones, the Enlightenment led to a renegotiation of cultural relations between the capital and the provinces which served to reinvigorate provincial culture.[45] It is true then that metropolitan cities increasingly formed an integrated network and metropolitan culture had a widening international role. But if the metropolis proposed itself as the arbiter of

European ideas and manners, it was the hinterland which disposed what this meant in cultural reality.

Ideas for comparative research

As we have suggested and the following chapters will confirm, it would be difficult to argue that there was a single model of metropolitan influence in early modern Europe. Not only are there different types of capital city and hinterland, but the relationship between them varies markedly whether we examine the demographic, or economic or cultural dimension. That relationship may also have altered over time – from the fast growth phase of metropolitan expansion to the mature status of established primacy. Yet to describe such a rainbow of effects in a largely qualitative way cannot take us very far, particularly when we are trying to understand the role and impact of these great cities across Europe. For this purpose we need to pursue a different approach, attempting to identify some of the fundamental defining variables in the relationship between capitals and their hinterlands. One way forward might be through a comparative programme of quantitative research which would enable us to construct a typology of causes and effects in the growth of capital cities and thence to understand more clearly their place in European development.

Such an approach relies on a simple principle: we should no longer consider the political economy of the eighteenth century, from Cantillon to Adam Smith, as the conclusion of our analysis, but as a point of departure; not to confirm our empirical observations, but as a list of indicators, which may be measured, approximately, but in a way which will help us to make comparisons. This returns to an old practice which dates back to William Petty's *Five Essays in Political Arithmetick* (1687), in which his 'Comparison between London and Paris in 14 particulars' provides one of the first systematic surveys of the question.[46] The theoretical schemes of the political economists allow us to choose those strategic indicators which particularly illuminate the economic process. Following Cantillon and Smith, one might suggest four indicators, though this list is by no means definitive or exclusive. In what follows these indicators are examined, initially in the light of French documentation, to suggest the opportunities for comparative study.

The first concerns the state. A regional study of royal finances offers one way of accessing the urban economy, especially that of the capital city. The question of the redistribution of royal fiscal revenues posed in social and political terms deserves to be reconsidered from the economic point of view. In 1677 64 per cent of the funds raised in Languedoc went to the French king, 3 per cent to notables living outside the province and 33 per cent to Languedocian élites mainly living within the cities of the province. One might interpret these figures as an index of redistribution working to the benefit of the province's towns.[47] What happens when we look at the royal capital? Precise calculations are impossible, but can one estimate the order of magnitude? In regard to the tax levies, this is relatively easy using fiscal records. In 1779 Paris paid 87 million livres in direct and indirect taxes, while the whole kingdom paid 476 million livres: in other words, the capital, comprising 2 per cent of the French population, contributed 18 per cent of taxation. How was this redistributed? Undoubtedly there were four massive channels of redistribution: state building works, the operations of the royal household, military costs and wages and honours distributed locally to royal officials. In all such cases there are rich archives which could be exploited from this point of view. For other countries, it would be important to check if sources of the same kind exist for their capitals, which would permit at least rough comparative calculations to be made. At the same level, that of the state, another possible measure might be taken by exploiting the opportunities created by specific historic events. At Versailles when the king left town from 1715 (after the death of Louis XIV) to 1722, and then finally after 1789, the community was not erased from the map, but its population fell each time by exactly a half; a clear measure of the dynamic effects of the presence of the Court.[48] What happened to Naples at the time of Italian unity? What occurred at Budapest and Vienna on the break-up of the Austro-Hungarian empire? What protects these towns, up to a point, from absolute decline? What underpins their relative autonomy with regard to their functioning as a capital?

The second indicator concerns rents. In France at least two sources are available. The first is the extent of property owned by townspeople in the countryside. Leases and transfers of property which appear in land registry records enable us to gain an idea of the radius of property ownership reaching out from towns and of changes over time. One might therefore take samples of the proportion of landed property owned by Parisians in the region. Fiscal registers (of the *vingtième* on real estate) enable us to estimate the revenue (initially fiscal) of landowners. Such a research undertaking would be considerable, proportionate to the size of the town (in France the limit of research so far has been Toulouse, a tenth the size of Paris). Similar sources seem to exist for Portugal. What about elsewhere in Europe?[49]

Thirdly, élite consumption had a multiplier effect whose importance did not depend solely on the scale of the revenues but on their appropriation. The aristocratic landowner could choose to live three months in London and nine months on his estates, or contrariwise three months in his country house and for the rest of the year in his London residence. He might prefer to train horses rather than support a large household. He could choose to buy all the luxury products he needed in London or he might prefer that they came from Paris. The studies of material culture and the social geography of consumption underline the variations in time and space of these forms of activity which one might well suppose were different at Madrid, Berlin, Naples and Budapest. Comparative analysis of them would help contribute to our understanding of the differential functioning of the economies of European capitals.[50]

Our last variable concerns production. In pre-industrial economies their relative development can be measured more precisely by the complexity of the phases of production than by the total volume of output.[51] It is important, therefore, to compare the local scale of the division of labour. Directories, dictionaries of trades, guild archives and tax records furnish the material for a lexical enquiry. Volumes of employment are less significant than the degree of occupational specialization, an index of the technical division of work. The meaning of the data comes from geographical or chronological comparison. Was the division of labour similar between the sixteenth and eighteenth centuries in London, Paris, Madrid, Budapest and Warsaw, and no less important in the hinterlands of those great cities?

One might conceive, furthermore, of another complementary programme of work, which would consider less the specific indicators we have discussed and more the processes in aggregate and their impact, so far as they occurred in time and space. Some sociologists at the present time are concerned with the way in which individuals transform the social capital at their disposal into intellectual capital (for instance, how the socio-economic level of the family determines educational success) or their intellectual capital into economic or social capital. The question can be transposed to the urban economy. The rising metropolitan cities have at their disposal capital which is by definition political. By what process did they succeed (or not succeed or succeed imperfectly) in transforming this into economic capital? For Warsaw, Maria Bogucka in Chapter Ten presents the following sequence of developments stemming from the city's political function: the augmentation of the capital's role in Poland's overseas trade; growing mercantile wealth and the accumulation of capital; the development of a textile industry as well as a consumer goods industry oriented towards the local nobility; and the growth of financial activities.[52] These processes, either simultaneous or closely related, seem so evident that they apparently do not deserve further investigation. However, they did not occur in all capital cities and, even where they did, not in the same order. This might suggest that such developments were not as logical or as straightforward as they appear. The Parisian sequence would seem to be the opposite of the Polish one: political power was transformed firstly into financial and banking power – for almost technical reasons related to the determination of the national treasury to avoid as much as possible the cost and risk of transporting coins from the provinces. It is the power of money which enables Paris steadily to enlarge its control over the foreign and internal exchanges, then over the country's burgeoning industrialization. To better understand this process we need to look at institutional changes together with economic developments (including the centralization of capital markets) and social ones. Under the Directory and the First Empire the expansion of Paris' power took place through the physical displacement (via migration) of bankers and entrepreneurs who left the provinces to take up residence in the capital.[53] It would also be helpful to include some investigation into collective attitudes for, paradoxically, it is in the capital cities that the economic élites can most easily evade the attentions of the state.

Fixing on the same processes spatially we can return to the notion of the hinterland. As we saw earlier, there is a danger in defining *a priori* the *arrière-pays* of a town. Can we really talk about the hinterland of the capital being the whole state together with its colonial dependencies? In the economic world this is only true in one respect, that of tax collection. But for all the rest, at least before the formation of a national market, the picture is largely artefactual. As we noted above, most of the linkages are lateral or class selective, without much spatial substance and frequently subject to negotiation. Moreover, as we showed earlier, metropolitan cities belonged to a class of town whose spatial relationships were the most diverse and extensive. Open to both local and international contacts and networks, they had the function of gateway cities. In this respect the notion of the hinterland must, to be meaningful, be given a precise definition. In economic terms we might, therefore, define the hinterland of a metropolitan city as the area which functioned in unison with it, which reacted identically or closely to its impulse. There is a need, then, to narrow down these regions, to see economic developments in a spatial context and, in evaluating the various factors affecting metropolitan development, to give greater weighting to those which cross both time and space, such as price convergences and the diffusion of innovations.[54] In the early modern period, at least, the main hinterland of the capital was the adjoining region and this must be the focus of future research.

* * *

Capital cities of the seventeenth and eighteenth centuries were significant players in the reshaping of Europe's economy, society and cultural order. Though most of that impact, as we have argued, was concentrated on the regional hinterlands, there are signs by the close of our period that in some countries state capitals were more crucial in advancing a sense of national identity, even promoting a measure of national integration, than the state itself. Across Europe capital cities in the early modern period seized the commanding heights of the urban system whence, despite repeated economic and political revolutions, they have still to be deposed. They did not, of course, enjoy effortless superiority. In the nineteenth century urban industrialization increasingly challenged their economic primacy, while in some countries, notably Britain, there was a degree of cultural and political decentralization to regional centres. From the later nineteenth century, however, the growth of the modern national state has once again entrenched their ascendancy and primacy.

Notes

1. P.M. Hohenberg and L.H. Lees, *The Making of Urban Europe 1000-1950* (London, 1985), p.229; Abbé Expilly, *Dictionnaire géographique, historique et politique de la France*, vol.5 (Paris, 1768), 399; G.B. Hill, ed., *Boswell's Life of Johnson*, vol.3 (Oxford, 1934), 178; E. François and E. von Westerholt, *Berlin au XVIIIe siècle. Naissance d'une capitale* (Nancy, 1988); W. Petty, *The Economic Writings of Sir William Petty* (ed. C.H. Hull, New York, 1964), vol.2, 501-32, 537-40; *Philosophical Transactions of the Royal Society of London*, vol.3 (London, 1723), 455-8.

2. P. Bairoch et al., *La Population des villes européennes 800-1850* (Geneva, 1988); see also J. de Vries, *European Urbanisation 1500-1800* (London, 1984), esp. pp.140-2.

3. A.L. Beier and R. Finlay, eds, *London 1500-1700: The Making of the Metropolis* (London, 1986), pp.3, 39; P. Benedict, ed., *Cities and Social Change in Early Modern France* (London, 1989), p.24; D.R. Ringrose, *Madrid and the Spanish Economy 1560-1850* (London, 1983), p.23; see below, chapter 8; for the other cities see Bairoch, *Population*.

4. As a sample: F.C. Lane, *Venice, A Maritime Republic* (Baltimore, 1973); B. Pullan, ed., *Crisis and Change in the Venetian Economy in the 16th and 17th Centuries* (London, 1968); J. Heers, *Gênes au XVe siècle* (Paris, 1961); H. van der Wee, *The Growth of the Antwerp Market and the European Economy (14th to 16th centuries)* (The Hague, 1963); J.A. van Houtte, 'Declin et survivance d'Anvers 1550-1700', in *Studi in onore di A. Fanfani*, vol.5 (Milan, 1962), 705-26.

5. P. Clark and P. Slack, *English Towns in Transition 1500-1700* (London, 1976), p.83; see below, chapter 7; Benedict, *Cities*, p.24.

6. R. Cantillon, *Essai sur la Nature du Commerce en Général* (trans. and ed. H. Higgs, London, 1931), pp.15, 17.

7.   Hohenberg and Lees, *Making*, p.107; J.H. Bater, *St Petersburg: Industrialisation and Change* (London, 1976), pp.17-18; see below, chapter 10; H. Diederiks, 'The Netherlands, the Case of A Decentralised Metropolis (14th-19th Centuries)', in E. Aerts and P. Clark, eds, *Metropolitan Cities and their Hinterlands in Early Modern Europe* (Leuven, 1990), pp.86-7.

8.   Beier and Finlay, *London*, p.12; Ringrose, *Madrid*, p.68; see below, chapter 5; A. Daumard and F. Furet, *Structures et relations sociales à Paris* (Paris, 1961); A. Jansson, *Börder och bärkraft: Borgare och kronot jänare; Stockholm 1644-1972* (Stockholm, n.d.), p.326; J. Söderberg, U. Jonsson and C. Persson, *A Stagnating Metropolis: The Economy and Demography of Stockholm 1750-1850* (Cambridge, 1991), p.17; François and von Westerholt, *Berlin*; Diederiks, 'Netherlands', p.89.

9.   H. van der Wee, 'Reflections on the Development of the Urban Economy', *Urbanism Past and Present*, vol.1 (1975-6), 12.

10.   F. Opll, 'Cities and the Transmission of Cultural Values in the Late Middle Ages and Early Modern Period: the Vienna Example', paper given at the Crédit Communal Conference on European Cities and the Transmission of Cultural Values, Spa, May 1994 (proceedings forthcoming); Ringrose, *Madrid*, p.71; G. Rude, *Hanoverian London 1714-1808* (London, 1971), ch.3; N. Coquery, *De l'hôtel aristocratique aux ministères: habitat, mouvement, espace à Paris au XVIIIième siècle* (Université de Paris I, thèse, 1995); see below, chapter 7.

11.   Ringrose, *Madrid*, pp.68-9; L. Schwarz, *London in the Age of Industrialisation: Entrepreneurs, Labour Force and Living Conditions 1700-1850* (Cambridge, 1992), pp.41, 60-1. Ringrose, *op. cit.*, p.101; M. Sonenscher, *Work and Wages: Natural Law, Politics and the Eighteenth-Century French Trades* (Cambridge, 1989), pp.210-18.

12.   Hohenberg and Lees, *Making*, pp.151-9; Ringrose, *Madrid*, p.69; J.A. Davis, 'Resistance to change: élites, municipal government and the state in the development of the city of Naples (1750-1870)', in H. Diederiks, P. Hohenberg and M. Wagenaar, eds, *Economic Policy in Europe since the Late Middle Ages: The Visible Hand and the Fortune of Cities* (Leicester, 1992), p.90; Schwarz, *London*, pp.79-81, 84-5, 87-9; also J. Summerson, *Georgian London* (London, 1962); P. Pinon, 'A travers révolutions architecturales et politiques 1715-1848', in L. Bergeron, ed., *Paris, genèse d'un paysage* (Paris, 1989), pp.147-215; D. Roche, *The People of Paris* (Leamington, 1987), p.14.

13.   Schwarz, *London*, p.27; Ringrose, *Madrid*, p.101.

14.   P. Earle, 'The Female Labour Market in London in the late 17th and early 18th Centuries', *Economic History Review*, 2nd Series, vol.42 (1989), 328-53; P. Clark and D. Souden, eds, *Migration and Society in Early Modern England* (London, 1988), pp.35, 307; see below, chapter 2; C. Schiavoni and E. Sonnino, 'Aspects généraux de l'évolution démographique à Rome 1598-1824', *Annales de Démographie Historique, 1982* (Paris, 1982), p.103; Bater, *St Petersburg*, p.70.

15.   P.J. Corfield, *The Impact of English Towns* (Oxford, 1983), pp.71-2; see below, chapter 4; H.E.S. Fisher, *The Portugal Trade: A Study of Anglo-Portuguese Commerce 1700-1770* (London, 1971); Jannsson, *Börder*, p.338; see below, chapter 9; L. Bergeron, 'Paris dans l'organisation des échanges intérieurs français à la fin du XVIIIième siècle', in P. Léon, ed., *Aires et*

structures du commerce français au XVIIIième siècle (Lyon, 1975), pp.237-64.

16. Cf. M. Power, 'The East and West in Early Modern London', in E.W. Ives et al., eds, *Wealth and Power in Tudor England* (London, 1978), pp.167-85; L. Schwarz, 'Social Crime and Social Geography: the Middle Classes in London at the end of the 18th century', in P. Borsay, ed., *The Eighteenth Century Town 1688-1820* (London, 1990), pp.318-34; see also the interesting study by S.E. Whyman, 'Sociability and Power; the World of the Verneys 1660-1720', (unpubl. Ph.D. thesis, Princeton Univ., 1993), pp. 175-82.

17. For Dublin see below, chapter 4. See below, chapter 11; see for example P. Clark, *The Rise of British Clubs and Societies* (Oxford, forthcoming).

18. F. Braudel, *Civilization and Capitalism, 15th-18th century* (trans. S. Reynolds, London, 1981-4), vol.1, 557.

19. P. Brimblecombe, *The Big Smoke: A History of Air Pollution in London since Medieval Times* (London, 1987), p.72; T.J. Chandler, *The Climate of London* (London, 1965), p.147; C. Chalklin, *Seventeenth-Century Kent* (London, 1985), pp.147-8; J. Meyer, *Etudes sur les villes en Europe occidentale*, vol.1 (Paris, 1983), 39.

20. See below, chapter 2; Clark and Souden, *Migration*, pp.24, 274; Roche, *People*, pp.22-8; also J. Beaud and G. Bouchard, 'Le Dépôt des Pauvres de St Denis 1768-92', in *Annales de Démographie Historique 1974* (Paris, 1974), pp.127-43.

21. François and von Westerholt, *Berlin*; Roche, *People*, p.23; M.D. George, *London Life in the Eighteenth Century* (London, 1965), pp.120-45.

22. B. Campbell et al., *A Medieval Capital and its Grain Supply: Agrarian Production and Distribution in the London Region c. 1300*, Historical Geography Research Series, no.30 (1993); J. Chartres, *Internal Trade in England 1500-1700* (London, 1977); see below, chapter 5; S.L. Kaplan, *Provisioning Paris: Merchants and Millers in the Grain and Flour Trade during the Eighteenth Century* (London, 1984), pp.88-9; see below, chapters 8 and 3.

23. See below, chapters 3 and 6.

24. D. Roche, *La France des Lumières* (Paris, 1993); François and von Westerholt, *Berlin*; D. Roche, *Le Siècle des Lumières en Province. Académies et académiciens provinciaux* (Paris, 1978).

25. P. Borsay, *The English Urban Renaissance: Culture and Society in the Provincial Town 1600-1770* (Oxford, 1989); see below, chapter 3.

26. D. Defoe, *A Tour Through England and Wales* (London, 1962 edn), vol.1, 159, 168, 172; F. Opll, 'The Metropolis and its Hinterland: the Vienna Example (1600-1850)', (unpublished paper at the session on Metropolitan Cities and their Hinterlands at the International Economic History Congress, Leuven 1990); see below, chapter 8.

27. Clark and Slack, *English Towns*, p.62; *The Country Journal or the Craftsman*, 19 Feb. 1736/7; see below, chapter 7.

28. For the discussion see B. Hoeslitz, 'Generative and Parasitic Cities', *Economic Development and Cultural Change*, vol.3 (1954-5), 278-84; E.A. Wrigley, 'Parasite or Stimulus: The Town in a Pre-industrial Economy', in P. Abrams and E.A. Wrigley, eds, *Towns in Societies* (Cambridge, 1978), ch.12; and more recently *idem*, 'City and Country in the Past: a sharp divide or a continuum?', *Historical Research*, vol.54

(1991), 107-20.

29. P. Bairoch, *Tailles des villes. Conditions de vie et développement économique* (Paris, 1977), p.263; St Pierre, Abbé de, 'Avantages que doit produire l'agrandissement continuel de la ville capitale d'un Etat', in *Ouvrages de Politique*, vol.4 (Amsterdam, 1733), 102-164.

30. Beier and Finlay, *London*, pp.57-9; J. Landers, *Death in the Metropolis: Studies in the Demographic History of London 1670-1830* (Cambridge, 1993), pp.84, 178; P. Clark, ed., *European Crisis of the 1590s* (London, 1985), p.12; Benedict, *Cities*, p.24; Opll, 'Metropolis'.

31. Landers, *Death in the Metropolis*, esp. ch.3.

32. A. Lasseu, 'The Population of Denmark 1660-1960', *Scandinavian Economic History Review*, vol.14 (1966), 154; E.A. Wrigley, 'A Simple Model of London's Importance in Changing English Society and Economy 1650-1750', in Abrams and Wrigley, *Towns in Societies*, p.218; see below, chapter 2; A. Ferreira da Silva, 'Lisbon and its Hinterland in the 18th century' (unpublished paper at the session on Metropolitan Cities and their Hinterlands at the International Economic History Congress, Leuven, 1990).

33. Current work of the National Small Towns Project, Centre for Urban History, Leicester University; Söderberg et al., *Stagnating Metropolis*, pp.24-5; Clark and Souden, *Migration*, p.307; see below, chapter 2.

34. Wrigley, 'A Simple Model', in Abrams and Wrigley, *Towns in Societies*, pp.226-43; Ferreira da Silva, 'Lisbon'; J. Kudela, 'Prague and its Hinterland' (unpublished paper at the session on Metropolitan Cities and their Hinterlands at the International Economic History Conference, Leuven, 1990).

35. J. Delumeau, *Vie économique et sociale de Rome dans la seconde moitié du XVIième siècle* (Paris, 1957-9); see below, chapter 7.

36. J.M. Moriceau and G. Postel-Vinay, *Ferme, enterpris, famille. Grand exploitation et changement agricole, XVIIième-XIXième siècles* (Paris, 1992).

37. Ferreira da Silva, 'Lisbon'; J. Meuvret, *Etudes d'histoire économique* (Paris, 1971), pp.119-229.

38. P. Matthias, *The Brewing Industry in England 1700-1830* (Cambridge, 1959), esp. pp.21-7; Schwarz, *London*, ch.7; N. Raven, 'City and Countryside: London and the Market Town Economies of Southern England c. 1770-1856' (paper at the Economic History Conference, Nottingham University, 1994); *idem*, 'A Study of the Changes in the Occupational Structure of Four North Essex Towns 1700-1830' (Certificate dissertation, Centre for Urban History, Leicester University, 1990): Mr Raven is currently completing doctoral research on this subject at Leicester; P. Sharpe, 'De-industrialization and re-industrialization: women's employment and the changing character of Colchester 1700-1850', *Urban History*, vol.21 (1994), 81 *et seq.*; P. Clark, 'Small Towns in England 1550-1850: national and regional population trends', in *idem*, *Small Towns in Early Modern Europe* (Cambridge, 1995), p.118; Corfield, *Impact*, p.74; W.H. Crawford, 'The Evolution of Ulster Towns 1760-1850', in P. Roebuck, ed., *Plantation to Partition* (Belfast, 1981), pp.140-56.

39. B. Short, 'The de-industrialisation process: a case study of the Weald 1600-1850', in P. Hudson, ed., *Regions and Industries: a Perspective on*

the Industrial Revolution in Britain (Cambridge, 1989), pp.156-74.

40. Bater, *St Petersburg*, p.44; B. Blonde, 'Domestic demand and urbanisation in the 18th century: demographic and functional evidence for small towns of Brabant', in Clark, *Small Towns*, p.237; E. Pawson, *Transport and Economy* (London, 1977), pp.18-21, 136-8; see below, chapter 3.

41. J. Patten, *English Towns 1500-1700* (Folkestone, 1978), pp.109-10, 118; C. Chalklin, *The Provincial Towns of Georgian England* (London, 1974), pp.14, 20; Opll, 'Metropolis'; J. Dupâquier, *La Population rurale du Bassin Parisien à l'époque de Louis XIV* (Paris, 1979), pp.194-5; M. Reed, 'Cultural Role of Small Towns in England 1600-1800', in Clark, *Small Towns*, pp.129-32.

42. Dupâquier, *Population rurale*, p.194 *et passim*.

43. J. Brewer, *Party Ideology and Popular Politics at the Accession of George III* (Cambridge, 1976), p.149 *et passim*; A. Goodwin, *The Friends of Liberty: The English Democratic Movement in the Age of the French Revolution* (Cambridge, 1979); A. Forrest, *Society and Politics in Revolutionary Bordeaux* (Oxford, 1975); T. Margadant, *Urban Rivalries in the French Revolution* (Princeton, 1992).

44. Roche, *La France des Lumières*; Borsay, *English Urban Renaissance*; see below, chapter 7; Hohenberg and Lees, *Making*, p.151 *et seq.*

45. J. Barry, 'The Cultural Life of Bristol 1640-1775' (unpublished D.Phil thesis, Oxford Univ., 1985); *idem*, 'Bourgeois Collectivism? Urban Association and the Middling Sort', in J. Barry and C. Brooks, eds, *The Middling Sort of People: Culture, Society and Politics in England 1550-1800* (Basingstoke, 1994), ch.3; Clark, *The Rise of British Clubs*.

46. Cf. Petty, *Economic Writings*, vol.2, 530-2.

47. W. Beik, *Absolutism and Society in Seventeenth-Century France* (Cambridge, 1985), ch. 11.

48. A.L. Lavoisier, *De la richesse territoriale du royaume de France (1791)* (ed. J.C. Perrot, Paris, 1988).

49. G. Béaur, *Le Marché Foncier à la veille de la Révolution* (Paris, 1984), pp.11-30.

50. N. McKendrick et al., *The Birth of a Consumer Society* (London, 1982), esp. chs.1-2; J. Cruz, 'Elites, merchants and consumption in Madrid at the end of the Old Regime', in A.J. Schuurman and L.S. Walsh, eds, *Material Culture: Consumption, Life-style, Standard of Living 1500-1900* (Milan, 1994), pp.137-46; also ch. by E. Wohl, *ibid.*, pp.21-30; D. Roche, *The Culture of Clothing: Dress and Fashion in the 'Ancien Regime'* (Cambridge, 1994).

51. J.C. Perrot, *Genèse d'une ville moderne: Caen au XVIIIième siècle*, 2 vols (Paris, 1975).

52. P. Bourdieu and J.C. Passeron, *Reproduction in Education, Society and Culture* (London, 1970); see below, chapter 10.

53. Braudel, *Civilisation*, vol.2, 537 *et seq.*; L. Bergeron, *Banquiers, négociants et manufacturiers parisiens du Diréctoire à l'Empire* (Paris, 1978).

54. J. Hoock and B. Lepetit, eds, *La Ville et l'innovation. Relais et reseaux de diffusion en Europe, 14ième-19ième siècles* (Paris, 1987).

CHAPTER TWO

Urban Systems and Economic Growth: Town Populations in Metropolitan Hinterlands 1600-1850

Paul M. Hohenberg and Lynn Hollen Lees

The explosive growth of capital cities accounted for most of the net movement of people from countryside to towns in Europe during the seventeenth and eighteenth centuries. At a time when most cities stagnated in size, London and Paris by 1700 had reached the half million mark, while Madrid, Milan, Naples and Vienna each numbered over 100,000.

The long shadows cast by periodic wars, epidemics and famine seemed scarcely to reach these metropolises, the boom towns of the early modern period. Most of the capitals had by 1800, if not long before, become primate cities, settlements overly large in comparison to the sizes of lesser ranking cities within their region.[1] If rank-size distributions for the cities within the major states of western Europe are compared over time, most of them moved towards primacy by 1700.[2] Most strongly in England and Wales, but also in southern Italy, France, Portugal and Prussia after 1800, graphs of city populations according to their rank reveal the disproportionate size of capitals. This tendency toward urban primacy is all the more puzzling because it could be found within thriving economic systems, such as those of Britain and France, as well as economies in decline, for example, those of Spain and southern Italy. Capital cities could apparently sustain their growth in the early modern period, whatever the fortunes of the larger urban network within which they were located.

The mechanisms permitting this sustained growth force the historian's attention beyond the borders of the metropolis, which left alone could neither feed nor reproduce itself. Despite the imports provided by imperial ties and long-distance trade, cities relied heavily on nearby resources for people and food. Regional relationships were therefore central to the survival of the mega-cities of the early modern period. David Ringrose has provided a compelling analysis of the relationship between Madrid and the rest of Castile during the seventeenth and eighteenth centuries, showing how the demands of the capital for food, taxes and transport services so burdened the regional economy that its urban system declined. Madrid's landlocked location, combined with the deficiencies of local transportation and the power of its growing market, meant high grain prices and a stifling of demand for products other than basic foodstuffs and luxuries. Under these conditions the Spanish capital acted as a brake on local economic growth rather than a stimulus. Ringrose's explanation, which combines the use of central place theory and neo-classical economics with a good dose of geography, shows how urban growth was feasible even where it aggravated regional under-development.[3]

The case of capital cities within a thriving regional system has been given less attention. Using the case of London, E.A. Wrigley has argued forcefully for the stimulating effects of metropolitan growth on economic development, directing attention to demographic pressures and agricultural productivity. He has focused specifically, however, on national rather than regional exchanges.[4] More recently, George Grantham and Philip Hoffman have looked at the Paris region, focusing on its agricultural development, and Otto Büsch has mapped with some precision the economic geography of the territory around Berlin, each specifying some of the local exchanges that underlay metropolitan growth.[5] Although data on the precise local flows of goods, people and wealth are sparse, there is enough to help specify regional relationships in cases where capital cities apparently stimulated the growth of their hinterlands.

In this essay we will explore how large, northern European capitals sustained themselves between 1600 and 1850 and how their very size and expansion shaped the economies in which they were embedded. Our discussion will centre on two cities, London and Paris, although we will offer some data on Berlin and other capitals by way of comparison. While we emphasize the seventeenth and eighteenth centuries, we consider the early nineteenth century as well. Not only are more precise data on regional patterns of migration and local trade available for the end of our period, but in terms of economic development, the years between 1800 and 1850 deserve to be grouped with the earlier two centuries. The influence of railways and factory industry was minimal on the continent before 1850 and not advanced by that date even in the London region.

Paradoxes of metropolitan development

Capital cities in early modern Europe were closely tied through trade, administration, and migration into national networks of exchange and were becoming more integrated internationally. Yet their local linkages through a central place system of settlements were uneven, and in fact remain puzzling. We enumerate four paradoxes of development upon which our discussion will focus.

1. Metropolises exacted a heavy tribute from their surroundings in terms of goods, labour, and taxes; moreover, they appear to have provided relatively little by way of tangible exports to the region. Yet there is good evidence that the large cities exerted a strong positive stimulus on the surrounding economies, notably in agriculture.

2. Despite the intense economic activity within metropolitan hinterlands, and the high levels of population mobility triggered by growth of the capital and by active regional exchanges, the towns of these thriving agricultural regions remained small and showed little tendency to grow.

3. Students of urban systems attach significance to balance as an indicator of integration within the territory covered by the system. Yet early metropolitan regions combine strong evidence of integration with great imbalance in urban growth.

4. Rapid urban growth and great size make regular and heavy demands on the economic environment: for labour, materials, and capital for construction, as well as the subsistence of so many inhabitants. Yet the strong spurt of growth that gave rise to mega-cities often came early, while the sustaining improvements in agricultural productivity and regional integration were gradual.

In our discussion of these paradoxes we shall focus not only on population flows and agricultural progress, but also on two other sectors: transport and small-scale manufacturing. The first is quite clearly important, if only because transport costs help to define the region relevant to the support of the metropolis and set the limits to its sustainable size. The second relates to larger themes within our story: urban and regional employment, the composition of migrant streams, the relation between rural and urban production, and the major changes associated with proto-industrialization. We hope to show how, in developing European economies, metropolitan hinterlands were characterized by growing functional urbanization not reflected in the absolute size of local towns. Long before the era of automobile-triggered suburban sprawl, high mobility and decentralized specialization operated within metropolitan regions to advance the growth of giant-sized cities, which in turn intensified the development of their hinterlands.

Uneven growth in and around the metropolis

We begin with a look at population growth patterns within metropolitan regions. Table 2.1 sets out basic data on the sizes of European capitals and the principal towns in their regions between 1600 and 1850.[6] The row under each entry for a metropolis gives the percentage change in population between the prior date and the one for that column, with growth greater than 50 per cent in half a century shown in bold characters and declines in italics. While each city and region had its own special history of development, growth of capitals was generally faster in the seventeenth century than in the eighteenth, and it accelerated again after 1800. This is shown by the unweighted averages of growth rates for the nine capital cities given in the last row of the table. At the time when the growth rate of the northern European population was slowest, during the years 1650 to 1700, movement into the metropolis took place at a relatively strong pace. After 1700, when overall population growth rates accelerated, the relative amounts of migration into Paris, London, Berlin, Amsterdam, and Brussels slowed down.

Urban growth in metropolitan regions was concentrated in the capital cities. Metaphorically, one can speak of a great tree in whose shadow nothing grew. The extreme case was London and nearby counties, of course, where the largest towns reached only 2 to 3 per cent of the capital's size after 1600. Except for the urban systems of the Low Countries, which were multi-centred rather than headed by one multi-functional town, capital cities tended to be surrounded by small cities, rather than by large, competing centres. Paul Bairoch and Garry Goertz, who have analysed the demographic effects of big cities on nearby towns between 1500 and 1800 in Europe, argue that in any region, 'the presence of a large city puts a cap to possible growth'.[7] Beyond a distance of 30 to 40km, comprising a ring of suburban growth, a metropolis inhibits the creation of another city within a significant radius. In fact, they show that in Europe as a whole, the larger the central city the smaller the towns in its hinterland are likely to be. Distance too has a dampening effect on growth; they find that the nearer the subsidiary towns to a city over 100,000, the smaller their size. While capitals grew, nearby settlements remained relatively small. Capitals in expanding regions as well as those in decline exhibited this characteristic.

The growth of giant-sized cities exercised other distorting effects upon regional and national demographic patterns. In particular, the combination of high urban death rates with metropolitan expansion generated major migratory flows into the capitals. Wrigley has estimated that London's extraordinary population explosion in the late seventeenth and

Table 2.1 Selected Cities in Metropolitan Regions (estimated population in thousands)

Metropolis	City	1600	1650	1700	1750	1800	1850
Amsterdam		60	175	200	210	217	225
change, %			192	14	5	3	4
	Leiden	35	67	60	37	31	37
	The Hague	12	18	30	38	39	72
	Utrecht	25	30	30	25	32	48
Berlin		17	12	55	102	161	437
change, %			−29	358	85	58	171
	Magdeburg	40	5	10	18	36	72
	Frankfurt-a-O	13		9	9	13	31
	*Stettin	12	6	6	13	23	48
Brussels		50	69	80	59	66	132
change, %			38	30	−26	12	100
	*Antwerp	47	70	67	43	62	88
	Ghent	31	46	52	44	55	107
	Mechelen	11	20	20	18	20	30
	Mons	16	13	14	17	18	24
London		200	400	575	675	948	2236
change, %			100	44	17	40	136
	Colchester	8	10	10	9	12	19
	*Ipswich	4		8	10	11	33
	Oxford	5	9	8	8	12	29
	Reading			5	7	10	21
Madrid		57	130	125	135	168	281
change, %			128	−4	8	24	67
	Segovia	25	16	7	11	10	10
	Toledo	65	20	23	20	22	15
Milan		120	100	125	124	135	209
change, %			−17	25	−1	9	55
	Bergamo	24		25	27	24	24
	Brescia	36	25	35	30	32	41
	Cremona	36	15	22	24	23	31
	Piacenza	33	17	31	28	28	39

Table 2.1 concluded

Metropolis	City	1600	1650	1700	1750	1800	1850
Naples		275	176	258	322	430	409
change, %			−36	47	25	34	−5
	Avellino	3		8		11	13
	Benevento	7		8	10	14	16
	*Salerno	11		8	8	10	21
Paris		260	430	500	570	565	1053
change, %			65	16	14	−1	86
	Amiens	25	27	32	35	40	52
	Chartres			12	10	14	18
	Orléans	40		32	36	48	47
	*Rouen	65	82	64	66	80	101
Vienna		50	60	114	175	239	431
change, %			20	90	54	37	80
	Bratislava	9		10	25	28	42
	Brno	15	9	10	15	20	47
change, %, mean of nine metropolitan cities			51	69	20	24	77

Notes: When the two sources diverge, the table gives the average of the two estimates.
The chosen cities are the principal ones within 110km of the metropolis, 75km in the case of Brussels and Amsterdam.
*port city.

Sources: Paul Bairoch et al., *La Population des villes européennes de 800 à 1850* (Geneva, 1988); Jan de Vries, *European Urbanization, 1500-1800* (Cambridge, Mass., 1984).

early eighteenth centuries required the diversion to the capital of half the surplus births of England and Wales.[8]

During periods of modest total demographic increase, simply keeping a metropolitan population steady required the movement into it of a significant share of the net increase from rural areas. Using reasonable assumptions about average fertility and mortality rates, Jan de Vries has estimated the share of the rural surplus of births required to maintain the urban sector during the early modern period. Even before the accelerated urbanization of the later eighteenth century, in the century before 1750, the growing urban sector in both northern and southern Europe required the migration of at least 30 per cent of the surplus population born in the countryside. Because the absolute size of the rural population in northern Europe, according to de Vries's measurements, was significantly higher than that of southern Europe – in 1700-50, 56 million on average in comparison with 21 million – it is clear that northern cities had much more potential for growth.[9]

On average, urban populations were generally more mobile than rural. By 1650 the size and spatial organization of the urban sector in northwestern Europe brought significantly larger groups of people within easy migrating and trading distances of one another than in the south. Using measurements for size and for distance, de Vries has calculated and mapped an accessibility score for European towns at fifty-year intervals from 1500. While at that date Italian urban systems had the highest potential for interacting with large numbers of people, by 1600 northern areas around Paris and Amsterdam-London showed equivalent potential. By 1650 the area of the Low Countries, northern France and southwestern England had outstripped Mediterranean areas in the numbers of people living in towns within 20 km of one another. The urban sector and its marketing networks had become much more closely integrated.[10] It should not come as a surprise, therefore, that the largest capitals and the fastest metropolitan growth rates after 1600 are found in northern Europe. That area had a significantly larger population upon which cities could draw and a tighter urban network along which people could move in search of an urban residence. In a sense, the population that large Mediterranean cities managed to sustain, though less considerable, is even harder to account for.

Ultimately, the migration potential depended on rural surpluses, and here also northern capitals had a more mobile population on which to draw. English, Dutch and Scandinavian agricultural labourers had long been free, while legal changes during the era of the French Revolution and the Napoleonic period emancipated French, German and Austrian peasants from legal obligations to landlords. Spanish, south Italian and Hungarian peasants were still bound in quasi-servile relations, retarding their movement into the towns. Given the higher urban potentials of northwestern Europe and the relatively greater potential mobility of their rural populations, one would expect to find higher growth rates among the towns of northwestern Europe, which was in fact the case. Why, however, did migration in metropolitan hinterlands lead so strongly into the centre, rather than go to swell nearby towns? An exploration of migration paths is in order.

Migration into the metropolis

It is difficult to chart movement into the metropolis precisely, however, because few societies bothered to record the changing residences of their citizens, and even those that did generally lost track of the temporary movements of job-seeking servants and labourers. Censuses, applications for citizenship and marriage records have been used effectively to give glimpses of migratory flows, but each offers only a partial record of the vast numbers of people who moved in and out of early modern cities. Questions also arise regarding urban dwellers who lacked resident status and so might not be recorded. Discussions of migration, therefore, have to move from partial information to inferences about general patterns.

Standard accounts of migratory movements stress the step-by-step movement of people and the primacy of short-distance moves, especially among women, but this image of a regular, even flow of people does not fit well with the apparent stagnation of town populations within metropolitan hinterlands. Two considerations must be added. First, movement into capitals involved both long-distance migration and frequent shifts of residence by young, unsettled people. Second, there is the reality of rapid urban emigration; most towns within 100km of a capital were way-stations for many of their migrants. It is important to consider gross flows, as well as the net results. In sum, migration comprises many types of movement – temporary or seasonal as well as moves of longer duration – over a range of distances. Immigration into capitals exhibited in an exaggerated form tendencies observable also in smaller towns.

French demographers and historians have traced population movements in the Paris hinterland, and their combined efforts give a picture of the quantitative differences between moves into the capital and entries into other towns within the region. Within a radius of 110km of the French capital lay three major towns (Amiens, Orléans and Rouen), two medium-sized places (Chartres and Beauvais), plus around ten more with five to ten thousand inhabitants. Recent studies of migration in early modern France as a whole stress the relatively sedentary quality of the population, and the highly endogamous, stagnant populations of some towns.[11] For example, in Angers, a medium-sized town along the Loire, only 10 per cent of the females and 25 per cent of the males marrying during the eighteenth century were born outside the borders.[12] In contrast, along the Seine, west of Paris, about half of the people marrying in Meulan between 1740 and 1789 were not natives; most, however, were short-distance migrants. Only 11 per cent of the males and 6 per cent of the females had been born in places beyond the neighbouring departments.[13] Also, in Chartres and in Rouen about half of those marrying came from outside the town. Relatively high migration characterized towns in the Paris region, even though below the level of the capital.

For the larger places a good deal of that migration involved longer distances. Over 30 per cent of the immigrants dying in the Rouen hospital came from more than 80km distance, most of them from out- side Normandy.[14] Even more migrants flooded into Paris, and they came from longer distances. By 1790, a census of the Popincourt section showed that 67.9 per cent of the adults had been born outside the capital; large contingents came from the north and east while significant numbers represented the Massif Central, the Pyrenees, Corsica and Europe outside France.[15]

The towns of the Paris basin thus constituted a region of compara- tively high mobility, but one in which urban growth was largely confined during the seventeenth and eighteenth centuries to the capital. While Paris increased from 300,000 to 550,000 inhabitants, the small towns of the region registered only tiny gains, and Rouen, Amiens and Orléans grew by only a few thousand people between 1600 and 1800. Yet figures for net growth underestimate mobility because they miss the large volume of temporary movement and the regular emigration out of towns of all sizes. Bardet calculates that, during the later seventeenth and eighteenth centuries, 26 per cent of couples marrying in Rouen would leave the city before their deaths, and emigration was probably more likely for those who did not marry in the town.[16] Cities near the capital combined a high volume of migration with low growth through the medium of emigration, Paris serving as the central attraction in an asym- metric system of constant movement in and out. Abel Chatelain has estimated that one in six Parisians during the early nineteenth century was a temporary resident, many merely seasonal visitors.[17] The many roads out of the capital led masons back to the Creuse and Cantal, servants to Châteaudun, day labourers to the villages and fields of the Ile-de-France, apprentices to Beauvais and Amiens, infants to nurses in Meulan, merchants to Rouen or towns in the south west. Although these multiple movements into and out of towns cannot be quantified, they clearly were of great social and economic significance. Metropolitan regions were dynamic demographic systems in which even relatively static places played a role as way-stations and sometimes as destinations for those leaving capital cities.

Philip Benedict has re-examined and reworked data on the population of eighteenth-century France, and his findings shed light on regional patterns. In the generalities of Paris and Orléans, the lesser towns of 2–20,000 showed almost no growth (1 per cent) between 1700 and 1806, while urban population as a whole grew by 20 per cent and total population by 32 per cent.[18] The same pattern of change holds for the northern and eastern fringes of the Paris basin, the generalities of Amiens, Soissons and Châlons: smaller towns, 10 per cent increase; urban population as a whole, 15 per cent; total population, 20 per cent.

Behind these numbers, as we shall see, is a growing intensity of economic activity, above all in agriculture and related processing, trade and transport, along with sufficient urban functional strength to support the increased numbers of active population, since the metropolitan region shows no evidence of developing an underemployed or unemployed rural proletariat.

To picture migration systems adequately requires data on gross flows of population, as well as the net results. Unfortunately, the temporary, stepwise movements of people are virtually impossible to trace in surviving records. Emigration, far more than immigration, remains a little explored topic, as does the frequent temporary movement of servants and unskilled labourers. When multiple listings of inhabitants or registers of residents have survived, scholars can use them to trace patterns of entry and exit, as well as the turnover of population.[19] Recent research on mobility patterns in Castile also helps to chart the levels of migration obtaining in towns below the level of the national capital.

David Reher has traced both emigration and immigration during the 1840s for the town of Cuenca, a sleepy and small county capital, about 200km south east of Madrid. He calls it a place 'which had little to offer potential migrants and ... an excellent example of most Spanish towns on the central plateau'. While the stagnant population confirms Cuenca's lack of drawing power, annual in-migration averaged 14 per cent of the total population, and emigration averaged about 16 per cent. Although movement was heaviest among people aged 15 to 55, significant numbers of children and elderly folk also arrived there and periodically left. Migration involved people in all stages of the life cycle and family groups, as well as single workers. Female adolescents looking for work as servants flooded Cuenca, and then changed jobs or travelled to another place. Reher calculates that migration-related turnover among servants was more than 30 per cent per year! High rates of mobility concentrated in the lowest and highest status occupations; servants and day-labourers, professionals and administrators moved in and out of the town at significantly higher rates than did artisans or service workers.[20]

Cuenca, despite its small size, drew 25 to 40 per cent of its resident migrants from outside the province, including the territories centred on Toledo, Madrid and Ciudad Real, and Reher thinks that departing professionals 'may well have circulated among urban centres on the peninsula'.[21] Almost 2 per cent of Madrid's population in 1851 came from Cuenca province, so there were regular currents of in-migration to the capital from that town and its hinterland.[22] Cuenca also supplied wood and charcoal to the capital during the eighteenth century, and it lay on an overland route from Valencia to the capital. People as well as goods moved along this trail.

The examples of Paris and of Madrid both show that circulation within metropolitan urban systems involved much city-to-city migration, even when the net result was not growth. Both Zipf and Zelinsky regard large-scale inter-urban movements as a function of advanced industrial economies; their work and that of most scholars of migration under-estimates the extent of mobility between towns during earlier periods.[23] It is clear that a strong inter-urban network of migration was in place in metropolitan hinterlands by at least the seventeenth century. Consider the case of Berlin. During the later eighteenth century, approximately two-thirds of both the brides and the grooms marrying in two central Berlin parishes had been born in towns outside the capital. Not all were long-distance migrants, however. About one half of this group – thousands of servants, journeymen, clergymen and professionals – had moved to the capital from nearby towns with fewer than 3000 inhabitants.[24] In the more heavily urbanized Netherlands, migration between cities was also relatively high. Newcomers to Amsterdam from cities both in Holland and elsewhere in Europe made up 49 per cent of the immigrants into the capital in the eighteenth century.[25] Even in southern Italy, which had a much lower rate of urbanization, 17 per cent of the newcomers to Naples who married there during the later sixteenth century arrived from coastal towns in the south or from major centres of the Po valley.[26]

Inter-urban migration to capitals was intensified, of course, by the frequent political and economic upheavals of the early modern period. When Philip II moved the Spanish capital in the later sixteenth century, a host of courtiers, artisans and bureaucrats moved from Valladolid to Madrid.[27] Thousands of textile workers and other artisans left Toledo for the capital during the seventeenth century, after the economies of their home towns declined.[28] The expulsion of the Huguenots from France forced the exodus of a largely urban population to major Protestant cities all over Europe: Amsterdam, Dublin, London and Berlin were major beneficiaries. Dutch towns grew after Spanish attacks on Antwerp, and the economic woes of the smaller Brabantine cities in the later sixteenth and early seventeenth centuries sent migrants to Brussels as well as to towns outside the region.[29] The multiple political instabilities of early modern times, which were concentrated in the later sixteenth and early seventeenth centuries, set people in motion. Capital cities with their complex labour markets, numerous charities and large housing stock were favourite destinations.

In western and central European societies, however, migration is pre-dominantly a voluntary process, one in which individuals or families choose their route and area of settlement. Theorists of migration posit a fairly standard list of factors motivating and constraining their choices. Alongside village connections and kin networks, the larger structures of regional and national economies, in particular the size of cities, their distance from a migrant's place of origin, and the intervening opportunities between residence and possible destinations also intervene.[30] Capital cities clearly exercised an atypically strong pull on migrants over large areas, yet they were only one of many possible destinations, among them a nearby settlement or a metropolitan hinterland. We therefore need to relate population movements to the spatial patterns of economic activity around early modern capitals.

The economic geography of metropolitan regions

Diversity with local specialization came to characterize the economies of metropolitan hinterlands by the seventeenth century. In his tour of eastern England, Daniel Defoe noted the many different industries to be found just in Essex and Suffolk. He saw workers weaving says and bays, catching fish, outfitting ships, growing grain, raising cattle and poultry. Defoe remarked that in Essex, like the rest of the kingdom, 'as well the people as the land, and even the sea ... are employ'd to furnish ... the best of everything, to supply the city of London with provisions; ... corn, flesh, fish, butter, cheese, salt, fuel, timber, &c. and cloths also; with everything necessary for building, and furniture for their own use, or for trades'.[31] His *Tour*, first published in 1724 but also based on observations he made during the 1680s, describes a complex, regional economy centred on small towns, linked by roads and rivers to London. Small-scale industries flourished alongside specialized market-oriented agriculture.

In terms of the theory of urban systems, one would expect the growing density of population - clearly the case in the districts surrounding London and Paris - to increase the range of urban services offered in regional towns.[32] Two explanations can be offered that square the theory with the only modest growth in size of small towns during the period: functions could be added with an offsetting decline in the number of town residents employed in agriculture; or, improvements in transport and communication could extend the service reach of the capital and larger towns, as well as the penetration of goods from more distant proto-industrial areas. We can observe both processes at work in the metropolitan regions of western Europe.

Evidence that changes of the first sort were taking place in East Anglia is offered by John Patten. Using wills, lists of borough freemen and assorted census-like documents, Patten charted the changing occupations of town residents from 1500 to 1700. Even the smallest towns, with fewer than 500 people, increased the number of occupations practised, and one would expect the process to have continued after 1700. This increased economic complexity was not merely a function of growth: towns of any given size had on average more local specialities in 1700 than in 1500. Patten notes the expansion of distributive trades and of transportation, but only modest increases in manufacturing. The smallest market towns declined in favour of larger rivals, whose reach was extended by improvements in transportation and communication.[33]

Otto Büsch has documented the shift to services and away from manufactures for the towns of Brandenburg during the early nineteenth century, a time of rapid development and urbanization.[34] Even in Berlin and the larger towns of the region, the number of industrial workers, particularly in metals and textiles, failed to keep pace with population, while urban agricultural workers decreased absolutely. In fact, the substitution of more distant for local activity that affected certain types of manufactures in town and country could extend to certain services. Steven Kaplan's magisterial study of how Paris was provisioned in the eighteenth century notes that merchants and traders from the capital increasingly bypassed the organized grain markets of the region's towns to deal directly with producers or landlords.[35]

The fact that regional central places further specialized in services points to ongoing agricultural progress. The story of agriculture in metropolitan regions involves more than the supply of bread grains to the capital. Let us focus a moment on the Paris basin, whose physical setting was made for diversity. The land resembles a series of graduated, stacked bowls, whose surfaces appear as concentric rings of different soil types. No matter how strong the economic pressures to grow again, wooded areas and zones of natural meadows or rough pasture would remain. But local needs, as well as the Paris-dominated market, called for more than bread in any case. Draught animals played a major role in farming and transport, and land was needed to breed and rear as well as to rest them. There was demand for meat, milk products, wool, hay and oats. Suitable areas near Paris grew fruit, including wine grapes, in addition to garden crops.[36]

Since both industrialization and urbanization involve concentrations of people not engaged in food production, the productivity of agriculture with respect to land and labour has long been recognized as critical to both processes. Scholars have postulated and then searched for agricultural revolutions to parallel the big changes in population, settlement and manufacturing. While a transformation clearly took place in the long run, marked by the spread of convertible husbandry, its timing has proved elusive.[37]

One recent view holds that the principal growth of land yields in southern England came in the seventeenth rather than the eighteenth century, thus fitting in with the period of rapid growth for London.[38] Ann Kussmaul's work reinforces this conclusion. Using parish-level data for England on the changing seasonality of marriages, she posits major shifts in regional patterns of agricultural and industrial specialization by the period 1661–1740.[39] In France, on the other hand, the evidence relegates the full triumph of the new agriculture well into the nineteenth century, even in the favoured Paris basin. Yet productivity grew there during the *ancien régime* as well, as recent work by Philip Hoffman indicates.[40] The growth was secular and gradual, though not steady, and Hoffman sees the Paris market as the stimulus as well as the beneficiary. The positive urban influence looms even larger in George Grantham's cross-sectional study, based on data from the 1852 agricultural census.[41] As in earlier centuries, nearness to Paris contributed to measured productivity, as did access to markets generally. Aside from the pure economic stimulus of more favourable producer prices, agriculture near towns received direct inputs in the form of manure and harvest-time labour.

However central the food supply to the metropolitan region's economy, other products, including those whose production generated employment in small-scale enterprises, were no less so. Note the particular importance of wood. Its uses were endless, and the demand for fuel insatiable. If one recalls that aristocrats' game preserves and parkland took up considerable space in the region, the share of woodland must indeed have remained large, and the labour devoted to its management no less so. With so many structures, vehicles and objects made of wood, sawmills and woodwrights' shops must have been among the most common non-agricultural businesses, and artisans working in wood particularly numerous.[42] But other resources vital to the city also occupied manufacturing workers in the surrounding area: clay, sand and stone were worked, while rags collected in the towns helped locate papermaking nearby.[43] However strong the pull of agriculture or urban work on the labour market, compelling locational factors kept certain industrial activities in the metropolitan region. Nevertheless, the economic evolution of the regional economy acted to displace traditional craft activities from the capital, the surrounding towns and the villages and farms. Economic maturation meant a growing call on producers outside the region to supply ordinary manufactures.

It is clear that by the eighteenth century, manufacturing had become concentrated in proto-industrial regions outside the direct metropolitan hinterlands.[44] Paris was surrounded, but at a distance, by districts of high manufacturing activity. Wool was worked in the plains of the

Beauvaisis and Picardy to the north, as well as in Lower Normandy to the west and near Reims and Sedan to the east. Linen production was scattered through the west, while cotton became important around Rouen in the eighteenth century. As the old cloth regions in the north in Flanders and Artois gained new strength, the plains around Amiens gradually shifted to agriculture. The German situation was somewhat similar, with the difference that the plains around Berlin had no great manufacturing tradition, either urban or rural. Some distance away, however, were flourishing concentrations: in Saxony and the Harz and farther away in Silesia, Westphalia and Bohemia. In England, production of various types of woollen and linen cloth expanded unevenly during the seventeenth and eighteenth centuries in eastern counties, although there were changes in the local geography of production.[45] In the longer run, however, textile production in Essex and Suffolk also declined with the advance of Yorkshire districts. Signs of de-industrialization can be seen in specific parishes of the south east by the period 1661–1740. Ann Kussmaul notes that early industry in England 'lacked locational stability', and she has charted some of the complex transitions that took place in the London region.[46] In the Weald, an active proto-industrial area just south of the capital in Kent, Surrey and Sussex, iron, cloth and glass industries started to collapse in the later seventeenth century and were 'quite dead' by 1820.[47]

We often forget how much manufacturing large cities housed, although some royal manufactures of the absolutist period are neither gone nor forgotten. In the period that concerns us, this sector changed character more than it either grew or shrank, unlike the situation in smaller regional towns, where industrial decline was rather the rule. The transformation in the capital emphasized skill and quality at the expense of more ordinary goods for mass markets. Paris and London dominated the new clock and watch trades, rivalled only by Geneva, while London's silk and shoe industries atrophied in favour of provincial centres.[48] Berlin, on the other hand, appears at first glance an exception. The younger metropolis housed a thriving woollen industry in the first third of the eighteenth century, but this activity owed its existence directly to royal backing, notably a captive market for military uniforms.[49] Soon the production of ordinary cloth gave way to such finer goods as silk and printed calicos.

The economic growth within metropolitan hinterlands during the early modern period was compatible with the relocation of much industrial production to more distant regions. Agriculture, food processing, the production of building materials and transportation proved more solid bases for regional prosperity. They attracted and held certain types of workers, but were not major stimuli to migration and higher fertility as were textiles and metals, the major proto-industrial trades and leading sectors in factory-based industrialization.

Over the longer run, the growing economic specialization of regions ought to have shifted migration patterns by artisans toward industrializing districts and away from the capital and its hinterland. Fragmentary evidence suggests that this was indeed the case. When metropolitan populations around 1800 or 1850 are compared to those of a century earlier, they contain fewer males, fewer long-distance migrants and fewer artisans. Migration fields shifted along with the location of proto-industrial districts. Movement into the capitals became more heavily female over time. By 1850, more women than men lived in several European capitals. London had an excess of females as early as the 1730s, while Paris made this change around 1800.[50] This shift to a female majority seems to have happened earlier in the largest, most dynamic capitals than in the smaller, slower-growing ones, such as Madrid and Naples.[51] Moreover, in London, a sharp decrease in the proportion of apprentices residing in the City took place between 1600 and 1700, and far fewer travelled to the metropolis from the north of England. In the eighteenth century, as Peter Clark has argued, migration into nearby towns replaced much long-distance movement.[52] Diederiks's research on Amsterdam shows somewhat similar results. Around 1800 the proportion of migrants with industrial occupations dropped; fewer newcomers arrived from Scandinavia and most other parts of Europe. During the eighteenth century, Amsterdam's migration field contracted in the north and the south, while it expanded to the east.[53]

The demographic expansion of capital cities shifted in character in response to the changing economic geography of proto-industrialization.

Transportation in the London and Paris regions

The economies of flourishing metropolitan regions had a strong basis in relatively advanced transportation systems. When compared to other parts of England and France, the hinterlands of London and Paris supported more elaborate and better maintained road networks. Moreover, their riverine sites brought both easy access by water and a comparatively flat, easily traversed terrain.

In the case of London a relatively sophisticated network for land transportation can be documented from an early date. Not only was London tied to the main provincial towns by Roman roads, but the Highway Act of 1555 made each parish responsible for keeping routes servicing markets in good repair. John Ogilby published a survey of British roads in 1675 and noted 11 main highways out of London complemented by an extensive system of crossroads.[54] By the 1720s several new turnpikes had been built within 40 miles of the capital, and the number continued to multiply. Aldcroft judges that up until 1750 turnpike development mainly centred on London in order to link the capital to provincial towns.[55] The British road system of the mid-eighteenth century impressed both native and foreign travellers, who noted not only good quality but rapid improvement. Henry Homer gave high praise during the 1760s in his *Enquiry into the Means of Preserving and Improving the Publick Roads*: 'There never was a more astonishing revolution accomplished in the internal system of any country. The carriage of grain, coals, merchandize, etc. is in general conducted with little more than half the number of horses which it formerly was ... Everything wears the face of dispatch and the hinge which has guided all these movements ... is the reformation which has been made in our publick roads.'[56]

The relative ease and speed of land transport in the London region was supplemented by an improved network of waterways. Even before the canal-building manias of the period 1790–1830, southern rivers had been dredged, straightened and provided with flashlocks and later poundlocks to regulate water levels, and with towpaths to ease barge traffic. These improvements made the Thames navigable as far upstream as Oxford by the early seventeenth century, and they facilitated transport on two tributaries of the Thames, the Lea and the Wey. London's access by water dramatically expanded with construction of the Thames-Severn canal in the 1780s and the Grand Junction Canal completed in 1805. By the early nineteenth century goods could be sent to the capital via river from virtually anywhere in the country.[57]

The lure of the London market had driven much of this investment in inland transport, so the results were not surprising: a rapidly increasing volume of people and goods moving by land, sea and river into the capital. John Chartres and Gerard Turnbull have documented dramatic growth in passenger traffic into London, which by 1715 was also linked by about 800 stagecoach trips per week to other towns. During the next century, they estimate, passenger miles travelled between London and 37 major towns expanded by a factor of 30. At the same time, road transport services for both long and short hauls were well developed, particularly in the London region. Not only did a large range of cart and caravan services function within the Home Counties, but the amounts of goods carried mushroomed during the eighteenth and early nineteenth centuries.[58]

The Paris region was also relatively well endowed with roads and waterways. Using a government inventory of French roads published in 1824, Bernard Lepetit has compared the transportation network of the

various French regions. Not surprisingly, the Seine and adjoining departments had the highest density of roads, as well as the highest proportions
of paved highways.[59] More royal roads linking the major towns had
been built in the north than in other regions of the country, and water
transport was relatively well developed there too. The French government had lavished money on road building during the eighteenth
century and had extended to the entire country the obligation of male
citizens to give free labour annually to the roads in their district.
Although maintenance programmes languished, many new routes were
constructed, particularly in the north. Arthur Young, after making his
way along major highways in northern France during the 1780s, said
nice things about their condition, although he noted how much less
traffic they carried than those in the south of England. While other
contemporary commentators complained about poor maintenance,
scholars agree that the road network had improved during the eighteenth
century.[60] Although linkages between regions were weak, within regions
and around the major cities relatively dense transportation systems had
developed, and all were tied to Paris.[61]

It seems sensible to argue that in both the Paris and London regions
during the eighteenth century transportation increased in speed as well
as in reliability and probably became cheaper at the same time. Although
Szostak argues that these shifts were much more marked in England, the
evidence for improved transportation within both countries is clear, and
it therefore should have had similar effects.[62]

One can infer the economic consequences within the London and Paris
hinterlands: farmers as well as manufacturers should have found that
their markets widened simply because of the new ease of transportation,
thereby encouraging them to expand production. Food and raw
materials became easier and cheaper to obtain, easing supply problems
for both consumers and producers. With improved transportation, however, it was also easier for merchants to bypass local, smaller markets,
which lost out in favour of larger, better-located central places. Increased
competition from proto-industrial centres at a distance was felt by small
producers. Adam Smith's formula - growth via specialization - applied
also to the wealth of regions. Szostak links improved transportation to
pressures for industrialization within England; the case he develops may
well be expanded to apply to France and to include the agricultural
sector, which also benefited from faster and cheaper transport.[63]

The effect of local transportation systems within the hinterlands of
Paris and London therefore contrasted sharply with the situation
described by Ringrose for the hinterland of Madrid, where the capital
drained Castile of resources, providing little in return.[64] Lacking usable
rivers or good roads, Castile relied on pack animals despite the scarcity

of fodder. By contrast, the needs of London and Paris for people, food and commodities were complemented by the needs of a flourishing hinterland. Transportation provided the intra-regional linkages that kept flows of commodities and people in motion, enriching the entire system.

Intra-regional exchanges in metropolitan hinterlands

We have seen that metropolitan regions provided support for capital cities that went beyond the basic commodities and people needed to insure material viability. Skilled and semi-skilled workers provided services and diverse manufactured goods for local residents, including the gentry who lived variably in town and in the country. They also staffed a great variety of secondary activities, from paper and brick-making to diverse cottage occupations, whose output reached the metropolis. While these activities did not disappear over time, despite the intensification of agriculture, transport and other services, they did give way in many cases to goods from other, more concentrated locations. As large-scale proto-industrial production grew in areas chiefly to the north of Paris and London, the manufacture of textiles and iron within the region became unprofitable. In contrast, the growing metropolitan population with its insatiable demands for housing, fuel and food offered a strong market for specialized agricultural products and building materials. The result was a growing absorption of labour into activities such as horticulture, animal husbandry, brewing, milling, wood and stonecutting, tanning and hauling. Hundreds of small forms of production designed for the capital flourished in the smaller towns and villages of the metropolitan hinterland.

A mature metropolitan regional system fitting north-west Europe in the early modern period can be represented in stylized form by a variant of the von Thünen model, which we have drawn in Figure 2.1.[65] The zone nearest the city (II) houses intensive agricultural production and other activities requiring easy access, including the court or palace and aristocratic estates. Good road transport facilitated frequent travel between the centre and nearby satellite towns. The second ring (III) provides primary sources of grain and wood; these areas maintained relatively high productivity and full commercialization. Exchanges of animals and manure with the city contributed significantly to the local economy, for which low transport costs were of central importance. This zone would tend to export servants and import agricultural labourers, and its towns would remain modest in size although sophisticated in service functions. While pockets of industrial activity persisted, any proto-industry on a larger scale would be the exception. In the next more

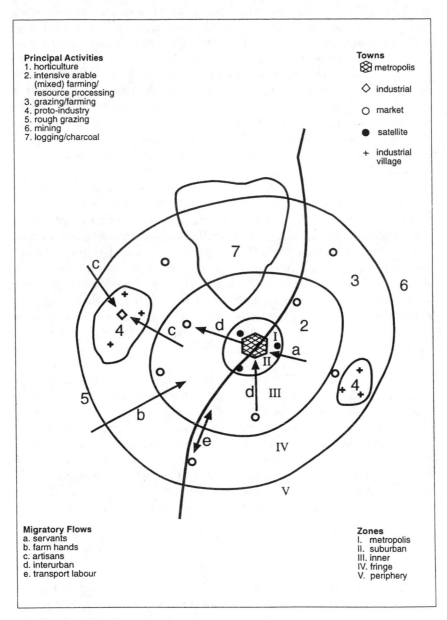

Principal Activities
1. horticulture
2. intensive arable
   (mixed) farming/
   resource processing
3. grazing/farming
4. proto-industry
5. rough grazing
6. mining
7. logging/charcoal

Towns
⊗ metropolis
◇ industrial
○ market
● satellite
+ industrial
   village

Migratory Flows
a. servants
b. farm hands
c. artisans
d. interurban
e. transport labour

Zones
I. metropolis
II. suburban
III. inner
IV. fringe
V. periphery

2.1   The metropolitan regional system

distant ring (IV), at the edge or even beyond the metropolitan region as we have defined it, the economy depends upon more extensive farming and grazing. Here proto-industrial concentrations and manufacturing towns appear. The towns are correspondingly larger than in rings II and III and more migrant workers came to them from remote upland districts. In this territory, towns competed with the metropolis for grain surpluses as well as artisans. Beyond the rings of metropolitan influence lie the poor uplands of the periphery (V), which continued a long tradition of exporting people, for example carters, rivermen and construction workers, as well as seasonal field hands. Their destinations could be either the metropolis, towns of the outer ring or the large farms within the capital's region.

This static model can be placed in motion by considering the direction of migratory flows over historic time. The continued growth of the capital drew servants from suburban settlements and other more distant points in zones II and III. Unskilled workers moved into the capital from these same territories, as well as from the upland regions of the periphery, to take up service jobs and work in construction. In contrast, migration into the capital by people of at least middling status originated in nearby towns and in major cities outside the region. Agricultural workers moved within the outer rings to the more specialized farming jobs in zones II and III, while growing numbers of service workers and craftsmen remained outside the metropolis to fill the growing demand in transportation and small-scale manufacturing. Intensive economic development, located in proto-industrial regions in zone IV and beyond, lured artisans away from migratory paths into the centre toward the growing industrial villages and towns. As a result, migrating craftsmen became less prominent in metropolitan labour forces while service workers and servants became relatively more plentiful. Sex ratios in the capitals shifted to clear female dominance. This rearrangement of migratory flows signalled the growth of metropolitan service industries at the expense of basic manufacturing, which was becoming more concentrated in proto-industrial regions.

Conclusion

In contrast to the deadening effect Madrid exerted on its hinterland, London and Paris formed the centres of thriving zones of mixed agricultural production and small-scale or material-producing manufacturing. With the metropolis nearby to provide an inexhaustible market, and with agricultural productivity rising, producers had growing incomes to spend on a variety of goods. Local towns became more functionally diverse over time, as demand rose for services and consumption goods. At the same time, improving transportation systems eased the movement of people, products and information that were necessary to support the array of interlocking central places. Although the strong pull of the capital meant that London and Paris captured the lion's share of permanent settlers, high levels of temporary migration and emigration meant that all of the towns experienced high rates of population turnover. While the growth of capital cities exerted pressure for continued urbanization, nearby towns became more functionally urbanized over time. During the seventeenth and eighteenth centuries, their local economies, as well as their links to local systems of distribution and exchange, became more sophisticated and specialized. The stagnation of their population counts is a poor guide to the dynamism of their economies. Within the hinterlands of Paris and London at least, a purely demographic standard for urbanization misses the many signs of economic vitality that underlay these metropolitan regions. Finally, we can fully grasp the regional dynamic only by including in our representation the proto-industrial nebulae growing at the fringes of the capital's hinterland and beyond.

Notes

1. Many theorists of city size distributions assume that the pattern of sizes in a developed, well-integrated economy would, when graphed on a logarithmic scale, conform to a lognormal distribution with a slope of -1. The rank-size rule, in which the populations of major cities are related proportionally to their rank in the urban systems, defines the standard against which primacy is measured. See G.K. Zipf, *Human Behaviour and the Principle of Least Effort* (Cambridge, Mass., 1949); B.J.L. Berry and F.E. Horton, *Geographic Perspectives on Urban Systems* (Englewood Cliffs, New Jersey, 1970); C.A. Smith, ed., *Regional Analysis*, 2 vols (New York, 1976).
2. J. de Vries, *European Urbanization 1500–1800* (Cambridge, Mass., 1984), pp.109–14, 119.
3. D.R. Ringrose, *Madrid and the Spanish Economy 1560–1850* (Berkeley, 1983); *idem* 'Towns, Transport and Crown: Geography and the Decline of Spain', in E.D. Genovese and L. Hochberg, eds, *Geographic Perspectives in History* (Oxford, 1989), pp.57–80.
4. E.A. Wrigley, 'A Simple Model of London's Importance in Changing English Society and Economy, 1650–1750', in P. Abrams and E.A. Wrigley, eds, *Towns in Societies* (Cambridge, 1978), pp. 215–44; *idem*, 'Brake or Accelerator? Urban Growth and Population Growth before the Industrial Revolution', in A. van der Woude et al., eds, *Urbanization and History: A Process of Dynamic Interaction* (Oxford, 1990), pp.101–12.
5. G. Grantham, 'Agricultural Supply during the Industrial Revolution: French Evidence and European Implications', *Journal of Economic*

History, vol.49 (1989), 43–72; P.T. Hoffman, 'Land Rents and Agricultural Productivity: The Paris Basin, 1450–1789', *Journal of Economic History*, vol.51 (1991), 771–805; O. Büsch, *Industrialisierung und Gewerbe im Raum Berlin/Brandenburg*, 2 vols (Berlin, 1971, 1977).

6. We are including Amsterdam in this list because of its size, political importance and dominant position in the Netherlands. While not technically a political capital, it played the role in the Netherlands of the principal city. For this list, regions have been defined by qualitative geographic criteria so as to minimize the presence of large urban centres with weak ties to the capital while including as substantial a share of the hinterland as possible. Except for the cases of Amsterdam and Brussels, hinterlands have a radius of approximately 110km; for capitals in the Low Countries we used a radius of 75km.

7. P. Bairoch and G. Goertz, 'A Note on the Impact of Large Cities on the Surrounding Cities, Europe 1500–1800', in E. Aerts and P. Clark, eds, *Metropolitan Cities and their Hinterlands in Early Modern Europe*, (Leuven, 1990), pp.48–57.

8. Wrigley, 'A Simple Model', p.218.

9. De Vries, *European Urbanization*, pp.203, 208.

10. *Ibid.*, pp.160–5.

11. J. Dupâquier, ed., *Histoire de la population française* (Paris, 1988) vols 2 and 3.

12. E. Le Roy Ladurie, ed., *La ville classique de la Renaissance aux Révolutions* (Paris, 1981), p.307.

13. M. Lachiver, *La Population de Meulan du XVIIe au XIXe siècle* (Paris, 1969), p.93.

14. M. Vovelle, *Ville et campagne au 18e siècle* (Paris, 1980), p.28; J.-P. Bardet, *Rouen aux XVIIe et XVIIIe siècles* (Paris, 1983), vol.1, 211, 213.

15. L. Bergeron et al., *Contributions à l'histoire démographique de la Révolution Française: Etudes sur la population française* (Paris, 1970), pp.49–55.

16. Bardet, *Rouen*, p.216.

17. A. Chatelain, *Les Migrants temporaires en France de 1800 à 1914*, 2 vols (Lille, 1976), vol.1, 565.

18. P. Benedict, 'Was the Eighteenth Century an Era of Urbanization in France?', *Journal of Interdisciplinary History*, vol.21 (1990–91), 207.

19. A. Perrenoud, *La Population de Genève, XVIe–XIX siècles* (Genève, 1979); J.-C. Perrot, *Genèse d'une ville moderne: Caen au XVIIIe siècle*, 2 vols (Paris, 1975).

20. D.S. Reher, 'Mobility and Migration in Pre-industrial Urban Areas: the Case of Nineteenth-Century Cuenca', in Van der Woude et al., eds, *Urbanization and History*, pp.168, 170–1, 185; *idem*, *Town and Country in Pre-Industrial Spain: Cuenca, 1550–1870* (Cambridge, 1990), p.257.

21. Reher, *Town and Country*, pp.262, 265.

22. Ringrose, *Madrid*, p.52.

23. Zipf, *Human Behaviour*; W. Zelinsky, 'The Hypothesis of a Mobility Transition', *The Geographical Review*, vol.61 (1971), 219–49.

24. H. Schultz, 'Land-Stadt-Wanderung im Manufakturzeitalter: das Beispiel Berlin', *Jahrbuch für Geschichte des Feudalismus*, vol.6 (1987), 281–2; see also *idem*, 'Bewegung und Entwicklung: demographische Prozesse in Städten des Spätfeudalismus', *Jahrbuch für Wirtschaftsgeschichte*, vol.3 (1988), 91–133.

25. H. Diederiks, *Een Stad in Verval: Amsterdam omstreeks 1800* (Amsterdam, 1982), p.120.
26. C. Petraccone, *Napoli dal Cinquecento all'Ottocento* (Naples, 1974), pp.114–19.
27. B. Bennassar, *Valladolid au siècle d'or: une ville de Castille et sa campagne au XVIe siècle* (Paris, 1967).
28. Ringrose, *Madrid*, p.57.
29. H. van der Wee, ed., *The Rise and Decline of Urban Industries in Italy and the Low Countries (Late Middle Ages-Early Modern Times)* (Leuven, 1988), p.278.
30. E.S. Lee, 'A Theory of Migration', *Demography*, vol.3 (1966), 47–57; R.N. Thomas and J.M. Hunter, eds, *Internal Migration Systems in the Developing World; with special reference to Latin America* (Boston, 1980).
31. D. Defoe, *A Tour Through the Whole Island of Great Britain* (Harmondsworth, 1971), p.54. More recent discussions of regional systems in England can be found in E.A. Wrigley, 'City and Country in the past: a sharp divide or a continuum?', *Historical Research*, vol.64 (1991), 107–20 and in J.A. Chartres, 'City and Town: forms and economic change in the eighteenth century', *ibid.*, 138–55.
32. H. Carter, *The Study of Urban Geography*, second edn (London, 1976), p.124.
33. J. Patten, *English Towns, 1500–1700* (Folkestone, 1978), pp.276–90.
34. Büsch, *Industrialisierung*.
35. S.L. Kaplan, *Provisioning Paris: Merchants and Millers in the Grain and Flour Trade during the Eighteenth Century* (Ithaca, N.Y., 1984).
36. A. Young, *Travels in France* (London, 1792), p.7.
37. We define convertible husbandry as the production of sustainable yields of grain sufficient to generate a good-sized surplus, coupled with the rearing of enough animals to work the land and to keep up soil fertility. Fodder crops are a key component, improving the soil as they grow and again when returned as manure.
38. R.C. Allen, 'The Growth of Labor Productivity in Early Modern English Agriculture', *Explorations in Economic History*, vol.25 (1988), 117–46.
39. A. Kussmaul, *A General View of the Rural Economy of England, 1538–1840* (Cambridge, 1990).
40. Hoffman, 'Land Rents'.
41. Grantham, 'Agricultural Supply'.
42. Van der Woude, *Urbanization and History*, p.8; evidence on this point is clear for the Berlin region. See Büsch, *Industrialisierung*, vol.1, 195.
43. The liveliness of these crafts in the south east of England is documented by Patten, *English Towns*, p. 169 and for Berkshire in M. Reed, ed., *English Towns in Decline* (Leicester, Centre for Urban History, 1986; Centre Working Paper no.1).
44. Proto-industrialization remains a controversial concept, one that has been heavily criticized; see for example D.C. Coleman, 'Proto-Industrialization: A Concept Too Many?', *Economic History Review*, 2nd Series, vol.36 (1983), 435–48. It has been used effectively in L.A. Clarkson, *Proto-Industrialization: The First Phase of Industrialization?* (London, 1985) and M. Gutmann, *Toward the Modern Economy: Early Industry in Europe, 1500–1800* (New York, 1988).

45. N. Evans, *The East Anglian Linen Industry: Rural Industry and Local Economy, 1500–1850* (Aldershot, 1985), p.128.
46. Kussmaul, *General View*, pp.127, 133.
47. B. Short, 'The de-industrialization process: a case study of the Weald, 1600–1850', in P. Hudson, ed., *Regions and Industries: A Perspective on the Industrial Revolution in Britain* (Cambridge, 1989), p.164.
48. D.S. Landes, *Revolution in Time* (Cambridge, Mass., 1983); D.R. Green, 'A Map for Mayhew's London: The Geography of Poverty in the Mid-Nineteenth Century', *The London Journal*, vol.11, (1985), 115–26; Henry Mayhew, *London Labour and the London Poor*, 4 vols (London, 1861–2 and New York, 1968).
49. L. Demps et al., *Geschichte Berlins von den Anfangen bis 1945* (Berlin, 1987).
50. R. Mols, *Introduction à la démographie historique des villes d'Europe du 14e au 18e siècle* (Gembloux, Belgium, 1954–6); R. Finlay, *Population and Metropolis: The Demography of London, 1580–1650* (Cambridge, 1981), p.142; Bergeron, *Contributions*, p.113.
51. Ringrose, *Madrid*, p.56; S. Martuscelli, *La Popolazione del Mezzogiorno nella Statistica di re Murat* (Naples, 1979), p.lxvi.
52. Finlay, *Population and Metropolis*; P. Clark and D. Souden, eds, *Migration and Society in Early Modern England* (London, 1987), p.270.
53. Diederiks, *Een Stad in Verval*, pp.129, 132.
54. H.J. Dyos and D.H. Aldcroft, *British Transport: An Economic Survey from the Seventeenth Century to the Twentieth* (Leicester, 1971), pp.30–2.
55. D.H. Aldcroft and M.J. Freeman, eds, *Transportation in the Industrial Revolution* (Manchester, 1983), p.41.
56. Quoted in Dyos and Aldcroft, *British Transport*, p.70.
57. *Ibid.*, pp.40–1, 105.
58. J.A. Chartres and G.L. Turnbull, 'Road Transport', in Aldcroft and Freeman, *Transportation*, pp.67–9, 85.
59. B. Lepetit, *Chemins de terre et voies d'eau: réseaux de transports, organisation de l'espace en France 1740–1840* (Paris, 1984), pp.53, 65.
60. Arthur Young, *Travels in France*; R. Szostak, *The Role of Transportation in the Industrial Revolution: A Comparison of England and France* (Montreal, 1991), pp.63–7.
61. B. Lepetit, *Les villes dans la France moderne (1740–1840)* (Paris, 1988), p.287.
62. Szostak, *Role of Transportation*, pp.68–72, 76–8.
63. *Ibid.*, pp.10–11.
64. Ringrose, *Madrid*.
65. J.H. von Thünen, *The Isolated State* (Oxford, 1966).

CHAPTER THREE

London and its Hinterland 1600–1800: the View from the Provinces

Michael Reed

The role and function of metropolitan cities have long been defined and appreciated. Alexandre le Maitre in *La Metropolitée ou de l'Establissement des villes capitales*, published in Amsterdam in 1682, gave three functions to metropolitan cities. They are the throne of the sovereign. They are the essential pivot in the mechanisms of exchange which for him were the essentials of urbanism, and they are the one place wherein is concentrated the glory, 'la valeur et la force d'un pays'.[1]

French kings from Henri IV onwards attempted to remodel Paris into the ideal capital city, from the planning of the Place Dauphine and the Place Royale to the development of the axis of the Champs Elysées, which reached the Butte de Chaillot in 1724 and the pont de Neuilly by 1772, by which time the northern fortifications had been demolished and the *grands boulevards* laid out.[2] In London, by contrast, the one great opportunity to replan the city, presented by the Great Fire of 1666, was allowed to slip by, not least for purely practical reasons: some 200,000 people had been made homeless by the fire and business was seriously disrupted. Squares, avenues and vistas in London depended for their conception and construction upon private builders and property owners, who were often constrained in their ideas by the amount of land which they owned or controlled, rather than upon state or crown direction. The last real opportunity for royal building upon the grand scale before the days of John Nash was lost when fire destroyed the ancient palace of Westminster in 1698. The site was quickly let off in small plots, and Wren's schemes for a royal palace came to nothing.[3]

If London lacked the monumentality and the architectural grandeur befitting 'la valeur et la force d'un pays', the last of Le Maitre's three roles of a metropolitan city, it more than made up for it by the key role it played across almost every facet of the economy and society of England in the other two, namely as the throne of the sovereign and as the central pivot in the mechanisms of exchange.

The role of London

London has always been by far and away the largest city in England.
According to Roger Finlay and Beatrice Shearer, in 1600 its population
was perhaps 200,000, and a little under 500,000 by 1700. By 1750 it
had reached 700,000 and by 1801 900,000.[4] No other town in England
has ever been able to approach it in sheer size. By 1700 it almost
certainly contained a tenth of the total population of England and before
1800 it was always at least ten times larger than the next English town.
All other English towns before the nineteenth century were small by
continental standards. Indeed, at least one commentator writing early in
the seventeenth century seriously suggested that England possessed only
one city, and that was London.[5] In 1700 only two English towns had
more than 20,000 inhabitants and these were Bristol and Norwich. By
1801 there were 15, but much of this growth had taken place after
1760 in towns in the midlands, south Lancashire and the West Riding of
Yorkshire. The nearest to London was Portsmouth, about sixty miles
away, and three more, Norwich, Bath and Birmingham, were each about
a hundred miles away. At the same time there were 29 towns of between
ten and twenty thousand inhabitants. Only three of these, Chatham,
Greenwich and Reading, lay within fifty miles of London, whilst a
further eight lay within a hundred miles. In other words, London in 1800
appears to be surrounded by a broad hinterland almost completely
devoid of large towns (see Figure 3.1). But this is an optical illusion, the
result of special factors making for the mushroom growth of the industrial towns of the north, an illusion heightened by the tendency of
economic historians to overlook the very substantial contributions of
small towns in general and those in the southeastern quarter of England
in particular to the economy of the seventeenth and eighteenth centuries.

London must be given a much wider meaning than just the old City of
London.[6] It was not a unified city but a series of *quartiers*. To the east
lay rapidly growing suburbs such as Wapping, Shadwell and Limehouse,
inhabited by those linked directly or indirectly to the sea, whether as
mariners or masters, manufacturers of ships' tackle, masts, spars, ropes
and cordage, as ship builders, or as processors of imported raw
materials such as sugar.[7] In 1700 three-quarters of England's overseas
trade passed through the Port of London and nearly half of all English
merchant shipping was registered there. By 1772 the proportion of
English overseas trade passing through London had fallen to two-thirds
of the total, but, and this in spite of the growth of Bristol, Liverpool and
Whitehaven, twice the trade of all the outports combined still passed
through London.[8] The City itself still had a large manufacturing
community, but was developing rapidly as a financial, commercial and

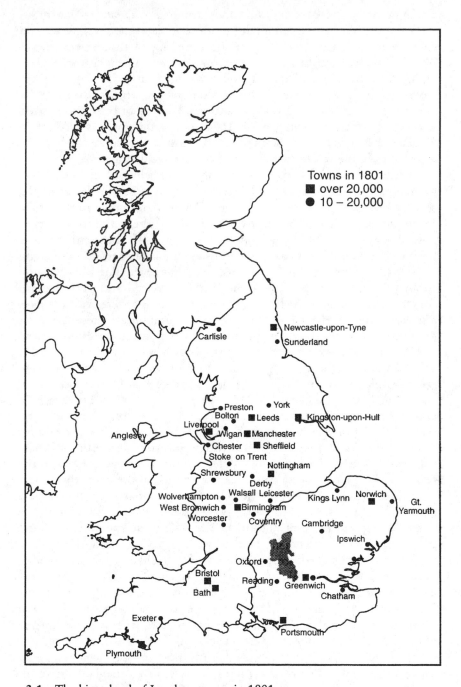

3.1 The hinterland of London: towns in 1801

trading centre. The Port and the City combined to create an enormous trading and imperial hinterland during the course of the seventeenth and eighteenth centuries. The dates of the founding of trading companies illustrate the geographical and chronological expansion of this hinterland.[9] The Muscovy Company was founded in 1553, the Levant Company in 1581, the East India Company in 1603, the Virginia Company in 1606, the Royal Adventurers Trading into Africa in 1662 and the Hudson Bay Company in 1670, whilst the voyages of Captain Cook and of Captain Vancouver had extended this hinterland to the other sides of the world by the end of the eighteenth century.

To the west of the City lay fashionable suburbs, which themselves grew rapidly after 1660, as new squares, Hanover Square for example, and Grosvenor Square, were laid out.[10] These were linked in their turn to Westminster, the seat of the royal Court, Parliament and the courts of law. The authority of Parliament was exercised at both national and local levels. It could levy taxes, determine religious beliefs and practices, at least their outward manifestations, and change the line of succession to the throne. It imposed a centralized currency and standardized weights and measures. At the same time it could interfere with the lives and property of named individuals or communities and indeed its authority was often sought as the final arbiter in quite personal affairs.

The king's justices, on circuit from the courts in Westminster, enforced a common law, and although a county and borough magistracy had considerable discretion in the administration of this law at local level, they were in the end accountable to the king's justices in London. The collection of national taxes, of customs and excise duties, created their own administrative patterns but the taxes themselves were returned into the Exchequer in London. It was through ministers and officials working from London that national defence was organized, even if the running of the local militia was left in the hands of the county gentry.

In these ways London, as 'the throne of the sovereign', imposed a considerable measure of uniformity across a wide spectrum of the national life, and the centrality of London from an administrative and political point of view can be studied without too much difficulty. The organs of state, Parliament, Exchequer, Treasury, King's Bench, Chancery and so on, through which this centrality was imposed, each had a sophisticated machinery, including record keeping upon a massive scale, a clarity of purpose and a distinction of function entirely lacking from the other metropolitan functions of London. Its role as the throne of the sovereign, and hence the final source of power and patronage, also meant that it attracted the largest concentration of wealthy people to be found anywhere in the country, implying a scale of demand for foodstuffs and manufactured goods out of all proportion to the actual numbers of people involved. Defoe, writing in the 1720s, refers again and again to the provisioning of London. 'This whole kingdom, as well the people as the land, and even the sea, in every part of it, are employ'd to furnish something, and I may add, the best of everything, to supply the city of London.'[11] It probably absorbed more than a half of the total coal production of the country until well into the nineteenth century. In 1736 nearly 70 per cent of all licensed dealers in tea and coffee in England, nearly 3500 of them, were to be found in London. By 1750 it was consuming at least ten million bushels of grain every year, 100,000 head of cattle and 180,000 pigs.[12]

By the beginning of the seventeenth century not only was London the largest market, it was also the most diversified manufacturing centre in England, a role it has continued to occupy down to the present. The medieval patterns of occupational · segregation were breaking down during the course of the sixteenth century, to be replaced by new ones. Thus silk weaving was established in Spitalfields by the beginning of the seventeenth century, long before the advent of Huguenot refugees. Clock and watch making became established in Clerkenwell, and pottery and glass making in Fulham, Vauxhall, Chelsea and Bow, whilst a number of big breweries were built in Southwark, on the south bank of the Thames. Booksellers congregated in Piccadilly during the course of the eighteenth century and one of them, Hatchards, is still there.[13] Even the most fashionable quarters of the West End of London needed large numbers of tradesmen, shopkeepers and craftsmen. A detailed survey of the Grosvenor estate made in 1789-90 reveals that 58 per cent of its inhabitants were engaged in 120 different trades, from muffin makers through bakers, cheesemongers, cabinet makers and carpenters to farriers, wheelwrights, stationers, watchmakers and a cow keeper.[14] Many of these trades furnished not only the town houses of the aristocracy and gentry who lived in the main squares and streets of the estate but also their country homes as well. By mid-eighteenth century the London upholsterers who had charge of these furnishings had changed from being craftsmen into interior decorators, the arbiters of fashion, matching furnishings, textiles, carpets and curtains, this process being one of the ways in which the fashions of the metropolis found their way into the rest of England.[15]

The manufacture to be found in London was small-scale, very diversified, and individual establishments were often highly specialized. It was said in 1805 that there were 112 steam engines in London, in 28 different trades.[16] In only three of these, however, public waterworks, brewing and founding and machine making, did the numbers of steam engines run into double figures. Obviously mechanization has scarcely begun, and in spite of short-term fluctuations there was to be little profound change in London's manufacturing basis much before the 1860s, save that in some trades its national dominance had been eroded. In 1700 it was often the only centre for some trades, silk weaving, for example. By the second half of the eighteenth century it had become only one amongst many centres, and some trades had left it for good, frame-work knitting, for instance, and shoemaking, and in any case it would appear that the proportion of London inhabitants engaged in manufac-ture fell during the course of the eighteenth century whilst the propor-tion in the professions, transport and distribution trades rose. Nevertheless, with all these provisos made, there were in 1851 373,000 of its inhabitants engaged in manufacture, making it the largest manu-facturing town in Europe, with 13.6 per cent of the United Kingdom population employed in manufacture, but 41 per cent of those engaged in government, the professions, banking and insurance.[17]

London was, however, much more than simply an immense vacuum-cleaner, sucking to itself the trade and produce of the rest of the country. It was often a source of venture capital and the *fons et origo* of innova-tion. The workshops of Thomas Savery were in Salisbury Court. Marine insurance was well established in London before the end of the sixteenth century, but begins in provincial centres – Bristol, Exeter, Hull, Liverpool and Newcastle – only during the course of the eighteenth century, and even then provincial practice was heavily dependent upon metropolitan example.[18] Other forms of insurance develop in much the same way. In February 1689 Mr Edward Bransby of Derby was robbed of five watches. He offered, in the *London Gazette*, a reward for information, to be sent either to his address in Derby or else to the coffee house of Mr Edward Lloyd, in Tower Street, London. This is the first known reference to the coffee house from which, by the 1730s, had emerged the principal source of information about shipping and of marine insurance underwriting anywhere in the world.[19] It hints at specialized ties between London and the provinces which were already well known and well established. The Sun Fire Office came formally into being in 1710. Almost immediately proposals were being made to appoint provincial agents, but it was 1721 before the first one, in Nottingham, was named. By 1730 there were at least 30, and by 1786 there were 123. By mid-century it was sending out fire engines, to Abingdon in 1752, Exeter in 1753 and one to Maidstone in 1757, on condition that the corporation provided another.[20] There was also in London by the early eighteenth century a well-developed capital market, with professional brokers, public quotation of prices and a permanent trading location.[21] A further specialized market made its first appearance in London in the 1680s.[22] The import of works of art was at that time in theory forbidden. The first auction of paintings took place in London in 1682. In 1695 an Act of

Parliament permitted the import of paintings upon payment of an *ad valorem* duty of 20 per cent. In 1721 this was changed to a duty according to size. The London art market was by this time well established, with professional dealers, and it continued to expand. Between 1722 and 1774 no less than 30,560 paintings were imported and paid customs duty. By the end of the eighteenth century paintings of foreign origin were in the possession of what may be called provincial middle-class collectors,[23] most of them transmitted via London.

London and its hinterland

If London has always headed the rank-size hierarchy of English towns it has also always possessed the greatest number of functions of any English town. All towns are multi-functional, and each function has its own hinterland. It is very rare for all the functions of any one town to coincide exactly, so that each town has a series of spheres of influence.[24] No sphere of influence is ever static, being subject to a continuous process of change over time and space, driven by changes in society, technology and even fashion, and no sphere of influence is ever a watertight discrete entity, sealed off by Chinese walls from a wider outside world. It may be possible to ascribe three spheres of influence to London: international,[25] national and regional. It fulfils the first two as the national capital and at the same time shares many functions at a regional and local level with both major and minor towns, these in their turn having their own spheres of influence, especially for everyday needs.

Unfortunately the objective and comprehensive sources which geographers and historians of the modern city use to analyse an urban hinterland[26] are not available before the middle of the nineteenth century and so analysis for the seventeenth and eighteenth centuries can be little more than a statement of a proposition illustrated with anecdotal evidence. Often the only feasible basis for discussion is a presence-absence matrix arranged as a scalogram,[27] but to construct such a scalogram for London would be a work of supererogation. A Westminster poll-book of 1749 lists 395 trades and a directory of 1791 lists 492.[28] Both sources are clearly incomplete. The evidence can be extended almost *ad nauseam*, but its accumulation can often do little more than emphasize the complexity and subtlety of the role of London in seventeenth and eighteenth century England.

In many respects almost the whole of England may be seen as the hinterland of London, but the 'pull' of the metropolis becomes weaker and weaker the greater the distance from it, although it was still considered worthwhile recording, for the benefit of Galloway cattle drovers, the distance to London, 330 miles, on the mileage panel erected in 1827 on the Mid Steeple of Dumfries. For the purposes of this chapter, however, the hinterland of London will be taken to be the southeastern quarter of England, and more especially the 16 counties bounded by Hampshire, Berkshire, Oxfordshire, Northamptonshire, Huntingdonshire and Norfolk, although this hinterland was of course much less precise than this delineation of boundaries would imply (see Figure 3.1).[29]

The structure of the hinterland

The economy and society of this narrower, regional London hinterland reflect centuries of human exploitation of the opportunities presented by its physical structures, in their turn based upon successive strata of limestones, chalk and sandstones, much altered by glacial action, both erosion and deposition. Some districts, the Sandlings of Suffolk for example, have open sandy soils. Others, such as the Weald of Kent, Sussex and Surrey, have heavy clays. Nowhere are there any hills over a thousand feet. Water supply is a problem only in certain isolated areas, the Breckland of Norfolk and Suffolk, for example.[30] Indeed an excess of water leading to extensive flooding is often the real problem. The terrain can often be difficult, especially in winter, when the roads of the Weald were impassable to wheeled traffic and its crossroads were said to be the worst in all England.[31] There are no deposits of coal or non-ferrous metals but there are large deposits of clay which have been used for making bricks and tiles since Roman times. Some parts of this hinterland were, and still are, heavily wooded, and again this resource has been exploited since early medieval times, whilst the numerous streams and rivers of the region have provided water power for centuries. These natural resources, their nature, location and distribution, have profoundly influenced the economy of the region and its relationships with London.

The structure and development of this hinterland is shaped by three closely interrelated factors: technology, energy and communication. It was well into the nineteenth century before the steam engine began to make serious inroads into the water wheel as the principal source of energy for English manufacture,[32] and it was upon the water wheel that the diversity of manufacture in southeastern England was erected. Most streams and rivers which had a sufficiently regular supply of water to power a mill were also the centres of manufacturing enterprises, since water mills, once erected, could change their function quite rapidly. The river Wey powered mills for flour, paper and gunpowder making.[33] The river Wandle, now running almost entirely underground beneath the suburban sprawl of Wandsworth, drove 40 mills in 1805, including calico, flour, snuff, oil, dyeing, paper, copper and iron works, together with a porter brewery.[34] The ironworks where Henry Cort perfected the puddling process was at Fontley, in Hampshire, powered by the river Meon. The mill where paper for banknotes had been manufactured since 1724 was at Laverstoke, also in Hampshire. There were silk mills at Braintree, gunpowder mills at Faversham, paper mills at Maidstone and a mill at Tewin, in Hertfordshire, for the grinding and polishing of optical glass.[35]

This manufacture and the exchange which supported it was sustained by a communication network the defects of which are better known than its merits. Water has always been the cheapest method of transporting bulk cargoes. Five important river networks gave access to the sea for more than half of England, and this before the first canal was built (see Figure 3.2). These are the Thames, the Severn, the Mersey, the Humber-Trent-Ouse network and that based upon the Great Ouse with its outlet through Kings Lynn. All save the Thames in fact drain outwards from the London hinterland but many of the difficulties which this physical factor might have created were overcome by the presence of a dense network of coastal ports. England has a long coastline in relation to its area, and coastal shipping has always been of the first importance, the tonnage of coastal shipping increasing almost four-fold between 1765 and 1826.[36] There were many thriving ports in the south east, stretching from Kings Lynn right round the coast to Lymington, in addition to inland ports like Wisbech, Spalding and Peterborough, where the Customs House dates from about 1700. They flourished as transshipment points for goods destined for inland shopkeepers drawn via London from America and the West and East Indies, with foodstuffs and raw materials for London as the return cargoes. The volume of traffic through Sussex ports increased five-fold during the course of the eighteenth century, whilst the average tonnage of ships doubled. Coal was the largest single import, increasing ten-fold over the same period, with grain the principal export.[37]

Many other rivers were navigable, in addition to the Thames. London drew much of its barley and malt from Hertfordshire along the river Lea, whilst the river Wey, made navigable from 1651, provided a moving highway for the transport of grain, timber and iron from the Weald of Surrey to the Thames and hence to London. The merchants of Abingdon objected to the building of Westminster bridge since they feared that it would obstruct their trade in grain by barge along the Thames to Queenhithe.[38] Guns cast at the Fuller family forge at Heathfield were sent by road to Maidstone and then by boat down the Medway.[39]

3.2   Navigable rivers in England about 1730

There is, however, a limit to the benefits which the use of navigable rivers alone can bring, not least because they are often not to be found where they are most needed. Only artificial waterways can fill the gap. The first artificial waterway to be built in England in the modern period was a three mile stretch linking Exeter to the sea. This was built in 1564–66, but was an isolated phenomenon, and the real Canal Age begins only in November of 1757 with the opening of the Sankey Brook Canal in Lancashire. By the end of the eighteenth century several million pounds had been raised, entirely by private efforts, to build about 700 miles of artificial waterway (see Figure 3.3). By 1858 this figure had reached 4250 miles.[40] Canals were to be found in most parts of the country, but the greatest effort was expended in linking three of the four great estuaries of England, the Humber, the Severn and the Trent. Where this network crossed, in the west midlands, lay the heart of industrialization. The canal network was used to transport bulky cargoes, especially coal, grain and building materials. Its contribution to the early stages of industrialization cannot be exaggerated. London, however, was at first linked to this network only by the circuitous route of the Birmingham and Warwick Canal and the Oxford Canal. It was only with the opening of the Blisworth tunnel in 1805 that London became directly linked into this canal system.

Road communication was certainly much better than contemporaries, concerned only with the bad news, would have us believe. The network of roads and bridges upon which road communication must depend was already well developed by 1500.[41] Indeed the main structure of the English road system, with its focus upon London, goes back to Roman times. The backbone of the inland transport system was an extensive network of carriers and their wagons, who, by the beginning of the eighteenth century, were providing a regular and generally fairly dependable service to almost all parts of the country. They seem very often to have had a real cost advantage over most inland waterways, being more reliable and running to a timetable, often from a regular departure point.[42] Navigation on inland waterways on the other hand was often interrupted by freezing in winter and drought in summer. Carrying services from London seem to have trebled between 1681 and 1838, with short-distance services growing most rapidly, not least because the southeastern quarter of England was poorly provided with canals.[43] This network of carriers was complemented by a stagecoach network which developed rapidly during the eighteenth century. By 1715 over 800 coaches a week were leaving London, covering over 67,000 passenger miles, a figure which had reached over a million miles in 1796. London for long remained the centre of coaching and it is the end of the eighteenth century before inter-regional coach links develop upon any

3.3   The canal network in England about 1800

scale.[44] Carriers and coaches departed from inns, and the great inns of eighteenth century London played a vital part in the chain of communication which linked London to its hinterland. Individual inns came to serve travellers to and from specific regions of England. The Bell in Friday Street served Gloucestershire, for example. To this they often added commercial and marketing functions. Thus the Half Moon in Southwark was the centre for buying and selling hops from Kent, inns in Aldersgate Street became the centre for the trade in meal from Bedfordshire and Hertfordshire, and there was a chamber for the buying and selling of Buckinghamshire lace in the George in Aldersgate.[45]

Individual stretches of road were improved during the course of the eighteenth century by the creation of turnpike trusts. The trust was set up by a private Act of Parliament, invariably for 21 years. The network of roads thus improved spread rapidly, at first following the traditional focus upon London, but by mid-century concentration upon the industrializing midlands and north was becoming apparent, a tendency which becomes ever more marked as the century draws to its close. By 1770 some 22,000 miles of road had been turnpiked. Knowledge of road-making techniques developed much more slowly however, and it was the first years of the nineteenth century before there were any significant advances. Nevertheless, turnpike trustees could, and did, improve the roads under their care by straightening and realigning them, by reducing gradients and by introducing signposts and milestones. At the same time the road surfaces themselves were gradually improved. The end result was a slow, unspectacular improvement in the condition of many miles of road in England, with a consequent improvement in the speed and comfort of travel.[46]

An Act of Parliament created a Post Office in 1660. There were at first six post roads, running from London to Chester, York, Exeter, Bristol, Great Yarmouth and Dover (see Figure 3.4).[47] The system thus established became increasingly reliable as time passed, so that the largest industrialist of the early eighteenth century, Ambrose Crowley, ran his Durham ironworks entirely by post from his house and warehouses at Greenwich.[48] This network, and a complementary network of byroads, was extended very slowly. The Royal Mail was first carried by stagecoach in 1784, and the Royal Mail coach quickly established an enviable reputation for speed and reliability.[49] By the early nineteenth century there were 220 Royal Mail coaches, covering between them something in the order of 12,000 miles a day.

One consequence of these improvements in communication was the growing integration, certainly from the last decades of the seventeenth century, of a 'national' market as opposed to a series of regional markets, most noticeably in grain and dairy produce.[50] There is however growing

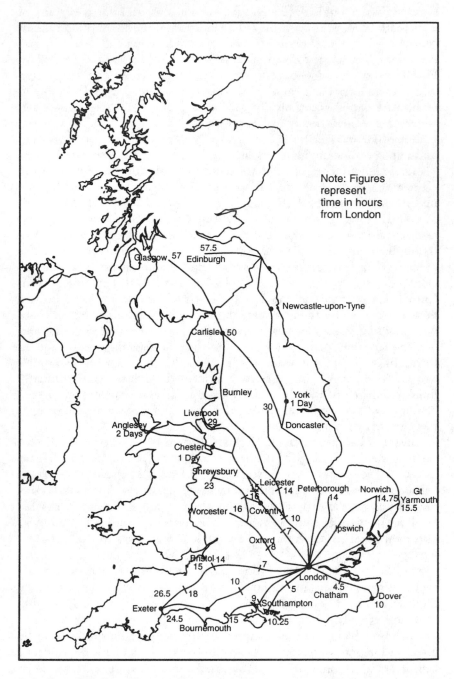

3.4 Royal Mail coach times from London

evidence to show that this development is paralleled by nascent regional specializations, both in agricultural produce generally and in manufactured goods,[51] and this specialization becomes more and more apparent as the eighteenth century draws on, with much of it being shaped by the demands of London. Thus the region between Chelmsford and Colchester in Essex developed specialist nurseries which were supplying seeds throughout the country by the end of the seventeenth century, and orchards supplying the London market with fruit were well established in the north Kent lowlands, from Gravesend to Sandwich, with Londoners going to pick hops in the Kentish hopfields by the same date,[52] whilst the making of silk buttons and silk twist was also established in Macclesfield by the end of the seventeenth century. It then grew very rapidly, becoming a serious rival to the London trade.[53]

Distance has a temporal as well as a spatial dimension. In 1754 the journey time between London and York was said to be four days. In 1761 it was three, in 1774 two and in 1776 the journey could be done in thirty-six hours, whilst the journey time between London and Edinburgh had come down from ten days in 1754 to three nights and two days in 1798.[54] England was shrinking rapidly by the end of the eighteenth century and this could only serve to accentuate and extend the pull of London, often with long-term effects upon the economy and society of places even at a considerable distance. Thus it was reported in the middle of the eighteenth century that the shopkeepers of Nottingham had begun in recent years to go to London themselves to buy their merchandise rather than buy it at the nearby Lenton fair, which was in decline as a consequence.[55] It was said of Malmesbury in 1805 that it had formerly been a considerable thoroughfare town on the road between London and Bath, but a new road made several years before meant that it was now less frequented than formerly,[56] whereas of Chipping Sodbury it was said in 1779 that the turnpiking of the Bristol to London road had brought much through traffic and buildings in the town had been greatly improved as a consequence,[57] while Yeovil was said to be large and populous, owing much to its situation on the great western road from London to Exeter.[58]

The economic impact of London upon its hinterland

The impact of London upon its hinterland has been apparent for centuries. The enormous demands of the London markets for food and raw materials gave a stimulus to rural change which it is impossible to exaggerate. Even by 1300 London and its markets dominated what has been called an inner, 'suburban', hinterland, extending for up to 50 miles around it, a hinterland in which agriculture had already become commercialized, with Henley-on-Thames an important collecting point for grain produced over a wide area for shipment down the Thames to London.[59] Following the von Thünen thesis,[60] it would be possible, were it not a gross over-simplification of an immensely complex and subtle process largely ignoring local diversity and the direction of the principal lines of communication, to construct concentric circles around London marking off its sources of supply according to the value of the merchandise concerned and the difficulties of transport. The phenomenon is nevertheless apparent. Thus fruit and vegetables were cultivated in Chelsea, Fulham and Hammersmith, then villages lying well beyond the built-up area of London. Further supplies came by water from Kent. Milk came from cows kept within the city itself, often in underground byres.[61] Hay, essential for the enormous numbers of horses then kept in London, was grown in many districts of Middlesex – Northolt, Hillingdon and Hayes, for example.[62] Grain for flour and for malt came from neighbouring counties and a number of big corn markets flourished in an arc around London: at St Albans, Hitchin, High Wycombe, Reigate, Farnham and Milton. Other supplies of grain came by sea, from the Norfolk and Sussex coastlands, for example,[63] whilst early in the nineteenth century Wisbech was the largest grain-shipping port in the United Kingdom.[64] Timber and wood, whether for fuel or as raw materials, came from the woods of the Weald and the Chilterns, again by water, this time along the Thames and the Wey, and fish came by pack-horse from Hastings. Butter and cheese came from Suffolk, Cheshire and Yorkshire, brought round the coast by water. London cheesemongers had established a 'factorage' at Uttoxeter before the end of the seventeenth century.[65] Horses and cattle, which could transport themselves, came from even further away, from Leicestershire, Wales and Scotland, whilst coal came by sea from Newcastle and wildfowl from the Fens.[66]

Efforts to meet the demands of London could bring profound long-term change to rural society. There was, for example, much enclosure in Oxfordshire, Buckinghamshire and Northamptonshire from the fifteenth century, with attendant rural depopulation, the emphasis being as much upon rearing cattle for the London market as upon raising sheep for wool. There is evidence from probate inventories to show that butchers were often also graziers, and the same source makes it clear that this could be a very profitable trade indeed. Defoe's comment, that all the gentlemen of the Vale of Aylesbury were graziers, although not all the graziers were gentlemen, encapsulates an observation of considerable economic and social complexity.[67] Cattle and sheep also provide the raw materials for tanning and hence for boot and shoe making, and again both of these trades supplied the London markets. Tanning was the leading manufacture in Steyning,[68] for example, and a probate inventory of 1706 lists London leather and London gloves. High quality, expensive gloves were also made in Woodstock in the eighteenth century,[69] but the development of this manufacture seems to have owed much to the building of Blenheim Palace, which was in due course open to the public, so that Woodstock, hitherto off the main lines of communication, came to depend upon the tourist trade for its prosperity. Brewing and tanning were the principal manufactures of eighteenth century Horsham, but there was also a large market where great numbers of poultry were bought and sold for London, whilst in 1756 it was claimed that only poor quality meat at high prices could be obtained in the town, the local farmers and butchers diverting the best direct to London.[70]

Lace-making was widely practised as a domestic manufacture in many towns and villages of Bedfordshire, Hertfordshire and north Buckinghamshire by the end of the sixteenth century. Its origins are obscure but it may well have been introduced by refugees from Flanders and Brabant, a number of whom were to be found in the towns in north Buckinghamshire from the middle years of the fifteenth century.[71] Olney, Newport Pagnell and Stony Stratford became important centres for this manufacture and for its marketing, which again was directed towards London. Straw-plaiting was another widespread domestic manufacture in Bedfordshire, with markets for the finished products at Tring, Hemel Hempstead, Hitchin and St Albans, where there were also clay tobacco pipe makers and numerous shoemakers.

At the same time, the woodlands of the region formed the basis for an extensive trade in timber, wood and in goods made from wood. The woods of Ruislip in Middlesex were supplying firewood to London as late as the 1870s. There was a flourishing woodware and hollow-ware manufacture at Cheshunt, in Hertfordshire. Defoe[72] describes vividly the trade in beechwood along the Thames from Marlow to London to make furniture, felloes for wheels and staves and handles for a wide range of tools and implements, whilst the beech woods of the hills surrounding High Wycombe formed the basis for a furniture-making industry whose most characteristic product is the Windsor chair. Other articles of furniture, beds for example,[73] were being made up in the woods of the Chiltern hills and sent off to London well before the end of the seventeenth century. Wood was also used to make brushes, broom handles and wooden spoons, and Chesham became a centre of this trade, whilst the making of wooden meat skewers from the wood of the spindle tree became a domestic trade in Marlow. Wood was used extensively to make charcoal, and charcoal, particularly from the alder tree, was one of the ingredients of gunpowder. There were water-powered gunpowder mills at Waltham Abbey and at Faversham. The Evelyn family was involved in gunpowder mills at Wotton and the East India Company had set up its own powder mill at Chilworth by 1625.[74] Charcoal was also used in iron furnaces and forges, and although the Wealden iron industry was in decline in the eighteenth century there was still an ironworks near Hindhead as late as 1767, and the last iron forge in the Weald, at Ashburnham, closed in 1813.[75]

Paper making was established in the region by 1497. The paper mills themselves were often converted corn or fulling mills and operations were usually upon a small scale, with only one vat in each mill. They were powered by the rivers and streams of the region and supplies of linen rags were drawn from London, which also served as the market for the finished product. By the end of the eighteenth century paper making was both important and widespread throughout the region, and paper makers were to be found in many towns and villages, including High Wycombe, Catteshall, Stoke next Guildford, Thetford and Maidstone, whilst the river Tillingbourne in Surrey was lined with paper mills.

Clockmakers were numerous in several villages in the London hinterland, in Swalcliffe, in north Oxfordshire, for example, and in Charlbury, where glove makers held stalls in the market place in the early eighteenth century, and where lived Larkum Kendal, who made the chronometer for Captain Cook.[76] Shefford, in Bedfordshire, had several clockmakers by the end of the seventeenth century, and several Bedfordshire boys served their apprenticeship in London, and London-trained apprentices settled in Bedfordshire. The greatest of English clockmakers, Thomas Tompion, was born in Northill in 1639, whilst Thomas Russell, born in Hampshire in 1667, was apprenticed in London in 1682 and eventually settled in Wootton, in Bedfordshire.[77] The clockmakers of Clerkenwell seem, from the end of the seventeenth century, to have drawn their supplies of parts from south Lancashire, developing themselves into assembling and marketing specialists.[78]

The making of paper, lace, boots and shoes, furniture, clocks and wooden spoons may well lack the excitement of the cotton industry, coal mining or iron founding, but their contribution to the totality of economic performance must not be under-rated.[79] They were almost always manufactures carried on at a small, domestic scale, making use of locally grown, reared or quarried raw materials and local sources of energy, either human or animal muscles or the vagaries of wind and water power. They were as likely to be found in the country as in the town, although marketing was more likely to be organized from a town than from anywhere else. It is as marketing and service centres as much as centres of manufacture that the towns in the hinterland of London flourished in the eighteenth century. Marketing itself undergoes significant institutional changes during the course of the eighteenth century. In the first half of the seventeenth century there were 283 places with markets in the 16 counties which make up the southeastern quarter of England.[80] By 1792 this number was reduced to 253, a decline of just over 10 per cent.[81] The places themselves had not disappeared, but their formal markets had ceased to function in the face of competition from shops and private transactions, often carried out in inns. It is clear from probate inventories that shops from the second half of the seventeenth century onwards were carrying an astonishingly wide variety of goods, drawn from America and the Indies almost as a matter of course, and almost always through the Port of London. Their contents often ran into several thousands of pounds, their nutmeg, tobacco, rice, brandy and sugar, together with thousands of yards of cloth of the most varied kinds, the silent, matter-of-fact evidence of the rise of the Atlantic economy.[82] Shops of this kind were to be found in the smallest towns and in villages. One substantial shopkeeper of Brill also had a shop in Thame, and another in Olney not only had a shop as part of his house but another in the market place in Olney and a third in Newport Pagnell[83] and Samuel Lucke, mercer of Steyning, had a shop in Steyning and another in New Shoreham at the time of his death in 1706.[84] A consumer society was well established and expanding rapidly by the second half of the seventeenth century.[85]

The social impact of London upon its hinterland

Over and beyond its economic pull, London also exercised what may be called a socio-cultural pull. It was always the source for the best quality furniture, glass and ornaments, for fashionable clothes, for unusual or exotic foodstuffs and the greater the distance from London the more specialized the goods and services sought from the capital. Thus the Shuttleworths of Gawsworth in Lancashire bought their spices once a year in London in the early seventeenth century.[86] Gloucester Corporation bought its fire engine in London in 1648[87] and Sir Thomas Haggerston, from his home in Northumberland, sent his sword to be dressed in London.[88] The Banks family of Revesby Abbey in Lincolnshire bought their asparagus plants in the capital and had them brought down into the country by the wagon to Chesterfield.[89] Sir John Harpur had three marble chimneypieces sent down from London to his country house at Calke, in Derbyshire, in September 1701.[90] Hornbeam sets, oranges, lemons, chocolate and tea were also sent down from London; his wine, however, came by sea to King's Lynn and then overland. William Blathwayt supervised the building of his country house at Dyrham in Gloucestershire almost entirely by post from London and bought much of the furniture in the capital, although his embossed leatherwork came from The Hague.[91] A London 'season' was well established by the end of the seventeenth century, partly as a consequence of the practice of Parliament meeting annually after 1689. Those who could afford it came in large numbers to see and be seen, to go to the play, to buy books and wine and to admire the latest fashions in clothes. 'Those who could afford it' were from the upper echelons of society, the aristocracy, the landed gentry and wealthy provincial merchants. They were often accompanied by servants who, if contemporary accounts are to be believed, were just as interested in the latest fashions as their masters and mistresses.[92] The Sir John Harpur just mentioned had a house in London and went there for four or five months almost every year. He and his family went to London in his own coach. His cook and housekeeper travelled by the public stagecoach, whilst three or four housemaids went by the carrier's wagon. Thus were the social niceties preserved, and thus too were memories and impressions of London life transmitted throughout the country and through almost every level of society.[93]

What may be called the fashionable pull of London had yet another side to it. Almost all of the Huguenot silk weavers who settled in Canterbury in the last decades of the seventeenth century had by the end of the century moved to London to be nearer to the centre of fashion and hence of profit,[94] and Josiah Wedgwood felt compelled to open a London showroom, first of all in Greek Street and then from 1797 in St James's Square. The rooms in Greek Street were taken in 1774 in order to put upon public show the service he had had made for Catherine the Great. Admission was by ticket only, but the event was a huge success, not least, it was said, because almost all of the owners of the 1282 country seats delineated on the service came to see it.[95]

Investment in East India Company and South Sea Company stock was by no means confined to Londoners, and provincial tradesmen were both creditors and debtors of Londoners. John Bache, a wealthy Birmingham ironmonger, had £500 in South Sea stock at the time of his death in 1719. James Britain, a linendraper of Wisbech, owed money in King's Lynn, Norwich, Manchester and Glasgow as well as London at the time of his death in 1722 whilst George Bayley, bargemaster of Fillingdon in Berkshire, was owed £60 17s. 2d. for malt by the malt factor at Queenhithe in 1728.[96] Maurice Thompson died at Haversham, in north Buckinghamshire, in 1680, leaving personal estate valued at £17,776. Almost the whole of this was made up of debts due to him, including some in New England and Barbados, and investments in the East India Company and the Guinea Company.[97]

The monopoly of printing and publishing exercised by the London

Stationers' Company was allowed to lapse in 1695. Provincial book-sellers and publishers quickly made their appearance, although from the first they were primarily concerned with the publication of newspapers. By 1730 there were about twenty provincial newspapers, of which several were well established. By the end of the eighteenth century book-sellers and printers were to be found in over 300 English towns. Nevertheless, London remained the centre of the publishing industry, and even when provincial printers did produce anything they often thought it worth their while to offer their books for sale in London.[98] Thus Thomas Gent's *History of Ripon*, published in 1733, was adver-tised as being for sale in Ripon, Knaresborough and Paternoster Row in London, whilst *Antiquitates Sarisburiensis*, printed in Salisbury in 1771, was to be sold there as well as from shops in Ludgate Street and Lincoln's Inn Fields. Readers in London subscribed to books published in the provinces, and provincial readers to books published in London. Few antiquarian or historical works were published in the last decades of the eighteenth century without a subscription from Richard Gough, who eventually became Director of the Society of Antiquaries, or from Thomas Pennant, who lived in Anglesey. James Simmons,[99] born in Canterbury in 1741, was apprenticed to a London stationer and returned to his native city in 1767, eventually becoming mayor, and, in 1806, the year before he died, Member of Parliament. He founded the *Kentish Gazette*, which included a London newsletter giving Court and society news, and in 1778 he began to publish Hasted's *History of Kent*. Subscribers included Joseph Banks of Soho, Lancelot Brown of Hampton Court, a Literary Society in Exeter and Thomas Pennant.

Those districts of the south east which enjoy easy and ready communication with London have always been popular with wealthy merchants, lawyers and government officials as a place in which to buy a country estate, from that Elias de Scaccario who almost certainly gave his name to Chequers at the end of the twelfth century, through Judge Jeffreys who had built a substantial country house in Bulstrode by 1686, and the Rothschilds who bought up much of central Buckinghamshire in the middle years of the nineteenth century, down to the present. Samuel Whitbread built a country house at Southill, in Bedfordshire, in 1795, and Lord Hardwicke built Wimpole Hall in Cambridgeshire in the 1740s. William Hobbs, a London apothecary, bought Great Hundridge in 1681, and a West India merchant, William Freeman, rebuilt Fawley Court at the end of the seventeenth century.[100] Sir Richard Glyn bought an estate in Dorset in about 1770, and his son, Sir Richard Carr Glyn, rebuilt the mansion house, Gaunts. Defoe remarks on several occasions upon the numbers of 'handsom large houses, being chiefly for the habitations of the richest citizens, such as either are able to keep two houses, one in the country, and one in the city; or for such citizens as being rich, and having left off trade, live altogether in these neighbouring villages, for the pleasure and health of the latter part of their days',[101] in such places as Walthamstow, Wansted, West Ham, Eltham, Peckham, Camberwell, Carshalton and Wimbledon.[102] Twickenham became particularly popular as a country retreat, more especially after Alexander Pope took up residence there in 1719, and Clapham was described in 1779 as a large straggling village about three miles from London with many handsome houses belonging to the gentry and citizens of London.[103]

Thus the immediate hinterland of London came to acquire an adventitious population of wealthy residents whose main preoccupations lay in the capital rather than locally. These new, or sometimes returned, residents often brought with them London craftsmen to build their new houses. Winslow Hall, in Buckinghamshire, was built for William Lowndes, Secretary to the Treasury and born in Winslow, in 1699. He employed a London mason and three craftsmen of the Board of Works who had worked with Sir Christopher Wren on St Pauls.[104] This movement from London into the country was echoed by well-to-do provincial townsmen, so that several towns of the London hinterland came to have their own wealthy suburb, as Great Baddow for Chelmsford, for example, and Wood Green for Witney.

These socio-cultural ties are particularly difficult to consider as a whole, since they are so multifarious and so all-pervasive, but it must be emphasized that the hinterland of London here being discussed was by no means an homogeneous whole. There was considerable physical diversity, even at a parish level, and much variation in economic and social structures, with some districts much more clearly and obviously influenced by London than others. A group of parishes in north Oxfordshire, for example, including Claydon, Cropredy, Clattercote, Mollington, Wardington and Prescote, betray almost no London influence. They were profoundly rural, with no manufactures and no charities founded by boys born in the village, who had gone to London, prospered in trade and left money to found schools, repair roads or establish other charities in their native villages, a phenomenon to be found in many towns and villages throughout England. Even here, however, the proprietors turned to Parliament to enclose their open fields in the second half of the eighteenth century, and Richard Gostelow, who died in 1621, son of a yeoman of Prescote, married as his second wife Katherine Hawes, the widow of a London haberdasher, hinting at personal links which lie beyond the reach of the historian.[105] There are yet more subtle links. The Pavement Commissioners of Southampton advertized in the London newspapers in 1770 for contractors to undertake the actual work,[106] and the Canterbury Pavement Commissioners consulted the Surveyor of the City of London in 1787 about repairing the streets of their city.[107]

The hinterland on the ground: the case of Buckinghamshire

It is clearly impossible to discuss in detail the history of all 16 counties in the south east of England. However by considering one, namely Buckinghamshire, we may be able to shed some light on the general experience of the near hinterland of the capital.

Buckinghamshire divides fairly clearly into two natural or physical regions. The north of the county is characterized by a series of broad river valleys and low rounded hills. There was much enclosure here during the fifteenth and sixteenth centuries, both for sheep for their wool and for cattle to supply the London market. At the same time a number of parishes, Padbury and Thornborough for example, remained un-enclosed until the very end of the eighteenth century. The chalk hills of the Chilterns lie in the south of the county. They form a series of steep hills and valleys, lying generally north west to south east, the hills them-selves covered with clay with flints, and often densely wooded. Here is a sheep-corn economy based in small enclosed fields. At the same time there is considerable woodland coppicing, to supply furniture, broom staves, hop poles, firewood and bark for tanning. The commercial exploitation of the Chiltern woodlands to supply the London markets was well established long before the beginning of the seventeenth century.[108]

By 1600 there were 19 places in Buckinghamshire which for one reason or another may be said to qualify as towns (see Figure 3.5).[109] They were all very small. In 1600 the largest was High Wycombe, with a population of about 2000. The next was Chesham, with about 1700, and the next two largest were probably Amersham and Newport Pagnell, with populations of about 1300 inhabitants each. There was some rearrangement in the hierarchy of these towns and, within their own terms, considerable population growth during the course of the next two centuries, but even by the time of the first census of 1801 High Wycombe, town and parish, had only 4200 inhabitants, Chesham just under 4000 and Aylesbury, the county town, just over 3000. The evolu-tion of the economic specializations of each of these towns is unique, a function of that growing regional and local specialization which charac-terizes the hinterland of London in the eighteenth century, and it would be tedious to recite them all here, not least because the documentary evidence before 1798 is so fragmentary and disjointed. In that year a

3.5   Buckinghamshire towns

survey of men aged between 15 and 60 was taken as part of anti-invasion preparations.[110] This Posse Comitatus also gives occupations. Comparison with the totals of the 1801 census shows that on average some 20 per cent of the total population is listed, and so it would appear to offer a fairly reasonable picture of the occupational structure of the county at the time and of its towns in particular.

It is clear that agriculture is the largest single occupation within the county, but manufacturing and distributive occupations were both common and widespread. The woollen textile industry had not disappeared entirely and there was some small pottery manufacture. Needles were made at Long Crendon and there were copper mills at Wraysbury. Many villages had shopkeepers and several had carriers and drovers, whilst bargemen, bargemasters and wharfingers were to be found in the villages along the Thames. Olney was the centre of lace making and marketing: it had 29 lacemakers and seven lace dealers. Woodworking trades were centred in Amersham, where there were ten carpenters and 11 turners, in Beaconsfield, which had 13 carpenters, eight sawyers, two broom makers and a timber merchant, and above all in Chesham, which had 31 turners and 18 carpenters, as well as two spoon makers. High Wycombe had 33 chairmakers. The woods of the Chilterns had created their own specialisms. Boot and shoe making was widespread, with no fewer than 77 shoemakers in Chesham. There were 16 papermakers in High Wycombe and 75 in Wycombe parish and 62 in Wooburn. The four smallest places in the county at the end of the eighteenth century, Little Brickhill, Brill, Fenny Stratford and Ivinghoe, had each of them fewer than a thousand inhabitants and fewer than 30 occupations. Their claims still to be considered towns at this time must be very doubtful. Chesham and High Wycombe lie at the other end of the scale. Each had more than 50 occupations and some were present in sufficient numbers to make it clear that they were working for more than a purely local market.

Buckinghamshire itself lacks any underlying homogeneity. Patterns of growth and decline, change and stability are themselves subject to considerable fluctuations, influenced by technological developments at national level, especially in transport. Improvements in communication 'spaced out' viable points of exchange. Little Brickhill and Fenny Stratford are less than three miles apart, and lie about half way along Watling Street between Stony Stratford and Dunstable. Any advantages which this situation might have brought to them disappeared as improvements in road transport made them redundant, this road being the first to have a properly constituted turnpike trust, set up in 1706, so that by the end of the eighteenth century they had both lost all pretence to urban status. Such improvements also enhanced the 'pull' of London, and this in its turn provided a positive stimulus to the development of a market-orientated agriculture and the growth of workshop manufacture. The profits from both of these reinforced consumer demand and with it the role of towns as marketing and distributing centres. The pace of change accelerated during the nineteenth century when first of all Slough, Bletchley and Wolverton suddenly began to grow very rapidly with the coming of the railway in the 1830s and 1840s and then Amersham and Beaconsfield when the network filled out at the end of the century.

It is important to stress that there is nothing unusual about Buckinghamshire. The other counties forming the hinterland of London are no less varied in their physical makeup and natural resources than Buckinghamshire, and, like Buckinghamshire, they also possess a network of towns which, certainly from 1660 onwards, flourished as exchange centres for the provision of a range of services and manufactures, often on a small scale, but sufficient, not only for their own needs and those of the inhabitants of their own hinterlands, but also to supply the voracious and insatiable London market. The eighteenth century houses, town halls and market places of towns like Ampthill, Abingdon, Berkhamsted, Newbury, Thame, Henley-on-Thames, Petworth, Chichester and Lewes are silent testimony to the prosperity of the south-eastern quarter of England in the eighteenth century.

Conclusion

The problems of unravelling London's relationships with its hinterland are especially difficult and complex in the increasingly dynamic economic and social world of seventeenth and eighteenth century Britain. By the time of the reign of George I the lives of growing numbers of Englishmen – and Scots and Welsh – were shaped – in what they wore, drank and ate, in how they decorated their homes, in what they read and said, what they produced or traded at market or in the shops, when and how they travelled and communicated – by the innovative impact of the capital. Yet for most of the British Isles that influence remained sectorally limited, socially selective – strongest among the upper classes – and locally uneven. There were many other powerful influences at work shaping British society, not least growing regional differentiation, commercialization and urbanization.

It was in the south east of England, broadly defined, that the metropolis, from the high Middle Ages, had its most powerful effect, helping to design the demographic and economic landscape. Here, as we have seen, the provincial view of the capital was largely positive, with buoyant London demand for foodstuffs and manufactured goods dovetailing with and reinforcing the structural capacities of the region – its energy resources and raw material supplies, its workshop crafts, its communication networks, its pattern of small towns. Reverse flows of investment capital, wholesale and imported merchandise and fashionable consumer wares flowed into the towns and countryside of the region. By 1750 many sectors of society in the Home Counties, and not just the better-off, had been incorporated in some way into the metropolitan sphere of influence; many districts, although as we have seen not all, had a complex web of economic and social relationships with the capital. The towns of the region, although never large, nevertheless prospered, decking themselves out with new town halls and assembly rooms, with classical façades on their main streets, and not only the county towns like Maidstone and Chelmsford but also market centres like Cranbrook or Winslow. If there was a price to pay it was largely demographic: the constant efflux to the capital of young people, notably young women, many of whom quickly died there in the early eighteenth century from smallpox and other virulent infections. Metropolitan mortality patterns also spread into the region. All of these relationships and interactions were particularly intense in the penumbra of suburbanizing villages and towns within ten miles of the capital.

By the late eighteenth century, however, the view from the provinces was changing. New regional capitals such as Birmingham and Manchester and rapid urban growth in the Midlands, the North and in lowland Scotland created new patterns of economic, social and cultural concourse. After 1800 the country's middle classes became less interested in the capital. In the south east relations with the capital may have become less beneficial. Even if the metropolitan mortality effect was less invasive, the costs of economic exchange with the capital increased. Agricultural specialization for the London market combined with mounting competition from the industrializing regions led to the decline or relocation of many traditional craft industries, undermining the mixed economy of the south east and creating an over-dependence on agricultural employment. The slump following the end of the wars with France led to a catastrophic increase in poverty in the Home Counties. The region and many of its towns were increasingly locked into below-average growth rates, localized industries and structural poverty, conditions which persisted until after the end of the First World War.

Notes

1. Le Sieur Alexandre le Maitre, *La Métropolitée* (Amsterdam, 1682), pp.9,

28, 55.

2. A.E.J. Morris, *History of Urban Form*, 2nd edn (London, 1979), p.165, and see H. Ballon, *The Paris of Henry IV* (Cambridge, Mass., 1991).

3. J. Summerson, *Architecture in Britain* (London, 1953, 1977 edn), p.273.

4. R. Finlay and B. Shearer, 'Population Growth and Suburban Expansion', in A.L. Beier and R. Finlay, eds, *London 1500-1700* (London, 1986), 45.

5. R. Burton, *The Anatomy of Melancholy* (1621, Everyman's Library edn, London, 1932), vol.1, 92.

6. For a discussion of the importance of defining what is meant by London when estimating its population see V. Harding, 'The Population of London, 1500-1700: a review of the published evidence', *London Journal*, vol.15 (1990), 111-28.

7. See M.J. Power, 'The East London Working Community in the Seventeenth Century', in P.J. Corfield and D. Keene, eds, *Work in Towns, 850-1850* (London, 1990), and M. Power, 'Shadwell: The Development of a London Suburban Community in the Seventeenth Century', *London Journal*, vol.4 (1978), 29-46.

8. C.J. French, ' "Crowded with traders and a great Commerce": London's Domination of English Overseas Trade 1700-1775', *London Journal*, vol.17 (1992), 27-35. For an account of the technological stagnation of the Port of London in the eighteenth century, see R.C. Jarvis, 'The Metamorphosis of the Port of London', *London Journal*, vol.3 (1977), 55-72.

9. See C.T. Carr, ed., 'Select Charters of Trading Companies, 1530-1710', *Selden Society*, vol.28 (1913).

10. See L. Stone, 'The Residential Development of the West End of London in the Seventeenth Century', in B.C. Malament, ed., *After the Reformation* (London, 1980), pp.167-212.

11. D. Defoe, *A Tour through England and Wales* (1724-26, ed. G.D.H. Cole, London, 1928), vol.1, 12. Burton, *Anatomy*, vol.1, 92, wrote of London, 'sola crescit decrescentibus aliis', but Defoe knew better than this, see *Tour*, vol.1, 15, where he wrote 'the present encrease of wealth in the city of London spreads itself into the country'. For a general account of the role of London in the early eighteenth century see P. Earle, *The Making of the English Middle Class: Business, Society and Family Life in London, 1660-1730* (London, 1989), esp. p.17 *et seq.*

12. J. Chartres, 'Food Consumption and Internal Trade', in Beier and Finlay, eds, *London*, pp.168-96, and see also G. Rude, *Hanoverian London, 1714-1808* (London, 1971), p.20.

13. *Survey of London*, vol.29 (1960), 252.

14. *Survey of London*, vol.39 (1977), 86 *et seq.*

15. P. Thornton, *Seventeenth Century Interior Decoration in England, France and Holland* (London, 1978), pp.99-104.

16. A.E. Musson, 'Industrial Motive Power in the United Kingdom, 1800-1870', *Economic History Review*, 2nd Series, vol.29 (1976), 415-39.

17. L.D. Schwarz, *London in the Age of Industrialisation* (Cambridge, 1992), pp.1, 23, 31-40.

18. H.A.L. Cockerell and E. Green, *The British Insurance Business, 1547-1970* (London, 1976), pp.4-5.

19. D.E.W. Gibb, *Lloyd's of London* (London, 1957), pp.6-7, 34-38.

20. P.M.G. Dickson, *The Sun Insurance Office, 1710-1960* (London, 1960),

pp.31, 39, 66-7. The policy register begins in 1710. Devonshire policies begin to appear in 1723. S.D. Chapman, ed., 'The Devon Cloth Industry in the Eighteenth Century. Sun Fire Office Inventories of Merchants' and Manufacturers' Property, 1726-1770', *Devon and Cornwall Record Society*, vol.23 (1978), xxiv.

21. D. Hancock, ' "Domestic bubbling": eighteenth century London merchants and individual investment in the funds', *Economic History Review*, 2nd Series, vol.47 (1994), 679-702.

22. I. Pears, *The Discovery of Painting* (New Haven, 1988).

23. J.H. Druery *(Historical and Topographical Notices of Great Yarmouth* [London, 1826] p.80) records that Mr Isaacs, a London picture dealer, sold some paintings to a Yarmouth inhabitant. He then goes on to list pictures owned by other Yarmouth inhabitants, including Dutch land scapes and a Poussin, as well as works by Crome and Gainsborough.

24. Cf. H. Carter, *The Towns of Wales* (Cardiff, 1966), pp.80, 105-13 and R. Northam, *Urban Geography* (New York, 1975), pp.98, 122.

25. London was supplying the colonies in America, its 'detached suburbs', with a wide range of manufactured goods by the end of the seventeenth century. See N. Zahedieh, 'London and the colonial consumer in the late seventeenth century', *Economic History Review*, 2nd Series, vol.47 (1994), 239-61.

26. H. Carter, *The Study of Urban Geography* (London, 1972), esp. ch. 6, pp.88-114.

27. H. Carter, *Introduction to Urban Historical Geography* (1983), p.89. For examples of such a scalogram see J. Patten, *English Towns, 1500-1700* (Folkestone, 1978), pp.273, 283.

28. Rude, *Hanoverian London*, p.25.

29. This area is slightly larger than the Home Counties discussed in P. Garside, 'London and the Home Counties', in F.M.L. Thompson, ed., *The Cambridge Social History of Britain 1750-1850* (Cambridge, 1990), vol.1, 471-540. The hinterland of London as defined in J.A. Galloway and M. Murphy, 'Feeding the City: Medieval London and its Agrarian Hinterland', *London Journal*, vol.16 (1991), 3-14, does not include Sussex, Hampshire or East Anglia. They should clearly be included by the sixteenth century. D. Keene, 'Medieval London and its Region', *London Journal*, vol.14 (1989), 99-111 uses a less precise definition, namely up to about fifty miles from London as an inner, 'suburban', zone, with a wider, more diffuse region lying beyond. *The Oxford English Dictionary* defines Home Counties as Middlesex, Surrey, Kent and Essex. This is clearly too restrictive.

30. For the agricultural regions of this hinterland and their underlying geological structures see ch.7-10 of J. Thirsk, ed., *The Agrarian History of England and Wales*, vol.V.1 (Cambridge, 1984).

31. A. Young, *General View of the Agriculture of Sussex* (Newton Abbot, 1970 edn), p.417.

32. See Musson, 'Industrial Motive Power'.

33. M. Alexander, 'The Mills of Guildford', *Surrey Archaeological Collections*, vol.74 (1983), 91-9.

34. *Victoria County History (VCH), Surrey*, vol.2 (1905), 255.

35. W.B. Johnson, *The Industrial Archaeology of Hertfordshire* (Newton Abbot, 1970), pp.21, 177.

36. D. Gerhold, 'The Growth of the London carrying trade, 1681–1838', *Economic History Review*, 2nd Series, vol.41 (1988), 392–410, esp. 405.

37. J.H. Farrant, 'The Seaborne Trade of Sussex, 1720–1845', *Sussex Archaeological Collections*, vol.114 (1976), 97–120. See also his 'The Harbours of Sussex', *Sussex Industrial History*, vol.15 (1985-6), 2–11.

38. P. Carron, 'The Building of the First Bridge at Westminster, 1736–1750', *Journal of Transport History*, vol.3 (1957-8), 111 *et seq.*

39. D. Crossley and R. Saville, eds, 'The Fuller Letters, 1728–1755', *Sussex Record Society*, vol.76 (1991), xxiv.

40. P. Deane, *The First Industrial Revolution* (Cambridge, 1965), p.77, and P. Deane and W.A. Cole, *British Economic Growth 1688–1959*, 2nd edn (Cambridge, 1967), p.238.

41. D.F. Harrison, 'Bridges and economic development, 1300–1800', *Economic History Review*, 2nd Series, vol.45 (1992), 240–61.

42. See M.J. Freeman, 'Introduction', in D.H. Aldcroft and M.J. Freeman, eds, *Transport in the Industrial Revolution* (Manchester, 1983), p.13.

43. See Gerhold, 'London carrying trade'.

44. J.A. Chartres and G.L. Turnbull, 'Road Transport', in Aldcroft and Freeman, eds, *Transport in the Industrial Revolution*, pp.64-99.

45. J.A. Chartres, 'The Capital's Provincial Eyes: London's Inns in the Early Eighteenth Century', *London Journal*, vol.3 (1977), 24–39.

46. See W. Albert, *The Turnpike Road System in England, 1663–1840* (Cambridge, 1972), esp. p.158 *et seq.*, and E. Pawson, *Transport and Economy* (London, 1977), esp. p.301 *et seq.*

47. K. Ellis, *The Post Office in the Eighteenth Century* (London, 1988), p.3.

48. M.W. Finn, ed., 'The Law Books of the Crowley Ironworks', *Surtees Society*, vol.167 (1952), and see A.G. Linney, 'Crowley's Wharf Greenwich', *Transactions of the Newcomen Society*, vol.16 (1935-6), 149-50.

49. P.S. Bagwell, *The Transport Revolution from 1770* (London, 1974), p.45.

50. Cf. J.A. Chartres, 'The Marketing of Agricultural Produce', in Thirsk, ed., *Agrarian History*, vol.V.2 (Cambridge, 1985), ch.17.

51. It is one of the principal conclusions of A. Kussmaul, *A General View of the Rural Economy of England, 1538–1840* (Cambridge, 1990), that the later seventeenth century is the key period in the development of regional specialization and market integration.

52. See Thirsk, ed., *Agrarian History*, vol.V.1, 215, 273-6, 282.

53. C.S. Davies, *A History of Macclesfield* (Manchester, 1968 edn), pp.122 *et seq.*

54. W. Jackson, *The Development of Transportation in Modern England* (London, 1962 edn), Appendix 5.

55. C. Deering, *Historical Account of the Ancient and Present State of the Town of Nottingham* (Nottingham, 1751), p.91. Many of the goods for the Lenton fair came via Gainsborough: see I.S. Beckwith, 'The River Trade of Gainsborough, 1500–1850', *Lincolnshire History and Archaeology*, vol.2 (1967), 3-20.

56. J.M. Moffat, *The History of the Town of Malmesbury* (Tetbury, 1805), p.154.

57. S. Rudder, *A New History of Gloucestershire* (Gloucester, 1779), p.671.

58. J. Collinson, *The History and Antiquities of the County of Somerset*, vol.3 (Bath, 1791), 203.

59. See Galloway and Murphy, 'Feeding the City', and Keene, 'Medieval London'. For an earlier account see F.J. Fisher, 'The Development of the London Food Market, 1540-1640', *Economic History Review*, 1st Series, vol.5 (1935), pp.46-64, and see now P.J. Corfield and N.B. Harte, eds, *F.J. Fisher, London and the English Economy, 1500-1700* (London, 1990).

60. See R.C. Richardson, 'The Metropolitan Counties: Bedfordshire, Hertfordshire and Middlesex', in Thirsk, ed., *Agrarian History*, vol.V.1, 245.

61. Cf. *The Times*, 2 January 1798.

62. *VCH Middlesex*, vol.4 (1971), 30, 76, 116.

63. See C.E. Brent, 'Urban Employment and Population in Sussex between 1550 and 1660', *Sussex Archaeological Collections*, vol.113 (1975), 35-50.

64. C. Taylor, *The Cambridgeshire Landscape* (London, 1973), p.254.

65. R. Plot, *The Natural History of Staffordshire* (London, 1686), p.107. On p.121 he records that the best clay for making pots for glass houses was to be found at Old Swynford. It was conveyed to London either by wagon or else by wagon to Bewdley, down the Severn by barge to Bristol and then on by sea.

66. *Philosophical Transactions of the Royal Society*, vol.19 (1695-97), p.343.

67. Defoe, *Tour*, vol.2, 14.

68. J. Pennington and J. Sleight, 'Steyning Town and its Trades, 1559-1787', *Sussex Archaeological Collections*, vol.130 (1992), 164-88.

69. *VCH Oxfordshire*, vol.12 (1990), 364.

70. *VCH Sussex*, vol.6 (1986), part 2, 172.

71. E.g. *Calendar of Patent Rolls, 1429-1436*, p.550.

72. Defoe, *Tour*, vol.1, 299.

73. M. Reed, ed., 'Buckinghamshire Probate Inventories, 1661-1714', *Buckinghamshire Record Society*, vol.24 (1988), 103-4.

74. *VCH Surrey* (1905), vol.2, 315-8, and A.J. Haslefoot, *The Industrial Archaeology of South-East England* (Newton Abbot, 1978), p.61.

75. Haslefoot, *Industrial Archaeology*, p.87; C.W. Chalklin, *Seventeenth Century Kent* (London, 1965), p.137; H.C. Tomlinson, 'Wealden Gunfounding: An Analysis of its Decline in the Eighteenth Century', *Economic History Review*, 2nd Series, vol.29 (1976), 383-400, and B. Short, 'The De-industrialisation process: a case study of the Weald, 1600-1850', in P. Hudson, ed., *Regions and Industries* (Cambridge, 1989), pp.156-74.

76. *VCH Oxfordshire*, vol.10 (1972), 127, 225.

77. C. Pickford, 'Bedfordshire Clock and Watchmakers, 1352-1880', *Bedfordshire Historical Record Society*, vol.70 (1991), 8-13.

78. See Schwarz, *London*, pp.38-9.

79. On the manufactures of the southern counties in general see J.R. Wordie, 'The South: Oxfordshire, Buckinghamshire, Berkshire, Wiltshire and Hampshire', in Thirsk, ed., *Agrarian History*, vol.V.1, esp. pp.346-57.

80. A. Everitt, 'The Marketing of Agricultural Produce', in Thirsk, ed., *Agrarian History*, vol.IV (Cambridge, 1967), 466-592.

81. Chartres, 'The Marketing of Agricultural Produce', pp.406-502.

82. Reed, 'Probate Inventories', pp.20, 289, etc., and J.A. Johnston, ed., 'Probate Inventories of Lincoln Citizens, 1661-1714', *Lincoln Record*

Society, vol.80 (1991), 9, 56, 122, etc.

83. Public Record Office, PROB.3 32/188. Buckinghamshire Record Office DA/Wf/73/227.
84. Pennington and Sleight, 'Steyning Town'.
85. See generally J. Thirsk, *Economic Policy and Projects* (Oxford, 1978); N. McKendrick, J. Brewer and J.H. Plumb, *The Birth of a Consumer Society* (Bloomington, 1982); L. Weatherill, *Consumer Behaviour and Material Culture in Britain, 1660-1760* (London, 1988), and C. Shammas, *The Pre-Industrial Consumer in England and America* (Oxford, 1990).
86. J. Harland, ed., 'Home and Farm Accounts of the Shuttleworths of Gawthorpe Hall, Lancashire', *Chetham Society*, vol.35 (1856), 212.
87. *VCH Gloucestershire*, vol.4 (1988), 268.
88. A.M.C. Forster, ed., 'Selections from the Disbursement Books of Sir Thomas Haggerston, 1691-1709', *Surtees Society*, vol.180 (1969), 45.
89. J.W.F. Hill, ed., 'Letters and Papers of the Banks Family of Revesby Abbey, 1704-1760', *Lincoln Record Society*, vol.45 (1952), 141.
90. Derbyshire County Record Office, D 2375 M 277/5.
91. K.M. Walton, 'An Inventory of 1710 from Dyrham Park', *Furniture History*, vol.22 (1986), 25–80, and see B. Murison, 'Getting and Spending: William Blathwayt and Dyrham Park', *History Today*, vol.40(12), (1990), 22–8.
92. McKendrick et al., *Birth of Consumer Society*, pp.21, 56 et seq.
93. Derbyshire County Record Office, D 2375 M 277/6, 277/7 (no pagination).
94. N.K. Rothstein, 'Canterbury and London: the Silk Industry in the late Seventeenth Century', *Textile History*, vol.20 (1989), 33–45.
95. *Survey of London*, vol.29 (1980), 71, and McKendrick et al., *Birth of Consumer Society*, pp.121–2.
96. Public Record Office, PROB.3 19/47, PROB.3 22/64, PROB.3 28/5.
97. Reed, 'Probate Inventories', pp.146–8.
98. See J.P. Feather, *The Provincial Book Trade in Eighteenth Century England* (Cambridge, 1985) *passim*.
99. F.H. Panton, 'James Simmons: A Canterbury Tycoon', *Archaeologia Cantiana*, vol.105 (1988), 215–42.
100. G. Tyack, 'The Freemans of Fawley', *Records of Bucks.*, vol.24 (1982).
101. Defoe, *Tour*, vol.1, 6.
102. *Ibid.*, vol.1, 168–9.
103. C. Burlington, *The Modern Universal British Traveller* (London, 1779), p.59.
104. J. Lees-Milne, *English Country Houses: Baroque, 1685–1715* (London, 1970, 1986 edn), pp.31–4.
105. *VCH Oxfordshire*, vol.10 (1972), 160 et seq.
106. J. Stovold, 'Minute Book of the Pavement Commissioners for Southampton, 1770–1789', *Southampton Record Series*, vol.31 (1990), 6, 18–19.
107. Panton, 'James Simmons'.
108. See Reed, 'Probate Inventories', pp.x–xx, and *idem*, *The Buckinghamshire Landscape* (London, 1979), *passim*.
109. M. Reed, 'Decline and Recovery in a Provincial Urban Network: Buckinghamshire Towns, 1350–1850', in *idem*, ed., *English Towns in Decline, 1350–1800*, Centre for Urban History, University of Leicester,

Working Paper no.1 (Leicester, 1988).
110. I.F.W. Beckett, 'The Buckinghamshire Posse Comitatus, 1798', *Buckinghamshire Record Society*, vol.22 (1985).

CHAPTER FOUR

Dublin 1600–1700: a City and its Hinterlands

Raymond Gillespie

The growth of Dublin

To account for the growth of large metropolitan cities in early modern Europe historians have resorted to a wide range of explanations. Most important has been that which links the growth of capital cities with the emergence of the modern state. Such an explanation has been used to account for the rise of large cities, such as Madrid and Paris, whose main function was political rather than economic or social. These cities, it is suggested, can only have been parasites, contributing little to their hinterlands in developmental terms but rather dominating them both economically and culturally. They sucked in wealth for conspicuous consumption by the political elite and provided nothing in return by way of economic stimulus. They also impoverished cultural life, repressing local developments, such as provincial printing, by state censorship, or dominating the market for cultural artefacts by their sheer size. At first sight such an explanation fits the dramatic growth of Dublin during the course of the late seventeenth and early eighteenth centuries. The rapid growth of eighteenth-century Dublin, both in terms of population and influence, is well known. Between 1700 and 1800 the city's population rose by about 1.1 per cent per annum and, after London, it was the most important city in the British Isles.[1] In the century before 1700 Dublin's rate of growth was even more spectacular. In 1600 it was a small town, probably comprising between 15,000 and 20,000 persons (certainly less than 1.3 per cent of Ireland's population) and was smaller than most English provincial centres.[2] Luke Gernon, who visited the city in the 1620s, recorded that the medieval town was largely unchanged. The town was 'most frequented more for conveniency than for majesty' and it 'resembleth Bristol but falleth short'.[3] Over the century the population was to grow at a rate of about 1.5 per cent per annum, which outshone even London's growth of about 1 per cent per annum over the same period. By 1680, according to a contemporary estimate, 9 per cent of Irish people lived in Dublin, in comparison with London's share of 7 per cent of the English population. The anonymous calculator also ventured to observe that, comparing Dublin with London, 'men live alike in these two cities'.[4] Thus the bookseller John Dunton's comment that by 1699

Dublin, although it was 'twelve times less than London, is yet the biggest next to it in all our dominions', is not a surprise.[5] Comparisons with London were not the only ones being made. One contemporary in 1686 placed Dublin in the top 12 European cities and in 1687 Sir William Petty compared it favourably with Paris, London, Amsterdam, Venice and Rome and declared it to be far in advance of any English provincial town.[6]

It was not only in terms of its population and cultural expansion that Dublin seemed to fit the pattern of a 'parasitic' political city, but its functions also changed over the seventeenth century, making it appear, for the first time, to be the political capital of a kingdom of Ireland. The sixteenth and early seventeenth centuries had seen a dramatic shift in social and political relations within Ireland. In the early sixteenth century gaelic and gaelicized Ireland was an amalgam of small lordships each with its own lord, economic arrangements and political structures.[7] Dublin was little more than the chief city of the English Pale concentrated on the eastern seaboard of the country and the extent to which its authority could be exerted on other parts of the island varied dramatically over time. In the course of the century the influence of the Dublin government expanded into other areas of the island through a combination of local agreements, plantation schemes and more informal colonization. The nine years war between 1594 and 1603 resulted in the decisive defeat of an alliance of lordships under Hugh O'Neill, Earl of Tyrone. After 1603 the royal writ ran throughout the whole country. The increased power of the central administration resulted in an enhanced parliament centralized in Dublin. In the sixteenth century 12 out of the 28 known venues of meetings of the Irish parliament had been outside Dublin. After 1603 no meeting was held outside the capital.[8] The courts also experienced a growth in business as a result of the extension of the Dublin administration's authority. The number of decrees handed down by the Court of Chancery, based in Dublin, expanded more than threefold between 1570-74 and 1635-39. A considerable portion of this was additional business resulting from the colonial expansion of the central government. Between 1603 and 1609 Chancery decrees to cases coming from Ulster and Connacht rose from 50 to 715 and the fines in Common Pleas over these years rose from 208 to 903.[9] The city was also the academic centre of the country after the founding of Ireland's only university, Trinity College, there in 1592. As with the courts the number of admissions to the College grew from 118 in 1637-40 to 367 in 1696-99, with the proportion of Ulster students rising from 4 per cent to 20 per cent over this period.[10]

However, the nature of royal authority in the localities was limited. The status and wealth of the new settlers in newly opened up regions depended on Ireland being seen as a centre of colonial exploitation and they resisted the interference of the central administration in that exploitation.[11] They used the institutions of the central government, such as the courts, only when necessary and notwithstanding the growth in the business of government, Dublin remained a relatively ineffective administrative centre. It lacked many of the symbols of power such as a vice-regal court which would act as a centre for social life and characterize the city as a capital. Sir William Brereton, visiting Dublin Castle, the seat of government, in 1635 was surprised at how modest it was. The House of Lords was 'a room of no great state or receipt' and the Commons 'but a mean and ordinary place'. The Council Chamber was 'a very plain room'.[12] The appointment of Thomas Wentworth, Earl of Strafford, as Lord Deputy of Ireland in 1632 was to change this situation. One of Wentworth's aims for the government of Ireland was to recreate the reality of an Irish kingdom, as envisaged in the 1541 act which had established a separate crown for Ireland and placed it on the head of the King of England. The centre of Wentworth's new entity was to be Dublin. Wentworth regarded himself as the King's representative in Ireland in a way no earlier Lord Deputy had done. In 1639, objecting to comments about him by a lawyer, he retorted that the lawyer had 'traduced his person and in him his Majesty himself whose character and image he was'.[13] Such a government required the trappings of power within the city and Wentworth began to develop these. He laid down a stringent code of court etiquette governing the actions of the courtiers which seems not to have existed in Ireland before.[14] The appointment of John Ogilby as Master of the Revels in February 1638 meant that an important court office was established in Ireland for the first time. Ogilby, a dancing master from Gray's Inns Lane in London, had come to Ireland between 1633 and 1635 to become a member of Wentworth's household and seems to have been given the brief of developing regular drama in the city which had been non-existent before this.[15] In terms of the physical fabric of the castle, Wentworth began rebuilding. Brereton commented that Wentworth had recently built 'a gallant and stately stable, as any I have seen in the king's dominions' and he had also constructed a brick building on the north side of the castle to house a proposed new symbol of the existence of an Irish kingdom: a mint.[16] This, however, was never established.

These initiatives began a transformation of the city from an essentially medieval town into a recognizably modern capital city. Wentworth's newly created vice-regal court began to attract the Irish nobility with its gaming, drama and eating. New trades, characteristic of the demands of conspicuous consumption, began to appear in the town's admissions to freedom. Between 1636 and 1640 silk dyers, bonelace makers, spurriers, vintners and box makers are documented for the first time. Older trades attached to the gentry also increased in importance. Of the 24 goldsmiths admitted to freedom between 1600 and 1640, ten were admitted between 1636 and 1640. Tailors also became more common with 56 being admitted during the late 1630s as opposed to an average of 18 over each five year period from 1600 to 1635. More gentry seemed to think it worthwhile becoming freemen of the city, with twice the average number of earlier years being admitted in the late 1630s.[17] The increased importance of the city gave rise to a spate of rebuilding to match its new-found status. Brereton's comment that 'this city of Dublin is extending its bounds and limits very far, much addition of building lately and some of those very fair and stately and complete buildings' is also borne out by the admissions to freedom. Between 1636 and 1640 more than half of all the plasterers who came to Dublin in the early seventeenth century were admitted to freedom along with nearly three quarters of the bricklayers and a third of all the joiners and carpenters.[18]

This process of transforming the physical and cultural environment of the city was short-lived and so had little impact outside Ireland, but the foundations of one of the main bases for the growth of the late seventeenth century had been laid. The increasingly unstable political situation in the late 1630s and the outbreak of war in 1641 meant that the development of a capital city was arrested. The experience of the city during the direct government of Ireland from London in the 1650s was not a pleasant one. It lost the vice-regal court which had become part of the economy and society in the 1630s, and trade restrictions imposed by the Cromwellian regime proved to be a serious challenge to the city's merchant community trying to rebuild its economy. More significant were the levels of taxation imposed on the city during the 1650s. Ireland as a whole was overtaxed in comparison to other areas of the British Isles during the 1650s, but Dublin city was more heavily taxed than most areas of Ireland. According to the monthly assessment set for 1657, Dublin city paid £82.7 per thousand payers of the 1660 poll tax. Dublin county paid £55.2 per thousand poll tax payers and the adjoining county of Kildare paid £42.6.[19] Discontent with these levels of taxation was no small factor in the Dublin revolt of the army in February 1660 which ultimately led to the restoration of Charles II. The Declaration which emerged from that revolt denied the right of the Rump Parliament to legislate for Ireland and in particular denied it the right to levy taxation without the consent of an Irish parliament. The Corporation of Dublin endorsed this view.[20] Among the English settlers a sense of Dublin as the capital of a Kingdom of Ireland was growing stronger. The local influence of the settler landholders was considerably reduced under the Cromwellian regime through a combination of high taxation, fines for delinquency and the presence of the army in the localities.[21] As a result the authority of the Dublin administration, and hence the status of the city as a political and administrative capital, grew in the late seventeenth century.

The arrival of the King's deputy, the Duke of Ormond, in the city in July 1665 was an event of some splendour in comparison to the arrival of Wentworth in the 1630s. Ormond was greeted by four masques along his route into the city, the last being one of Bacchus at the gate of Dublin Castle itself.[22] The message was clear: there was confidence that the vice-regal court would quickly re-establish itself and this would be of fundamental importance in the shaping of the late seventeenth century city. It was necessary to demonstrate in a tangible form the power of the newly restored monarchy and the government in Ireland; as Ormond later remarked to his son, 'It is of importance to keep up the splendour of the government.'[23] Ormond considered the possibility of building a new vice-regal palace but funds did not permit this and instead he contented himself with refurbishing the Castle. As a result the late seventeenth century saw considerable rebuilding in Dublin Castle, a process which was hastened by two fires in 1671 and 1684. The administrative functions of the Castle were also reorganized. Meetings of parliament were transferred to Chichester House and the prison was also moved out of the Castle, which was now to be a centre for the Viceroy only. The Privy Council also moved to a newly constructed chamber on Wood Quay and the old Council Chamber became the Lord Deputy's residence. A description of the Castle in 1678 by Robert Ware referred to the rebuilding by the Earl of Essex following the fire of 1671 as 'a beautiful form of a fair building unto which you ascend by a noble staircase'.[24] The rebuilding after the 1684 fire made further improvements so that by the 1690s the Castle could be compared by John Dunton with Whitehall. He added 'and indeed the grandeur they live in here is not much inferior to what you see in London if you make allowances for the number of great men at court there'. The same point was made by the French traveller Jouevin de Rochefort at the end of the 1660s when he noted that Ormond 'has a fine court and a suite altogether royal, among them are several French gentlemen'.[25] It was not only the Castle which was reshaped. Other signs of sociability began to become more prominent in the city. Theatre, for instance, expanded dramatically in the late seventeenth century. The appointment of John Ogilby and Thomas Stanley as joint masters of the revels in 1663 linked the growth of theatre with the vice-regal court which provided a stimulus for such entertainment.[26] Other features of the society are more difficult to quantify. Coffee houses had become important by the 1680s not only as centres of business but also as a means of disseminating news. The intellectual life of the city was guided by the Dublin Philosophical Society, founded in 1683, and modelled on the Royal Society in London.[27]

Thus late seventeenth-century Dublin was becoming an effective centre of government with its own institutions, such as a vice-regal court, and its status as a legal centre was also enhanced. All the Irish law courts based in Dublin saw a marked growth of business in the late seventeenth century. The number of fines entered in Common Pleas increased by almost two and a half times between 1665–69 and 1695–99, with decrees from the Court of Exchequer increasing four-fold over the same period. Only Chancery business seems to have slowed down in the 1690s after an increase in the previous two decades.[28] The growth in the status of Dublin even gave rise anew to the old claim of the Archbishop of Dublin to be primate of all Ireland, a title usually held by the Archbishop of Armagh. The Privy Council had ruled in 1634 that in the case of the Church of Ireland Armagh was to be the superior see; by 1679 the Catholic Archbishop of Dublin, Peter Talbot, felt that the city was now important enough for him to claim the primacy of all Ireland for the see of Dublin, but Rome ruled against this.[29]

All of this evidence seems to suggest that Dublin conforms to the model of a rising political centre, associated with state building, which promoted not economic expansion but rather encouraged conspicuous consumption. The consequence of this should have been economic stagnation in the hinterland of the city. Dublin, however, does not fit this paradigm neatly. Although possessing all the trappings of the capital of a kingdom its status was, at least in part, colonial, which leads to problems in the definition of a hinterland and the measurement of the effects of the growth of the city on that area. The definition of a hinterland for the city is difficult given the paucity of sources for the seventeenth-century city, but one way of exploring the problem is to examine the origins of the Dublin population in the seventeenth century.

The demographic dimension

The demographic background to seventeenth-century Dublin was similar to that of most other European capitals. In the main, the city experienced a surplus of deaths over births throughout the seventeenth century. While the survival of parish records is poor it is possible, nonetheless, to indicate the broad outlines of the population trends. In the extramural parish of St Michan's, for instance, burials outstripped baptisms by over two to one during the 1630s. In the parish of St John, at the core of the medieval city, burials outstripped baptisms by 1.3 to one, although the register seems to be defective before 1638.[30] At the beginning of the eighteenth century the picture was little different. The bills of mortality between 1712 and 1718 reveal that burials exceeded baptisms in the city as a whole by almost 2.5 to one, with fevers and smallpox being the largest killers. Rather over half the burials occurred in the under-16 age group.[31]

The growth in Dublin's population therefore came about through immigration. Some of this inflow certainly came from the adjoining Irish counties but the importance of this source of population growth varied considerably over time. In the sixteenth century, of the 59 aldermanic families of the city only 11 originated in England, 14 from the city itself and the remainder from the surrounding countryside. Certainly from the 1680s, when estimates of Irish population by region are possible, the growth rates of population in the counties near Dublin were significantly lower than in other areas of the country, suggesting migration into the city.[32] However, Dublin could not afford to rely on its Irish hinterland alone for its supply of people. Irish population was low, although growing fast mainly through immigration, and the ready availability of land at low rents meant that it was difficult to attract men to live in towns, a point illustrated by the failures of many attempts by settlers to establish towns in other parts of the country.[33]

One rather crude way of measuring the relative importance of Dublin's Irish hinterland compared with other sources for the city's population growth is to examine the religious composition of the city's inhabitants over time. Migrants drawn from the surrounding countryside would usually be Catholic while immigrants from England tended to be Protestant. In the early part of the seventeenth century Dublin was, in the main, a Catholic city, and there is no evidence to suggest that significant numbers of Catholics converted to Protestantism. Archbishop Bulkeley's visitation of 1630 recorded only two parishes, St Werburgh's and St John's, as having a Protestant majority.[34] This would suggest that the inflow of migrants up to this time was largely from surrounding Irish counties. As a result of this Catholic dominance the sixteenth-century experience had almost inextricably intertwined the city and its privileges with Catholicism. While Catholics did not hold the mayoralty after 1612, they still remained prominent in the Corporation and held the office of sheriff on a number of occasions before 1641. It took the purging of the Cromwellian regime to break the connection between the Catholics and the government of the city.

The 1641 rebellion in Ulster and the rapid spread of this throughout the island saw an initial dramatic increase in the number of Protestants in the city. The violence resulting from sectarian tensions exacerbated by economic crises caused many of the Protestant minority in the countryside to flee to the city for protection. Conditions in the city became increasingly difficult during the 1640s. Dublin's trade ground to a halt as a result of a parliamentary blockade at sea, and the war in its hinterland had effectively stopped trade between the city and surrounding areas. From 1647, when the city surrendered to the parliamentary commander, Michael Jones, matters improved but this advance was curtailed by the outbreak of plague in the city in 1650 and 1651. Renewed immigration into the city during the 1650s boosted the population again. As a result of the developments of the 1640s and 1650s Dublin had become a decisively Protestant and English style city. In the poll tax of 1659 about 73 per cent of the inhabitants were described as 'English'.[35] This proportion was maintained into the eighteenth century despite the dramatic growth of the last part of the century. There are indications that this dramatic late seventeenth-century population growth was mainly the result of immigration of Protestants from England. The largest guild of the city, the Merchants Guild of Holy Trinity, had fallen on such hard times through the decay of trade in the 1640s that in 1648 it had to dispense with one of its clerks whom it could no longer afford. By the late 1670s the Guild had become so large that it could no longer meet in its old Guild Hall and it was proposed to build a new one. A large proportion of such Guild members would have been Protestant since freedom of the city, only available to Protestants, was normally a prerequisite of membership of the Guild.[36]

The religious composition of the city's population by the end of the seventeenth century also suggests that the main source of Dublin's population growth was not from within Ireland but from Britain or elsewhere. The growth of dissenting congregations, which were drawn mainly from England or Scotland, in the later seventeenth century points to immigration. By 1700 Dublin could boast four Presbyterian congregations, with another at Clontarf near the city, as well as three Baptist congregations, a scattering of Independents and a Jewish synagogue.[37] There was also a substantial Huguenot community of about 2000 families in the city according to James Verdon, rector of East Dereham in Norfolk who visited the city in 1699. They had been given one of the aisles of St Patrick's Cathedral in which to set up their church and in 1687 the Corporation decreed that French Protestants should be admitted to the city free of all taxes for five years. By 1716 there were four congregations of Huguenots in the city.[38] A smaller, though much more significant, community within the city were the Quakers, of which there were about 200 families by 1685. The Quaker community had three meeting houses in 1692 when a new large meeting house was built in Sycamore Alley to accommodate all the Quakers of the city.[39] While such groups may not have been approved of in England, in Ireland where

Protestants were in a minority, differences in theology and practice between various Protestant groups were often ignored and the colonial ethos of Dublin was more congenial to dissent than many English cities. Thus the Chester Quaker Joseph Haddock found it more politic in 1685 to serve his apprenticeship to a linen draper in Dublin than to remain at home. At the other end of the social spectrum, the Quaker Anthony Sharpe, one of the largest woollen merchants in late seventeenth-century Dublin, was also an immigrant from England having left Gloucester after suffering persecution there.[40] The Quaker community was important to the development of the city's trade since it provided a truly national organization of contacts through which trade could be conducted. Ulster Quakers, for example, were prominent among the early developers of the linen trade, the finished cloth being shipped by Dublin Quakers.

More detailed evidence suggests that the Dublin immigrants came in particularly significant numbers from northern and western England and Wales. The Welsh in Dublin met for 'a feast' on St David's day, 1671 followed by a sermon preached by a Welshman; and in the same year the men of Chester and Cheshire met in St Werburgh's church for a sermon preached by Samuel Hinde in celebration of the fact that the mayor for that year, the shoemaker John Totty, was a Chester man.[41] That Chester should have been a place of origin for a group of Dublin immigrants is not surprising given the strong trading connections between Dublin and Chester in the sixteenth century. Chester was but one example, since Dublin's attractions for immigrants from areas other than its local Irish hinterland brought in a wide range of settlers. For example, the expansion of the Dutch economy overseas in the early seventeenth century saw the arrival of a significant number of Dutch families in Dublin which, although it was an expanding trading centre, had little in the way of shipping – an element which the Dutch could provide. Over 40 per cent of the heads of Dutch families identified in seventeenth-century Ireland lived in Dublin. Indeed so rapid was the growth of Dutch influence in the early seventeenth-century trade of Dublin that in 1632 Sir Philip Perceval felt that they were about to monopolize it. Rumour circulated in Dublin that the Dutch were proposing to purchase the farm of the Irish customs which was held by the Duchess of Buckingham.[42]

This immigration to the city as a result of economic pulls was central to its demographic growth. From the 1650s the Corporation consciously tried to attract English settlers into the city. In 1651, for example, the Corporation invited English manufacturers, traders and artisans to settle in Dublin and the traditional guild restrictions were lifted to admit newcomers.[43] Similar, though less generous, terms were offered regularly throughout the late seventeenth century. Landlords also were offering incentives to attract the right sort of tenant to their newly developing estates. In the 1670s, for example, the Earl of Meath, by agreement with his tenants, released the estate giving the satisfactory tenants longer leases: 40 per cent of the new leases were for 31 years and 51 per cent were for 41 years. He also built facilities for new markets. After the Williamite wars new incentives were given in the form of leases for lives which were renewable for ever. Nine of these leases are known on the estate before 1691 and 131 were granted between 1691 and 1701.[44] The Earl was clearly concerned to tempt an appropriate tenantry to his estate and in 1683 he was even attempting to encourage families from Yorkshire to settle there. Such moves certainly had some impact, especially in attracting highly skilled settlers to the newly developed estates, such as those of the Earl of Meath and the Corporation, around the city.[45] In the Earl of Meath's liberty to the west of the city weaving became an important occupation. While there is no conclusive evidence that the Earl encouraged this development it does represent the reversal of the normal pattern of a European city of the industrial centre being at the east of the city and some intervention is highly probable. In the area around Oxmantown Green, developed by the city, the parish registers record a very wide range of skills, both craft and industrial.[46] One indication of the success of this type of activity is that over the century differentials in wage rates between Dublin and England (as measured by the Phelps-Brown/Hopkins index) did not widen over the century as would be expected if Dublin lacked skills.[47]

The city and its economic hinterlands

What such a detailed investigation of Dublin's demographic history for the seventeenth century reveals is that the definition of its hinterland is not an easy matter. In particular that hinterland, as defined by population movements, was not confined to Ireland but was focused on the Irish Sea, drawing influences from both Ireland and north-west England into the city. This reality meant that Dublin's influence on its hinterland was complicated by the fact that the forces at work in shaping that hinterland were not contained within one set of economic or social conditions. In particular Dublin's position as a port was crucial as it acted not only as a centre of government for Ireland but as a centre of interchange between the various cultural and economic hinterlands within which it operated. In economic terms Dublin provided a channel through which the produce from the commercial exploitation of its Irish hinterland could be exported to markets elsewhere in its other hinterland of north-west England. Over time its share in Irish trade expanded significantly. In 1616 Dublin accounted for 20 per cent of the customs revenue of the kingdom. By the 1630s this had risen to 30 per cent and by the 1660s about 40 per cent of customs revenue was generated from Dublin port. As trade became more specialized and complex in the late seventeenth century so it became attracted to the capital with its specialist services so that by the end of the century Dublin accounted for 50 per cent of customs revenue.[48]

The impact of such a growth in trade on the north-west England part of Dublin's hinterland remains to be investigated. The availability of large numbers of Irish cattle and sheep in this area, for example, may well have had local dietary implications. At any rate by 1640 Chester, at least, was dependent on the Dublin trade for its survival.[49] Within the Irish hinterland of Dublin significant changes were seen. Many of the English merchants who traded through Dublin established agents in the city's Irish trading hinterland, which was growing in line with the political status of the city. Christopher Lowther, a Whitehaven merchant who traded extensively with Dublin, expanded his business into Ulster in the 1630s when he established an agent at Belfast to purchase beef.[50] The structure of Dublin's export trade in the early seventeenth century shows what may be described as a colonial export trade concentrating on unprocessed staples and the consequences of asset-stripping newly acquired estates, such as timber exports. As early as 1611, for instance, a report on the Irish customs recorded that Dublin's principal exports were corn, hides, linen yarn and wool and among its principal imports were linen and woollen cloth, groceries and silks. By 1626, when Dublin exported almost 28 per cent of all Irish exports by value, the picture was similar. About 43 per cent of Dublin's export trade by value was in live cattle, another quarter in cattle products such as hides, tallow and beef, 10 per cent in sheep and wool, and 12 per cent in grain.[51]

Dublin, because of its access to an English hinterland, was of considerable importance to its Irish hinterland in providing a marketing structure for the output of a fast-developing region. Initially those services were rudimentary. Despite the fact that Dublin was mainly a trading port it had little in the way of a significant merchant community. Much of its trade was carried on in foreign shipping. Part of the reason for this small merchant community in the city was the colonial process which was under way in most of the rest of the island. Land was easily available at low prices and many Irish merchants used their cash surplus not to advance loans or to engage in further trade but to speculate in Irish land.[52] As the commissioners appointed to survey the state of Ireland in 1622 noted, 'the merchants here in all the cities of the kingdom do as they grow unto wealth withdraw themselves into the country and there settle upon farms and neglect their trade of merchandise in which they were bred.'[53] The problem was not unique to the merchants. As early as 1595 the Corporation resolved that so many of the inhabitants of the town were now living outside it that the cess of the city would also be imposed on them. In 1602 the by-laws of the city complained that craftsmen were withdrawing themselves into the country 'for more profit' and leaving a shortage of tradesmen in the town. By 1641 the merchant Thomas Wakefield, who was also mayor that year, had an estate in Wexford. The sheriff that year had land in Meath and at least one alderman claimed losses of land in counties Meath, Louth and Wicklow as a result of the rebellion.[54] Thus, while a significant portion of Irish trading wealth flowed through Dublin, the city itself did not retain a large portion of this wealth. In the 1634 subsidy, for instance, Dublin was assessed at only 2.4 per cent of the subsidy and in 1664 4.4 per cent of the subsidy was payable by the city.[55]

In the later seventeenth century the city was to be of more importance to its Irish hinterland. There are indications that after 1660, partly as a result of the growing status of the city within Ireland, the range of skills within the city began to grow. This is reflected in the creation of a large number of small guilds in the late seventeenth century which represent the break-up of the old medieval guilds into more specialist bodies. The Guild of St Luke the Evangelist covering cutlers, painters, stainers and stationers was founded in 1670, the felters in 1676. In the 1690s the curriers, brewers and maltsters all formed guilds and the joiners were granted a charter in 1701.[56] Some of these guilds reflect the demand for services by the gentry community in the city. The establishment of the Guild of St Luke, for instance, reflects the rise of the artist, particularly the portrait painter, in late seventeenth-century Dublin. Similarly the stationers' faculty in the Guild of St Luke also expanded over the century. In 1670 the faculty stood at five members, in 1676 at nineteen free and admitted brethren and by 1686 the number had risen to thirty-five.[57] The seventeenth century also saw the emergence of other specialist services. A significant merchant community also grew up in the late seventeenth-century city. The dramatic rise in land prices outside the city during the late seventeenth century meant that purchasing land there was no longer the attractive option it had been earlier in the century. As a result merchants tended to remain in the city, devoting their energies to urban land speculation, trade or other specialist skills. The Dutchman Christian Borr acted as a banker in Dublin and London in the 1630s and other settlers in the late seventeenth century set themselves up as bankers, providing mainly bills of exchange for merchants and landlords wishing to have their rents paid to them abroad.[58]

This growth of the range of functions provided by the late seventeenth-century city was of importance to the Irish economy as a whole. While the early seventeenth-century trade of Dublin had been dominated by raw unprocessed exports, its late seventeenth-century exports were rather different. By 1683 only half of the city's exports could be accounted for by butter, meat, hides and wool which had been the staples of the earlier part of the century.[59] In part this was a result of economic change in the island as a whole. The economy shifted from being a producer of staples to a more specialized economy concentrating on processed goods such as barrelled beef, butter and in some areas cloth. Regions within Ireland began to specialize to a much greater extent than before. This created a need for a more comprehensive marketing network, both national and international, for their produce and the late seventeenth century saw the dramatic growth of the urban network in Ireland.[60] In this context the overseas contacts of a growing Dublin merchant community and its access to services such as banking gave Dublin the edge in marketing much of this new output. Luxury goods, such as the fine linens produced in late seventeenth- and early eighteenth-century Ulster, could not be consumed locally because of the limited demand in the Irish market. The most likely market was London and the merchants of Belfast did not have the necessary contacts there or access to the credit mechanisms to conduct the transactions. By contrast the Dublin merchants had. By the end of the seventeenth century bleached linen cloth had become the single most important export through Dublin, the city handling over 70 per cent of national linen exports.[61] In this area Dublin's most serious rival was Cork which provided similar services for the Munster region and like Dublin its share of Irish trade also grew in the late seventeenth century at the expense of smaller ports.

By the early eighteenth century the range of services provided by the capital city to its Irish hinterland was unusually wide even by European standards. Dublin had become the unrivalled economic centre of the country through which most of the needs of the country were imported and through which most of its produce was exported. That had only been achieved because of Dublin's contact with a wider hinterland in north west England, especially Chester. The buoyancy of this market and the greater financial resources of its merchant community meant that it was in a position to stimulate developments elsewhere in the country, such as the Ulster linen trade. In doing so it promoted inter-regional trade and encouraged national economic integration.[62] In this way Dublin bound together its varying hinterlands in England and Ireland and promoted economic change in both areas. Thus Dublin managed to combine the role of economic stimulus with that of political capital by using its ambivalent status as both the political centre of the Kingdom of Ireland and financier of colonial activity.

The city's cultural role

While the economic experience of Dublin in the seventeenth century suggests that Dublin used its unique position as both a colonial centre and a political capital to act as an interchange between its different hinterlands, thus becoming an engine of change within Ireland, its success as an innovator in cultural life was more limited. The colonial element in Dublin's civic life saw its political future in a wider British imperial world and the cultural norms of that world were those of London and the royal Court. For visitors to Dublin in the late seventeenth century what was most impressive about the Tholsel, newly built to house the Corporation, was the symbols of loyalty to the crown with which it was decorated. The royal arms were placed at the centre of the exterior. In 1684 the Corporation erected on either side of the royal arms two eight-foot statues, one of Charles I and the other of Charles II. These were intended to be prominent since when first carved, by the Dutch sculptor William de Keysar, they were judged too small and an additional two feet in height was added. Inside the building there were portraits of the King; the Corporation paid £24 for a portrait of James II in 1689.[63] This theme of loyalty by the city to the crown extended to the Corporation regalia. In April 1661 the King conferred on the mayor of Dublin a cap of maintenance to be borne before him in processions together with a collar to be worn by the mayor. Similarly the city mace, also borne before him, and regilded in 1685 to match the new splendour of the Tholsel, had the royal arms emblazoned on it.[64] All this iconography distinguished the loyal city-dwellers from the potentially disloyal Irish in the surrounding countryside. It also demonstrated their anglicization, and therefore in the eyes of English and Anglo-Irish contemporaries, their civility. They were, as James Verdon noted, Christians rather than the heathens of the countryside. Similarly, the possession of a clock by a corporation was a sign of the distinct character of the town, in particular the difference between the rhythm of urban life, governed by the clock, and of rural life, governed by the weather and seasons. English towns had begun to acquire clocks by the middle of the sixteenth century and Dublin in so doing quickly asserted not only its modernity, but also its Englishness. The late seventeenth-century annals of Dudley Loftus noted under the year 1560:

> This year were set up three public clocks, the one in the castle another in the city and a third at St Patrick's church which were at the first setting up a very great pleasure to the people and became the subject of verses made on that occasion with much ease by putting the name of Ireland into the place of England which was the only difference between these and other verses which had been made in England upon the like occasion.[65]

The Tholsel clock surrounded as it was with the royal arms symbolized to Dubliners what was expected of them.

In cultural terms the domination of Dublin by the norms and standards of London is well demonstrated by the history of the theatre in the late seventeenth century. In the main the plays performed in Dublin theatres were those of the London stage. There were some significant exceptions. Mrs Philips' rhymed translation of Pierre Corneille's *Pompey* was first produced in Dublin in 1663 with much interest from London where it was printed later. Similarly the Earl of Orrery's *Altemira*, written in 1661, can claim to be the first 'heroic play' in a style later to be taken up by John Dryden. It was not until William Philips' *St Stephen's Green or the Generous Lovers*, written in 1697 or 1698, that the Dublin stage could boast of anything resembling an Irish play. Indeed most of the promising Irish playwrights of the next generation such as George Farquhar saw London as the centre of dramatic activity and were not attracted by a derivative centre such as Dublin.[66] In terms of literary patronage Dublin had little to offer as a status imprint on published work. As a result most seventeenth-century Irish manuscripts were published in London, leaving the Dublin presses idle for most of the seventeenth century. As James Verdon remarked, 'they have, moreover, a printing house which, I must own, is no great glory for them because they seldom print anything but news and tickets for funerals'.[67]

From outside Dublin at least some of the inhabitants of Ireland looked to the capital city as an arbiter of cultural standards. The heroine of the 1693 novel *Virtue Rewarded or the Irish Princess* compared some of the local gentry with one of her Dublin suitors: 'the breeding which he brought from Dublin, elevated him so far above them, in his discourse, his carriage, and all he did that they did look like our wild Irish to him'.[68] The diffusion of the norms of the capital became easier in the eighteenth century with the more regular meetings of parliament, and by the middle of the century a winter 'season' had emerged. The location of Trinity College, the island's only university, in the city gave it an added social cachet. The young Donough Clancy, from West Cork, not only wrote to his brother in the college for schoolbooks in 1639, but also looked forward to going to the college himself because 'I am very desirious to be brought up among gentlemen, to see fashions and all other kind of breeding.' He enclosed with his letter a number of Latin verses to show that he was 'as handsome a scholar as any of my age'.[69] From another perspective the cultural life of Dublin seemed decidedly inferior. English observers saw it as a pale reflection of London and as a dumping ground for undesirables who had no future in England. The colonial situation in Ireland offered scope for such men. It was these groups who were satirized in Richard Head's 1663 play *Hic et Ubique or the Humours of Dublin*. One of the themes of the play is a group of men travelling from Holyhead to settle in Dublin, including Bankrupt, Contriver, Hope Well and Trust All. Bankrupt, for instance, settles in Dublin where, with no previous experience, he sets himself up as a surgeon specializing in venereal diseases.[70] Perhaps it is not surprising that Dublin acquired a reputation as a centre for vice and the dissolute life. In the 1690s when, partly in imitation of earlier English development, the Societies for the Reformation of Manners were established in Ireland, they only established themselves in Dublin, Drogheda, Kilkenny and Maynooth. However, hope was at hand in the shape of the leaven of dissenters who resided in the city and who were among the godly. Archbishop Marsh of Dublin, for instance, expressed hope for the city, arguing that its inhabitants were 'very pious and do not want zealous leaders to bring them up to a good pitch of devotion', but he added that the surrounding rural population had little hope of reform.[71]

In a cultural sense the role of Dublin as a funnel between two hinterlands achieved rather less than in economic terms. This is not to say that an Anglo-Irish culture did not emerge in the eighteenth century, but that this culture was not shaped in Dublin, which stood in the shadow of England, but rather on the estates of landlords. There landlord-tenant relations and patterns of sociability shaped a culture which owed little to the direct influence of Dublin. What Dublin did do in cultural terms was to act as a meeting ground for each of these cultural traits, making it a world common neither to England nor Ireland. It is clear that at least some of the Irish rural gentry were unhappy in the city and when they did visit, it was for as short a time as possible. A six week stay in 1665 brought the comment from the usually urbane George Rawdon of Lisburn, 'I am weary of Dublin and long to be at home.'[72] Dublin became a city which had many of the characteristics of an English capital but was very untypical of the little-urbanized Irish landscape. James Verdon, the rector of East Dereham in Norfolk, in 1699 contrasted Dublin with the rest of eastern Ireland. All the towns were small and 'none so good [as Market Dereham] except Dublin, the people [there] are civilized and do like christians but in the country they are barbarous in all parts'.[73]

Conclusion

The history of Dublin and its varying relationships with its different hinterlands in the seventeenth century is a somewhat chequered affair. It does not fit into a simple model of a centre of conspicuous consumption which acted as a parasite on the surrounding region. Rather, it developed a diversity of functions during the seventeenth century which enabled it to act as a stimulus for economic change rather than a retardant. It was only possible to do this because of its unique position in having as its hinterland not only eastern Ireland but also northwestern England. This operation in two economically and culturally different hinterlands created tensions about the city's status and functions. At one level its growth was due to the expansion of the English state in the sixteenth and early seventeenth centuries which began a process by which the large number of gaelic and gaelicized lordships which made up Ireland in the sixteenth century were integrated into a new political and social order. Dublin as the medieval centre of the pale thus gained a new significance as a colonial capital through which the King's representative in Ireland, the Lord Deputy, could rule the country. Dublin, in this situation, was subservient to London. The Lord Deputy was appointed in London and received his orders from there. The wealth of Dublin was also based on its status as a colonial centre with the growth of its population being mainly dependent on immigration from England or Scotland. Its trade was also dependent on a set of economic and social arrangements under-pinned by a colonial land settlement and, especially in the early part of the seventeenth century, its trade was characteristically colonial, being composed mainly of raw unprocessed goods. Yet a second trend was also at work. The establishment of a colony in Ireland had built on the structures of the medieval kingdom already established in the city, the Viceroy, the Privy Council, the parliament and the courts, all of which argued for the existence of a separate and distinct kingdom with Dublin as its capital. That approach to urban development had begun in the 1630s under Wentworth but its heyday was in the later seventeenth century when the English settlers, traumatized by the events of the 1650s, turned to the constitutional idea of a separate Kingdom of Ireland co-equal to that of England. The development of the vice-regal court, the rebuilding of the city and the diversification of its trade and occupa-tional structure all derived from this understanding. Thus Dublin was a city which existed within a tension of two ideas about its status; neither that of a colonial capital nor, in reality, that of a metropolis of a kingdom equal to England in all respects. This is reflected in its relations with its hinterlands, dominated by one in cultural affairs yet expansionist in economic matters with the other.

In some respects this tension was the secret of Dublin's success in the seventeenth century. It became both a 'court' centre, including the centre for higher education in Trinity College, and a market and financial centre. It was not a parasite as a centre of government arising from the state building process in the seventeenth century could become. Its status as a colonial capital interacted with its role as the Irish metropolis to develop an extremely wide range of functions for a pre-industrial capital and hence invites comparison with London. It both fed off its hinterland and provided stimulation to it in the form of marketing services and provided the stimulus to commercialization and integration into a wider economy for areas such as Ulster. The price of success in blending those roles was high in terms of its confused identity. It was neither an English nor an Irish city. In some ways Dublin fell between the standards of its two hinterlands, north-west England and eastern Ireland. It could, in the final analysis, be like neither region and that is the source of its unique and elusive personality.[74]

Notes

1. D. Dickson, 'The place of Dublin in the eighteenth century Irish economy', in T.M. Devine and D. Dickson, eds, *Ireland and Scotland, 1600–1850* (Edinburgh, 1983), pp.177–92; *idem*, 'The Demographic Implications of Dublin's Growth, 1650–1850', in R. Lawton and R. Lee, eds, *Urban Population Development in Western Europe* (Liverpool, 1989), pp. 178–89.
2. L.M. Cullen, 'The growth of Dublin, 1600-1900', in F.H.A. Aalen and Kevin Whelan, eds, *Dublin City and County* (Dublin, 1992) p.277, note 2.
3. C. Litton Falkiner, ed., *Illustrations of Irish History and Topography* (London, 1904), p.350.
4. *Calendar of State Papers, Domestic 1686-7*, pp.91–3.
5. Dunton's letters are printed in E. MacLysaght, *Irish Life in the Seventeenth Century*, 3rd edn (Dublin, 1969), Appendix B. The quotation is on p.376.
6. W. Petty, *The Economic Writings of Sir William Petty* (ed. C.H. Hull, Cambridge, 1899), vol.2, 225–6.
7. R. Gillespie, *The Transformation of the Irish Economy, 1550–1700* (Dundalk, 1991), pp.3–4, 20–3, 24–9.
8. T.W. Moody, F.X. Martin and F.J. Byrne, eds, *A New History of Ireland*, vol.9 (Oxford, 1984), pp.602–6.
9. Public Record Office of Ireland (PROI), RC6/1; Trinity College, Dublin (TCD), Ms 2512.
10. TCD., Ms Mun V/23/1.
11. For example R. Gillespie, *Colonial Ulster* (Cork, 1985), pp.206–12.
12. Litton Falkiner, *Illustrations of Irish History*, pp.380–1.
13. Quoted in M. Perceval-Maxwell, 'Ireland and the Monarchy in the Early Stuart Multiple Kingdom', *Historical Journal*, vol.34 (1991), 288–9.
14. British Library (BL), Add. Ms 29587, ff.24–25v.
15. For this see W.S. Clark, *The Early Irish Stage* (Oxford, 1955), pp.26–32.
16. Litton Falkiner, *Illustrations of Irish History*, p.381; J.B. Maguire, 'Seventeenth Century Plans of Dublin Castle', *Journal of the Royal Society of Antiquaries of Ireland*, vol.104 (1974), 11.
17. The evidence is conveniently summarized in B. Fitzpatrick, 'The Municipal Corporation of Dublin, 1603–40' (Ph.D. thesis, TCD, 1984), Appendix 3.

18. Litton Falkiner, *Illustrations of Irish History*, p.385; Fitzpatrick, 'Municipal Corporation of Dublin', Appendix 3.
19. The taxation figures are in C.H. Firth and R.H. Rait, eds, *Acts and Ordinances of the Interregnum* (London, 1911), vol.2, 1243-4 and the poll tax payers are from S. Pender, ed., *Census of Ireland c.1659* (Dublin, 1939).
20. *The Declaration of Sir Charles Coote* (London, 1659 [1660]); J.T. Gilbert, ed., *Calendar of the Ancient Records*, vol.5 (London, 1895), 129-80.
21. For example R. Gillespie, 'Landed Society and the Interregnum in Ireland and Scotland', in R. Mitchison and P. Roebuck, eds, *Economy and Society in Scotland and Ireland, 1500-1939* (Edinburgh, 1988), pp.38-47.
22. T. Carte, *History of the Life of James, First Duke of Ormond*, vol.2 (London, 1736), 313; *Calendar of State Papers, Ireland, 1663-5*, p.651. This episode is Ormond's return from a brief spell in London. For his first entry into the city in 1662, *Calendar of State Papers, Ireland, 1660-2*, pp.563-4. Compare these with Wentworth's rather subdued entry into Dublin described in BL, Add. Ms 29587, ff.19-20.
23. Historical Manuscripts Commission, *Report on the Manuscripts of the Marquis of Ormond*, New Series, vol.7 (London, 1912), 189.
24. The history of the rebuilding of the Castle can be followed in Maguire, 'Seventeenth Century Plans of Dublin Castle', pp.8-11 and R. Loeber, 'The Rebuilding of Dublin Castle: Thirty Crucial Years, 1661-1690', in *Studies*, vol.69 (1980), 45-69.
25. MacLysaght, *Irish Life in the Seventeenth Century*, pp.385-6; Litton Falkiner, *Illustrations of Irish History*, p.413.
26. Clark, *The Early Irish Stage*, pp.43-8.
27. K.T. Hoppen, *The Common Scientist in the Seventeenth Century* (London, 1970), chs.1-3.
28. PROI, RC 6/2-3, RC 12/2, 23; TCD, Mss 2512-3.
29. P. Talbot, *Primatus Dubliniensis* (ed. W.E. Kenny, Dublin, 1957).
30. J.Mills, ed., *The Register of St John the Evangelist, Dublin, 1619-99* (Dublin, 1906); H.F. Berry, ed., *The Register of the Church of St Michan's, Dublin, 1636-85* (Dublin, 1907).
31. BL, Add. Ms 21138, ff.62, 65; one other bill survives for 1683-4 in J.T. Gilbert, ed., *Calendar of the Ancient Records of Dublin*, vol.5, 610-12; Petty, *Economic Writings*, vol.2, 165-84.
32. C. Lennon, *The Lords of Dublin in the Age of Reformation* (Dublin, 1989), p.71; D. Dickson, C. Ó Gráda and S. Daultrey, 'Hearth Tax, Household Size and Irish Population Change, 1672-1821', *Proceedings of the Royal Irish Academy*, vol.82, sect. C (1982), 161.
33. For example, R. Gillespie, 'The Small Towns of Ulster, 1600-1700', *Ulster Folklife*, vol.34 (1990), 25, 26-7.
34. M.V. Ronan, ed., 'Archbishop Bulkeley's Visitation of Dublin, 1630', *Archivium Hibernicum*, vol.8 (1941), 57-62.
35. Pender, *Census of Ireland c.1659*, pp.363-73.
36. Dublin City Library, Gilbert Library, Pearse St, Dublin, Gilbert Ms 78, ff.119, 156.
37. The Presbyterian Church in Ireland, ed., *A History of Congregations in the Presbyterian Church in Ireland* (Belfast, 1982), pp.426-48; L. Hyman, *The Jews of Ireland* (Shannon, 1972), ch.2; I am grateful to Kevin Herhily for a figure for the Baptists.

38. BL, Add. Ms 4169, f.37; B. O'Mullane, 'The Huguenots in Dublin', *Dublin Historical Record*, vol.8 (1946), 110-20.

39. O. Goodbody, ed., *Guide to Quaker Records* (Dublin, 1967), p.33; J.G. Simms, 'Dublin in 1685', *Irish Historical Studies*, vol.14, no.55. (March 1965), 225.

40. O. Goodbody, 'Anthony Sharp: A Quaker Merchant of the Liberties', *Dublin Historical Record*, vol.14 (1955), 12-19.

41. Historical Manuscripts Commission, *Manuscripts of the Earl of Egmont* (London, 1909), vol.2, 25; J.T. Gilbert, *A History of the City of Dublin* (Dublin, 1854), vol.1, 30.

42. R. Loeber, 'English and Irish Sources for the History of Dutch Economic Activity in Ireland, 1609-89', *Irish Economic and Social History*, vol.8 (1981), 76-85; BL, Add. Ms 46920/A, ff.34-9.

43. Gilbert, *Calendar of the Ancient Records*, vol.4, 3.

44. Meath Papers, Kilruddery House, County Wicklow, Abstract of the Earl of Meath's Leases.

45. Gilbert, *Calendar of the Ancient Records*, vol.3, pp.xvii-xviii; Meath Papers, Oliver Cheyney's Letter Book, Cheyney to Meath, 17 March 1682/3.

46. Berry, *Register of the Church of St Michan's*.

47. Dublin price movements are given in L.M. Cullen, T.C. Smout and A. Gibson, 'Wages and Comparative Development in Ireland and Scotland, 1565-1780' in Mitchison and Roebuck, *Economy and Society in Scotland and Ireland*, pp.107, 109.

48. Kent Archives Office, Sackville Ms ON 4806; Sheffield City Library, Wentworth Wodehouse Mss, Strafford Letter Book 24/25, no.174; Bodleian Library, Oxford, Carte Ms 52, f.645; TCD Ms 672, f.238; *Calendar of State Papers, Domestic, 1686-7*, p.91; Public Record Office, London (PRO), Customs 15 (for 1699).

49. D. Woodward, 'The overseas trade of Chester, 1600-1650', *Transactions of the Historic Society of Lancashire and Cheshire*, vol.122 (1970), 32-42.

50. D.R. Hainsworth, ed., *Commercial Papers of Sir Christopher Lowther* (Gateshead, 1977), pp.2, 11, 12, 17 for example.

51. *Calendar of Carew Manuscripts, 1603-24*, p.175; PRO, CO 388/85/A15. The goods on the 1625 list have been valued at prices given in *Calendar of State Papers, Ireland, 1663-5*, pp.694-7 which represents the earliest wide-ranging price series.

52. Gillespie, *Transformation of the Irish Economy*, pp.21-2, 54-5.

53. BL, Add. Ms 4756, f.31v.

54. Dublin City Library, Gilbert Library, Gilbert Ms 42, ff.6, 33; TCD Ms 809, ff.306, 336, Ms 810, ff.134, 136, 138, 193, 238.

55. *House of Commons Journals, Ireland*, vol.1 (1753), 179-84; J. Walton, ed., 'The Subsidy Roll of County Waterford, 1662', *Analecta Hibernica*, vol.30 (1982), 51-2.

56. The fortunes of the guilds can most easily be traced in J.J. Webb, *The Guilds of Dublin* (London, 1929), pp.177-236.

57. M. Pollard, *Dublin's Trade in Books* (Oxford, 1989), p.39; J. Fenlon, 'The Painter Stainers Company of Dublin and London', in J. Fenlon, N. Figgis and C. Marshall, eds, *New Perspectives: Studies in Irish Art History* (Dublin, 1987), pp.101-8.

58. Meath Papers, Oliver Cheyney's Letter Book, Cheyney to Meath, 20

January 1682/3 which refers to bankers.
59. BL, Add. Ms 4759.
60. Gillespie, *Transformation of the Irish Economy*, pp.41–50.
61. Based on 1699 returns in PRO, Customs 15.
62. On Dublin's role in the eighteenth century economy see Dickson, 'The place of Dublin in the eighteenth century Irish economy'.
63. Gilbert, *Calendar of the Ancient Records*, vol.5, 271, 291, 319–20, 497–8.
64. *Ibid.*, vol.1, 42–3.
65. N.B. White, ed., 'The Annals of Dudley Loftus', *Analecta Hibernica*, vol.10 (1941), 236.
66. Clark, *The Early Irish Stage*, pp.52, 58–60.
67. BL, Add. Ms 41769, f.35. For the activities of the press see R. Gillespie, 'Irish Printing in the Early Seventeenth Century', *Irish Economic and Social History*, vol.15 (1988), 81–8. As William King, Archbishop of Dublin, wrote in 1716 'I believe we are as backward in Ireland as to architecture and indeed to all arts and sciences as to most countries in Europe nor is it any wonder it should be so considering we are a depending province ...' TCD, Ms 2533/271-2.
68. H. McDermott, ed., *Vertue Rewarded; or, the Irish Princess* (Gerrards Cross, 1992), p.20.
69. TCD, Mun P/23/407, 352.
70. Richard Head, *Hic et Ubique or the Humours of Dublin* (Dublin, 1663), *passim*.
71. T.C. Barnard, 'Reforming Irish Manners: the Religious Societies in Dublin during the 1690s', *Historical Journal*, vol.35 (1992), 805–38.
72. *Calendar of State Papers, Ireland, 1663–5*, p.590.
73. BL, Add. Ms 41769, f.40.
74. V.S. Pritchett, *Dublin* (London, 1991), p.21.

CHAPTER FIVE

Paris: First Metropolis of the Early Modern Period

Jean Jacquart

The largest western city

As Fernand Braudel observed, 'Paris is a city on its own',[1] compared not just with the other French cities that it had always completely over-shadowed, but, at least up to the second third of the seventeenth century, with the other cities of early modern Europe. What strikes us first of all is the longstanding character of this situation. Whereas Madrid and London did not experience spectacular growth until 1630 or even 1650, and Amsterdam did not become a metropolis until after 1600, the population of Paris had certainly reached or exceeded 200,000 by the end of the fourteenth century, prior to the Black Death, the economic depression of the late Middle Ages and the Hundred Years War. Although this extraordinary figure, derived from the 1328 census, has often been contested,[2] it is nowadays accepted by the great majority of medieval historians. With this uniquely large population, Paris, around 1320, was far ahead of the great economic centres of the day: Ghent, Bruges, Genoa and Venice.

The situation was unchanged at the start of the sixteenth century: four European cities then had 100,000 inhabitants, but just one, Paris, had more than 200,000. And the position was still the same when the Court moved to Versailles, though by that time Paris was closely followed by London, which by 1700 had taken the first place. The primacy of Paris had nonetheless lasted for over three hundred years. The city's population curve is as follows: 200,000 in about 1320; a little less than 100,000 at the worst point of the crisis (though it was still one of the largest cities in Europe); between 150,000 and 200,000 around 1500; at least 300,000, possibly more, at the start of the Wars of Religion; around 200,000 at the time of the terrible siege of 1590; more than 400,000 at the time of Richelieu; and 550,000 at the end of the eighteenth century.[3]

A quantitative gulf separated the capital from other French cities.[4] It seems that Rouen was still the second city of the kingdom at the start of the sixteenth century, though it was closely followed and soon to be overtaken by Lyon. According to R. Gascon, the latter counted 60-70,000 inhabitants around 1520, compared with 20-25,000 half a century earlier, before the great development of its fairs. The figure declined after the civil war, not recovering the level of 50,000 until around 1636.[5] Rouen certainly grew in the sixteenth century, but still barely exceeded 70,000 inhabitants around 1640. Such figures clearly have nothing in common with those for Paris.

Looking beyond France, the only city at all comparable with Paris in the sixteenth century was Naples. Its population at the start of the century is estimated at 150,000, rising to 210–220,000 in 1547 and to 280,000 at the start of the next century, before decreasing significantly under the impact of successive calamities in the second third of the century. The other great cities of western Europe were all around the 100,000 mark: Venice reached 150–160,000 between 1560 and 1600, Seville counted 120,000 inhabitants at its zenith around 1600, at the same time London had roughly 200,000 inhabitants, and Amsterdam rose above 200,000 after 1650.

The sources of power

What were the reasons for this long-established special position of Paris?[6] At the end of the Middle Ages, as in the sixteenth century, the city did not possess the international economic role of other contemporary but less populated centres. Paris hosted none of the great fairs so important in the commercial life of western Europe; nor was it a major centre for financial transactions and capital flows; nor was it among the great port cities, open to the outside world and new horizons. At the start of the sixteenth century, the Paris textile industry was not entirely ruined, but the city had never figured among the so-called *villes drapantes*, be it for the old or new textile sectors. This is not to say, of course, that these factors did not contribute, albeit in small doses, to the city's growth and dynamism.

Mention can also be made of its famous university, responsible for attracting students and teachers and for sustaining a whole range of related activities: copyists and illuminators, replaced after 1470 by printers, plus the population of landlords, landladies and bawds. But this alone could scarcely account for the city's extraordinary growth. J. Favier has estimated at 5000 the total university population in the fifteenth century[7] and, despite the reform of the colleges and the quality of the *modus parisiensis*, the situation is unlikely to have changed significantly during the next century.

A factor of greater importance was the status of Paris as capital of a kingdom long characterized by the progressive centralization of a range of powers.[8] At the start of the early modern period, the Court itself continued to move about depending on royal whim, the seasons, local resources and the fortunes of war; and the Loire valley châteaux and, during the Italian expeditions, Lyon, all kept the centres of power away from Paris. Yet the main institutions of the kingdom remained in the capital: the old Parlement of Paris, whose jurisdiction extended over more than a third of the royal domain, the Chambre des Comptes, the Grand Conseil, whose role grew in the sixteenth century, plus some of the services of the Chancellerie, even if the king retained those he needed to run the state. This institutional presence in Paris implied a concentration not only of office holders but also of an extensive auxiliary personnel of court clerks, officers, procurators and lawyers.[9] It also produced a constant coming and going of provincial officers and litigants responsible for generating service activities. The administrative framework is estimated to have required 5000 royal officers in 1515, with a further 8000 for the kingdom's 'administrative technostructure'. The capital alone accounted for a third of this total and, although the proportion tended to decline thereafter due to the creation of financial and legal venal offices in the provinces, when Colbert had a list of 46,047 office holders drawn up at the start of Louis XIV's reign, Paris still accounted for 11 per cent of the number and 38 per cent of their total venal value.[10] Development of the administrative and bureaucratic monarchy necessarily reinforced this longstanding presence of agents of the state, even though the dirty, crowded and unruly city was abandoned by the monarch and his entourage.

In 1528, two years after his return from captivity, François I announced in a letter to the Bureau de la Ville his intention to 'henceforth reside the greater part of the time in our fair town and city of Paris'.[11] That decision did not establish the Court in Paris permanently, but it did prefigure a renewed importance for the Ile-de-France and the return to Paris of many courtiers, along with their households and servants. It was Henri III, unsympathetic to the nomadic lifestyle of his predecessors, who really fixed the Court in Paris. By the eighteenth century, the tradition was well established and the creation of Versailles did not alter the situation, coming too late to slow the development of the capital.

Paris and its hinterland

Another factor of major importance was the position of Paris at the centre of a large region in which average population densities frequently reached or exceeded 40 inhabitants per square kilometre.[12] Conditions here were those of the *monde plein* of P. Chaunu, comparable to those in the Flemish and Tuscan countrysides. And although the enumeration of

1328 reveals wide variations in the number of households between different *pays*, the overall impression remains. What this meant was that, despite the wealth characteristic of many areas in the Ile-de-France, there always existed a population surplus in the countryside to serve as a reservoir from which to meet the demands of the city. The development of Paris, in fact, depended largely on draining human and material resources from an extensive zone of influence, a zone that itself tended to grow as the city expanded. It was as if, like in nuclear fission, beyond a certain critical mass – in this case a certain population size – the fact of satisfying the multiple needs of the Parisian population was itself enough to sustain economic activity and, by the same token, the range of urban functions. In fact, calculations to measure the flows generated by the actual existence of the city, like those made by R. Gascon for Lyon, leave no doubt as to the sheer scale of exchanges that must have occurred between the city and its hinterland. The growth of this hinterland over the centuries is visible on any map of the urban networks in early modern France.

The first point to note is that, from the start of the sixteenth century, it was necessary to travel 80–100 kilometres to find urban centres of significant size that were autonomous in relation to the capital. The map drawn by R. Gascon, based on a document of 1538, shows that the first major centres around Paris were the Gallo-Roman sites, episcopal sees and provincial capitals: Rouen, Amiens, Reims, Troyes, Orléans and Chartres.[13] Within this 100km circle, however, there were numerous towns whose population reached between eight and ten thousand inhabitants, a significant size for the period, and which, although they were satellite and relay towns, still had a life of their own that had not been smothered by the omnipresence of Paris.

The situation in 1725 was almost identical.[14] On the edges of the same circle were Rouen, Reims, Orléans, Amiens, Troyes, Chartres, Beauvais and Chalons, their populations ranging from 10,000 for the latter, up to 30,000 for Reims and 55,000 for Rouen; that of Paris was ten times larger. But, with the already striking exception of Versailles, the circle now contained no town with more than 6500 inhabitants. Indeed, when the 1725 figures are compared with those of the sixteenth century, it emerges that the satellite towns had tended to atrophy. Etampes had counted 2100 households in 1544, 1400 in 1725; Meaux counted 1500 in 1599 and 1140 in 1725. It was a pattern reproduced in numerous other small towns of the Paris basin.

The exchanges between city and hinterland

The Parisian hinterland in the sixteenth and seventeenth centuries was thus a 100km circle, within which occurred the bulk of the exchanges between the city and its surrounding *plat pays* or hinterland. Tentative figures and interpretations can be advanced. The first concerns the nature of relations and whether they were authentic exchanges or more akin to *prélèvements*. For, if goods and services seldom travelled exclusively in one direction, the exchange was certainly weighted heavily in favour of the city.

This was true to begin with of the human flows. Like all the cities of the day, Paris was a *mouroir*, a demographic 'black hole', accounting for disproportionately fewer marriages, fewer births and more deaths. The capital's population registers, a first-class source for analysis, have not survived, though references to epidemics and famines can be found in the press and the proceedings of the Bureau de la Ville. However, it is certain that the city required a large and constant flow of immigrants in order to maintain and increase its population. Using marriage or apprenticeship contracts and hospital records, Gascon estimates that between one and two thirds of Lyonnais were not born in the city. The documentary sources for Paris are poorer, but there are good grounds for thinking that the proportions were similar. Migrants to Paris, most of them seeking work in the artisanal and domestic service sectors, came predominantly from the Ile-de-France and the neighbouring provinces of Normandy, Val de Loire and Picardy. More than a third of apprenticeship contracts involved youths sent from outside the capital to learn a trade.[15] This flow from the regions swelled when poor harvests forced country dwellers to seek relief in the city, and it turned to a torrent when war raged in the *plat pays*. Conversely, the outbreak of an epidemic in the city produced an exodus, as those who could, like the narrators in the Decameron, sought safety in the countryside. Far more typical, however, was the steady influx of new Parisians, setting up to begin with in the *faubourgs*, where rents were lower and the semi-rural conditions came as less of a shock. Immigration was overwhelmingly a phenomenon of the poor, though present too were small farmers, notables, petty gentlemen and scholars, graduates in law or medicine from one of the provincial faculties.

In the period of interest here, two phases appear to have been marked by an acceleration of immigration to Paris: the first was between 1520 and 1560, to take broad dates, the second came in the aftermath of the Fronde. And, in both, the arrival of large numbers of newcomers from the provinces, most of them country dwellers, ill-adapted to city life and cut off from their roots, their traditions and their networks of sociability, posed hard-to-resolve problems. Arguably these as yet poorly integrated masses were a contributory factor in the disorders after 1570 and in the Fronde.

The migratory flow ran strongly towards the city, but it was not entirely unknown for the capital to send some of its inhabitants out into the hinterland, if only temporarily. This was the case of artisans hired for tasks that could not be entrusted to their village counterparts, master craftsmen employed on the construction of châteaux and churches, the lawyers who serviced the multitude of seigneurial courts, plus, of course, the itinerant pedlars who circulated around the fairs and markets. But it was always an unequal balance, with on the one hand a heavy and definitive influx, on the other a limited number of short-term movements.

Provisioning the capital

Even more important than the circulation of men was that of produce. The supply question was paramount in a society that was becoming more diverse, wealthier and more demanding, and whose needs were growing. Satisfying the material needs of a population of 200,000, 300,000 or 400,000 implied a considerable logistical effort to ensure regular arrivals in the Parisian markets of all the necessary produce.[16]

First and foremost was bread. On the basis of one *livre* of bread a day per person, the equivalent of 6300 tonnes was needed each year for a population of 200,000, 9400 tonnes for 300,000 and 12,600 tonnes for 400,000.[17] Part of these totals arrived in the form of deliveries by producers, and another part was sold on the capital's markets, but a significant proportion was 'imported' as ready-made bread, baked in a number of villages and *bourgs* around the capital: prominent among these were Corbeil and Gonesse (the latter counted between 140 and 160 bakers at the end of the sixteenth century).[18] The quantity of draught animals, carts and boats needed to transport all this grain, flour and bread is not hard to imagine. In normal circumstances, the rich farmland of the Ile-de-France produced enough to feed both the rural and urban populations. But even this 'drained' all the available breadstuffs in the 100km radius and, in the event of a bad harvest in the Paris basin, supplies had to be sought from further afield. In 1565, for example, agents sent by the city authorities sought the necessary extra supplies on markets in the Limagne, Brittany and the Bourbonnais. Use even had to be made of the Hanseatic merchants.[19]

Parisians, of course, did not live on bread alone. Large quantities of wine were consumed in the capital. Figures for 1637, that have often been used, indicate a consumption of 643,000 hl, which for 400,000 inhabitants represents 0.44 litres per person per day, 'including women and children'.[20] Dividing by three gives 320,000 and 480,000 hl for the other population estimates. But if large quantities of wine thus had to be transported, it was over short distances, since the bulk of the total came from the vineyards of Ile-de-France, the largest in the kingdom at this time. For the more discriminating drinkers, wines from the Loire and Burgundy were available, though it was not until 1720 that Beaujolais appeared on the Paris market.

If consumption of wine became more widespread in the sixteenth century, that of meat declined.[21] This was a consequence of the strong demographic growth which made it necessary to extend arable surfaces at the expense of pasture. The region close to Paris produced mainly sheep and lambs, reared on the fallow of the cereal-growing plains; cattle had to come from further afield, from the Brie Champenoise, Normandy and even Limousin. By contrast, the numerous watercourses of the region and the lakes of the Brie provided freshwater fish, complemented by smoked or salted cod and herrings.

The reasonable standard of living enjoyed by a significant proportion of the population, coupled with the adoption of tastes hitherto confined to the nobility, meant that Paris generated a demand for more sophisticated produce from its immediate surroundings: herbs and vegetables; fruits, like the peaches of Montreuil and Corbeil or cherries from Antony and Montmorency; fresh cheese, already a speciality of the Brie, and butter – that of Vanves was well known. The city was, in fact, surrounded by a ring of market gardens and smallholdings, cultivation of which was a valuable source of income for the villages that specialized in this production. What could not be produced locally came from further afield.[22]

In all, thousands of tonnes of foodstuffs of all kinds were absorbed by the city. The flow was almost entirely in one direction. Itinerant pedlars supplied the hinterland with the exotic products of the capital, such as spices, oils and dried fruits, but the quantities involved were insignificant by comparison.

Foodstuffs were not the only elements in this flow to satisfy the material needs of the capital. Heating at this time was exclusively by means of burning wood. Because of the high concentration of royal and seigneurial forests, woodland probably accounted for 20 per cent of the surface of the Ile-de-France region.[23] There were copses and plantations, heavy timber, essential for building and construction, as well as light wood and firewood. Yet, in spite of royal ordinances regulating forest husbandry and measures by the Bureau de la Ville to ensure regular supplies, the entire sixteenth century was marked by a serious shortage, responsible for a large increase in price. The result was an overworking during the first third of the century of woodland close to the city. The solution involved expanding the supply zone and, around 1545, timber from the Morvan first began to be floated down the valleys of the Cure and Yonne. The rivers Oise and Aisne and their tributaries were also used for transporting wood to the capital. By cutting Paris off from its distant suppliers, the civil wars caused a further price increase and prompted a reckless exploitation of woodland close to Paris. At the end of the civil wars, there was already talk of reforming the forests, a task that fell to Colbert.[24]

The growth of the city generated a high level of activity in the building sector. Besides timber, the capital imported large quantities of hardcore, stone, plaster and lime. Most of this came from local quarries – many of them at the gates of the city, in the Saint-Jacques and Saint-Michel *faubourgs*, at Belleville and Bagneux – and the remainder from Saint-Leu d'Esserent on the Oise.[25]

This provisioning of the city generated considerable traffic in the direction of the capital, the bulk of it within the 100km circle that delimited the Parisian hinterland. But allusion has also been made in the preceding pages to the material exchanges occurring in the other direction, from the city to its hinterland: exotic and costly produce, demand for which was extremely limited; a few manufactured goods, metalwork and textiles (when domestic and village production did not meet needs); some printed matter that will be discussed shortly. In all, it was little by comparison with the scale of the flow in the opposite direction. One thing the city did send in ever larger quantities to the surrounding area was the waste it produced. Disposing of the capital's waste was already a problem at the start of the modern period, one to which no satisfactory solution could be found. Liquid waste was either poured into the Seine or left to soak away into the ground. Solid waste accumulated in the streets, forming the grey 'crust' so often remarked on by visitors to the city; dusty in the summer, transformed by rain into a sticky slime, it always stank. A proportion at least of this mud was transported by cart to the outskirts of the city, but it was a long time before an effective waste disposal system was developed. The construction work and demolition in the city produced large amounts of rubble that were carried to worked-out quarries on the immediate limits of the city.

The terms of trade

Circulation of produce also meant circulation of wealth. Here, too, there was movement in both directions, but again with a clear advantage to the city. Paris in fact took resources from the countryside in two forms, first as food purchases, second in the form of four different types of payments. Payment to begin with to seigneurs living in the city, foremost among them the bourgeois owners of multiple fiefs on the path to enoblement, and to the great religious orders, deeply involved in the feudal-seigneurial system. They all exacted a series of rights from their dependents, whether on land, individuals or activities. Another payment was the tithe, returns from which often went to bodies in the city, such as the chapters, priories and abbeys. Payment also had to be made to urban landlords by village tenants for houses, vines and plots, but above all for the great farms owned by the religious houses, seigneurs, major office holders and increasingly, by ordinary bourgeois such as merchants and lawyers. Lastly, debt payments: indebtedness and the proliferation of mortgages weighed increasingly heavily on the peasant masses. To this has to be added taxation, the revenues from which went to the state but whose collection nonetheless involved and profited numerous intermediaries, most of whom, of course, were Parisians.[26]

Is this to say that everything went to the city? Manifestly not, for the countryside would quickly have been ruined. A part of what the city drew from the rural economy it redistributed in the region: by its purchases of farm output, by the wages paid in the countryside to labourers, grapepickers, servants and artisans, by paying the country dwellers working in the city who returned home with part of their earnings. Another form of redistribution was the purchase of land from country dwellers forced to sell. The proportion of land in the Ile-de-France owned by Parisians increased throughout the century.[27] The areas closest to Paris experienced the greatest concentration, with peasant property here subject to virtual expropriation. Similar conditions prevailed for 40 to 50 kilometres from the city walls, though declined thereafter. The crisis of the peasantry, that began in the second third of the sixteenth century and that the Wars of Religion exacerbated and the upheavals of the seventeenth century continued, was responsible for this immense transfer of property and funds. It is worth bearing in mind that the sums paid by the urban purchasers very often merely passed through the hands of the unfortunate vendors, before returning to repay urban creditors.

All these facts illustrate the degree to which the terms of trade were unfavourable to the countryside. The development of Paris, marked by the construction of houses, mansions, churches and convents, accompanied by better living standards, and one which so impressed visitors from the provinces and abroad, albeit amidst filth and stench, was in fact based on a systematic exploitation of the vast hinterland around the city.

Cultural domination

The control the metropolis exercised over its hinterland was not limited to material forms such as flows of produce, people and wealth; it was also cultural. By means of its clerics, men of law and printed output, the city imposed its values on the villages and *bourgs* of the surrounding region.

Not that the countryside made no contribution to the metropolitan culture. A large proportion of the capital's population originated in the countryside, albeit at one or two generations' remove, and many Parisians retained links with their region of origin, links indicated by ownership of plots of land or a share in a house; by a presence at the signing of a marriage contract; by acceptance of responsibility as godparents, and by testamentary bequests to country parishes. Yet these new city dwellers also brought with them to the city an element of peasant culture that permeated the scholarly and bourgeois culture to varying degrees. These rustic contributions are essential to an understanding of the work and success of Rabelais, for example, just as in the next century, Perrault's *Contes* and La Fontaine's *Fables* both drew on the rustic fireside story-telling tradition. Likewise, the dances performed by members of the Court were modelled on the jigs and reels of village entertainment. But, if these rustic inputs were important, it is necessary to stress that they were always adapted and transformed, 'civilized', both by and for the city dwellers.

The decisive advantage always lay with the latter. The sixteenth century witnessed an intensification of the so-called 'civilizing of manners' and reshaping of mentalities, with scholars, men of law and the authorities combining their efforts to edify the populace, in both town and country.[28] The troubles in the second half of the century interrupted this process, but it started again in earnest at the beginning of the seventeenth century, favoured by the new climate created by the strengthening of monarchical absolutism and the attitude of the Tridentine Church.[29] This period witnessed the foundation of the village schools and the introduction of catechisms and the Lazarist, Jesuit and Capuchin missions. It also saw the beginnings of the famous *Bibliothèque bleue* of Troyes, that was responsible for exposing large sections of rural society, by the intermediary of its literate members, to a normalized conception of social and human relations.[30] The influence of Paris over its hinterland is harder to measure in this field. Books seldom figure in the inventories of peasant households,[31] though brochures and almanachs, as well as religious images, are all known to have circulated.

In these conditions is it possible to speak of a parasitic metropolis, of a sort of vampire drawing its sustenance from the surrounding countryside and more distant provinces?[32] The monstrous capital was a common target for pamphleteers, notably at the time of the great popular revolts of the seventeenth century. The reality was, of course, rather different.

Exchanges, albeit unequal, have been seen to occur in both directions. It would be inappropriate to speak of *Paris et le désert français* at the start of the modern period.[33] Having said this, it is interesting to observe that, from the sixteenth century, Paris experienced all the problems faced by large cities in subsequent periods, such as the organization of provisioning, housing shortages, maintenance of public order and creation of an adequate system of public assistance and health.

State and city

The growth of the capital was a source of concern for the public authorities, not merely the municipal administration, which through its complex selection procedure was an expression of the Parisian bourgeoisie,[34] but also of the higher authority of the state, in a kingdom which since the Middle Ages had been evolving towards a form of centralized monarchy. The capital city aroused suspicion and a desire to control. Extensive powers continued to be delegated to the Paris municipality as regards streets, markets, town planning, regulation of trades, but the crown made sure it had the means to act when the situation required it, using its own institutions: the *prévot* of Paris and his lieutenants, the Châtelet, the Parlement, the Governor of the Ile-de-France; and, of course, through the direct intervention of the King's Council should the officers of these bodies show insufficient zeal. It is significant that the series of the registers of proceedings of the Bureau de la Ville begins in October 1499 with the suspension of the municipality following the collapse of the Pont Notre-Dame, by decree of the Parlement.[35] Whenever famine or epidemic threatened or an enemy was at the gates, the local city authorities were in effect bypassed by the royal courts and the King's Council. The creation of the Lieutenant General of Police in 1677 gave the monarchy an official it could depend upon, directly linked to the crown and invested with extensive powers.

Until then, the monarchy adopted a subtle mix of pressure and flattery to control selection of the representatives of the Parisian bourgeoisie, *échevins* and *prévots de marchands*. For the *échevins*, a balance was sought between the two great categories of notables, the merchants of the *Six-Corps* and the Royal Officers, but the office of *prévot* was increasingly monopolized by lawyers. Of the forty-five leaders of the Paris municipality in the sixteenth century, ten were members of the Parlement, seven were from the Chambre des Comptes, three from the Cour des Aides, six were *maîtres des requêtes* and five notaries and royal secretaries. In a century, just two merchants held the office, and one of these was in fact Claude Marcel, jeweller to Queen Catherine and closely linked to the Court. The King had for a long time made no attempt to hide his preferences, and it was not unknown for him to extend the mandate of a favoured *prévot*.[36] On every such occasion, though protesting against the illegality of the measure, the city acquiesced. Submission to the royal will did not preclude outbursts when circumstances allowed, as during the captivity of François I after the defeat at Pavia, during the Wars of Religion and in particular at the time of the Ligue, and again during the Regency of Louis XIV. These episodes are well known and require no further comment here, except to note that they invariably ended with the urban élites and populace coming back into line after their outburst.

The start of the modern period saw Paris firmly established in the role of metropolis. The problems that now confronted the city, the domination it exercised over an extensive territory, and its responsibility for the spatial organization of its hinterland, foreshadowed the phenomena produced by urbanization in subsequent centuries.

Notes

1. F. Braudel, *L'Identité de la France* (Paris, 1986), vol.3, 204.
2. The discussion is presented and summarized by J. Heers, 'Les limites des méthodes statistiques ...', *Annales de démographie historique* (1968), 57–8. The higher estimate is adopted by R. Cazelles and J. Favier in the volumes of the *Nouvelle histoire de Paris*; it is rejected, though without a convincing argument, by P. Chaunu, in *La mort à Paris* (Paris, 1978), pp.197–8. If it is agreed that the 20,000 houses of 1637–49 corresponded to 412,000 inhabitants, the '10,000 to 15,000' the author accepts for 1328 could presumably have held 200,000 inhabitants.
3. J. Jacquart, 'Le poids démographique de Paris et de l'Ile-de-France au XVIe siècle', *Annales de démographie historique* (1980), 87–95, reprinted in his *Paris et l'Ile-de-France au temps des paysans (XVIe–XVIIe siècles)* (Paris, 1990), pp.227–36. For the sixteenth century, J.P. Babelon, *Paris au XVIe siècle (Nouvelle Histoire de Paris)*, advances higher figures: 200,000 in 1500, 350,000 in 1550, 300,000 in 1565, back to 350,000 in 1588. For the seventeenth century, R. Mousnier, *Paris capitale au temps de Richelieu et de Mazarin* (Paris, 1978), pp.159–64.
4. On this point see the recent works of synthesis, *Histoire de la population française*, ed. J. Dupâquier, vol.2 (Paris, 1988), and *Histoire de la France urbaine*, ed. G. Duby, vol.3 (Paris, 1981).
5. R. Gascon, *Grand commerce et vie urbaine au XVIe siècle. Lyon et ses marchands* (Paris/The Hague, 1971), vol.1, 341–51, and O. Zeller, *Les recensements lyonnais de 1597 et 1636* (Lyon, 1983).
6. *Paris. Fonctions d'une capitale* (Paris, 1962), papers by R. Mousnier, C. Samaran and B. Gille.
7. J. Favier, *Paris au XVe siècle*, pp.72–4.
8. For the origins, see R.-H. Bautier, 'Quand et comment Paris devint capitale',

Bulletin de la société de l'histoire de Paris, 1978 (1979), 17–46.

9. P. Chaunu, 'L'Etat', in F. Braudel and E. Labrousse, eds, *Histoire économique et sociale de la France*, vol.1.1 (Paris, 1977), 193–5.

10. J. Meyer, *Le poids de l'Etat* (Paris, 1983), p.56 and map on p.55.

11. Letter from King to Bureau de la Ville, 15 March 1528, in *Registres des délibérations du Bureau de la Ville*, vol.2 (Paris, 1886), 17.

12. F. Lot, 'L'Etat des paroisses et des feux de 1328', *Bibliothèque de l'Ecole des Chartes*, vol.90 (1929), 51–107 and 256–315; J. Dupâquier, *La population rurale du Bassin parisien à l'époque de Louis XIV* (Paris, 1979); G. Fourquin, 'La population de la région parisienne aux environs de 1328', in *Le Moyen-âge* (1956), vol.62, pp.63–91; J. Jacquart, 'Le poids démographique'.

13. R. Gascon, 'La Ville', in Braudel and Labrousse, *Histoire économique et sociale de la France*, vol.1, 407.

14. Dupâquier, *La Population rurale*, pp.193–8.

15. Sample based on E. Coyecque, *Recueil d'actes notariés ...* , 2 vols. (Paris, 1905–29).

16. Mention should be made of the mass of information contained in N. de La Mare, *Traité de la police* (Paris, 1705).

17. An estimate of 1565 advances the figure of 60,000 *muids* per year (*Registres des délibérations* (Paris, 1892), vol.5, 518), while a report of 1637 mentions 84,000 *muids* per year; but these figures do not include the grain that was delivered directly. The traditional amount is 3 *setiers de Paris* per person per year.

18. J.P. Blazy, *Gonesse, la terre, les hommes* (Gonesse, 1982), pp.128–30.

19. Rich material is in *Registres des délibérations*, vol.5.

20. Document published by A.M. de Boislisle in *Mémoires des intendants sur l'état des généralités, I: Généralité de Paris* (Paris, 1881), pp.656–9.

21. The 1637 report mentioned above (note 17) gives the following figures: 368,000 sheep and lambs, 67,800 calves, 40,000 cows.

22. See the overview in Babelon, *Paris au XVIe siècle*, pp.302–13.

23. M. Devèze, *La vie de la forêt française au XVIe siècle*, 2 vols. (Paris, 1961).

24. M. Devèze, *La grande réformation des forêts royales sous Colbert (1661–1680)* (Nancy, 1962).

25. *La maison de ville à la Renaissance* (Paris, 1983), esp. contributions by F. Boudon and J.P. Babelon; J.P. Babelon, *Demeures parisiennes sous Henri IV et Louis XIII* (Paris, 1965); M. Le Moel, *L'architecture privée à Paris au Grand Siècle* (Paris, 1990).

26. In his study *Une province française au temps du Grand roi, la Brie* (Paris, 1958), E. Mireaux calculates the total income of the Brie at the start of Louis XIV's reign at 45.5 million *livres tournois*, of which seven million went to Paris (pp.213–24).

27. J. Jacquart, *La crise rurale en Ile-de-France* (Paris, 1974).

28. There is a large bibliography on the subject, including works by among many others N.Z. Davis, J. Delumeau and R. Muchembled.

29. J. Ferté, *La vie religieuse dans les campagnes parisiennes (1622–95)* (Paris, 1962).

30. R. Mandrou, *De la culture populaire aux 17e et 18e siècles* (Paris, 1964); H.J. Martin, 'Culture écrite et culture orale. Culture savante et culture populaire', *Journal des savants* (1975), 225–84.

31. Jacquart, *La crise rurale*, p.476; the books were mainly religious works, but

also included the history of France and romantic fiction: in 1603 a farmer from Villejuif had a copy of *Les amours de Clitophon*.

32. D.R. Ringrose, 'Metropolitan Cities as Parasites', in E. Aerts and P. Clark, eds, *Metropolitan Cities and their Hinterlands in Early Modern Europe* (Leuven, 1990), pp.21–38.
33. The title of the famous book by J.F. Gravier, first published in 1948.
34. The complex procedure for selecting the electoral body was controlled by the 1450 regulations, analysed by Babelon, *Paris au XVIe siècle*, pp. 266–7.
35. *Registres des délibérations*, vol.1 (Paris, 1883), 1.
36. The first instance occurred under Louis XI in 1464 and was followed by many others. See Babelon, *Paris au XVIe siècle*, pp.267–9.

CHAPTER SIX

A Capital City in the Feudal Order: Madrid from the Sixteenth to the Eighteenth Century[1]

José Miguel López García and Santos Madrazo Madrazo

Introduction

In recent years historians of early modern Europe have devoted unprecedented attention to the subject of urbanization.[2] Nevertheless, most of the works on this subject, through their eclectic incorporation of methodological perspectives derived from neoclassical economics, have given rise to theoretical constructions by and large devoid of social analysis. They have moreover depicted the urban development of Europe in excessively homogeneous and simplified terms.[3] Recent contributions of historical materialism to the study of the transition from feudalism to capitalism provide an alternative causal model. By integrating a wide range of differentiated variables, this approach highlights the peculiarities of diverse processes of urban development in relation to structural changes in distinct social formations beginning in the later Middle Ages.[4]

Within the feudal mode of production, the city was defined as a collective seigneury, that is, a complex system of resource organization which reproduced, both within its walls as well as in its hinterland, a specific economic structure. This structure linked shared rights in property to the fundamentally political processes of appropriation and exploitation inherent to feudal society. Finally, the collective seigneury was characterized by a substantial degree of autonomy within the broader political order.[5]

Several characteristics distinguished feudalism in Castile. The northern nobility's inability effectively to control the initial phase of territorial expansion (tenth to thirteenth centuries) led it to concede to the monarchy a leading role in the organization of the kingdom. It also gave rise to intense competition between the upper and lower levels of the aristocracy. Above all, it led to a constant restructuring of the nobility in relation to complex political organizations like urban councils, charged with appropriating social surplus from the productive classes. The result was a social dynamic subject to constant change. The extensive territory Castile incorporated by the late thirteenth century led to a marked imbalance between an abundant supply of land and a relative scarcity of labour. This situation in turn gave rise to a certain laxity in the feudal relations of production, as the nobility was obliged to exercise a measure of flexibility in regard to the productive classes in order to avoid further displacement of the peasantry toward the recently conquered south.

For these reasons the fundamentally political processes of feudal exploitation and accumulation were channelled through complex organizations and institutions, like collective seigneuries. These compensated for the original weakness of productive relations within the Castilian social formation. Urban seigneuries, the principal agents of feudalization of the peasantry, facilitated the emergence of different factions and modes of organization within the ruling class. Towns and cities functioned as centres of social exploitation through their absorption, mediated by the monarchy, of feudal rent. This power structure not only permitted the integration of the three organizational levels of the feudal class: local, seigneurial and royal; it also fostered the development of manufacture and merchant capital in the leading cities of Castile, thus consolidating by the end of the Middle Ages dense urban networks firmly embedded within the feudal state.[6]

As in much of the rest of continental Europe, fifteenth-century Castile suffered a pronounced seigneurial reaction. The feudal class increased both its representation in municipal government and its power over the productive classes. One consequence was a growing patrimonialization of civic office by the aristocracy and lesser nobility. The other side of this coin was the consolidation of the centralized feudal monarchy beginning with the reign of Ferdinand and Isabella, a process which culminated during the early modern period. Both changes favoured the growth of administrative and court cities. During what one could call the late feudal era these cities housed the ruling class along with the central organs of the absolutist state. Nerve centres of the late feudal order, they now absorbed a large portion of the surplus produced by the peasantry, not only through the feudal dues traditionally levied by cities, but also through the additional flow of resources known as 'centralized feudal rent'. Despite their defeat in the Comunero Revolt (1520-21), cities went on to strengthen their social, economic and political roles during the reigns of Charles V (1516-56) and Philip II (1556-98). Two developments in particular bear this out: by the end of the sixteenth century more than 60 per cent of the Castilian populace lived in towns and cities of more than 1000 inhabitants. Meanwhile, representation of the kingdom within the *Cortes* or parliament of Castile was limited to 18 cities, the clerical and aristocratic estates long having ceased to meet.[7]

However, in the same decade in which Philip II installed the Court in

Madrid (1561), the cities of Castile entered a period of growing difficulties. These included a profound de-urbanization, which lasted well into the second half of the seventeenth century. Students of this phenomenon have by and large offered monocausal explanations, highlighting demographic losses through epidemics, a decline in agrarian production, the collapse of urban industry thanks to the price revolution of the sixteenth century, the increasing fiscal demands of the crown and their burden on the areas under royal jurisdiction, the triumph of *rentier* ideals among the urban bourgeoisie or the uncontrolled growth of the capital city itself.[8] It is evident, nevertheless, that all these factors were inter-related. They were moreover, symptoms of the more general process of feudalization that Castilian society experienced during this period, and which consolidated the structural elements that in the long run determined the specific characteristics of its transition to capitalism.

The rest of this essay examines the trajectory of a single Castilian city and its territory during the late feudal era. It explores why Madrid grew so remarkably in this period, and how its exceptional status can be explained only by the feudal reaction experienced by the Hispanic monarchy during the 'Iron Century'. We will also show how during this era Madrid's territory suffered changes similar to those found in other Castilian hinterlands. These included processes of expropriation and dismemberment which in the long run favoured the different groups of the ruling class - aristocracy, court nobility, clergy and the feudal bourgeoisie - which took up residence in the capital city after the Court definitively settled there.

The Court's impact on the city

Around 1541, the population of Madrid and its hinterland was barely 50,000. The establishment of the Court in 1561 accelerated the city's growth so that by the end of the century Madrid, with (according to the latest estimates) some 85,000 inhabitants, was one of the twenty most populous cities in Europe. The removal of the Court to Valladolid in 1601 cut Madrid's population in half, but the Court's return in 1606 stimulated uninterrupted growth until 1629. By then Madrid had 130,000 inhabitants, making it one of the ten largest cities in Europe.[9] Stagnation set in in 1630, caused by catastrophic mortality and decreasing immigration. Madrid's population remained around 125,000 inhabitants until the end of the century. The eighteenth century opened with a new demographic crisis caused by the War of the Spanish Succession, which left the capital with 109,000 inhabitants. After 1714, Madrid regained its previous population level, which held steady until more accelerated growth in the 1730s caused by the relative decline of the death rate and changes in migration routes. By the middle of the century, Madrid may have had 150,000 inhabitants, and reached perhaps 190,000 by the end of the century. Furthermore, comparison of the demographic curve with that of the number of dwellings shows that the number of families per dwelling had tripled; from almost two families per dwelling at the end of the sixteenth century to almost five in fewer than two centuries.[10]

Figure 6.1 shows that early modern Madrid's physical growth passed through four stages. First, around the critical date of 1561, the city experienced notable expansion, especially towards the east along the Atocha and Alcalá roads. In the second stage – 1565-90 – the establishment of the Court accentuated the eastward expansion and stimulated the settlement of extensive zones in the north and south. The third stage, beginning in the seventeenth century, saw more moderate growth except in the northeastern part of the city, which grew by almost 25 per cent. Finally, in the eighteenth century, there was limited expansion in the north and south, much less marked than the growth under the Habsburgs.

The number of houses confirms these trends: from 2500-3000 houses in 1561 to 7100 in 1597, a spectacular increase caused by expansion during Philip II's reign and by the initial fragmentation of landed property. Excepting the years the Court spent in Valladolid (1601-06), which caused a substantial decrease in the number of inhabitants and inhabited buildings, the city's growth continued, reaching 9439 dwellings in 1623. In this year, property began to concentrate, while the height of buildings increased. By 1764, the date of the original *Planimetría General*, or map survey of urban property, the number of houses was down to 7557.[11]

Continuous migration fed the city's growth. Until well into the eighteenth century, 48 per cent of Madrid's population was between 16 and 40 years of age. The over-representation of adults was due to four factors: a high proportion of males in the population, low female marriage rates, a significant number of unmarried persons (more than 50 per cent of the population in the mid-eighteenth century), and finally, the small size of families, two thirds of which comprised a married couple and one child.[12] Given the high death rates, similar to those of other European cities, migration remained the motor propelling Madrid's demographic growth, compensating for the deficits generated by the imbalance between birth and death rates.

This migration, mostly male, was dual: on the one hand, a seasonal migration from Madrid's hinterland and New Castile in which female migration was more common, and on the other, a permanent migration

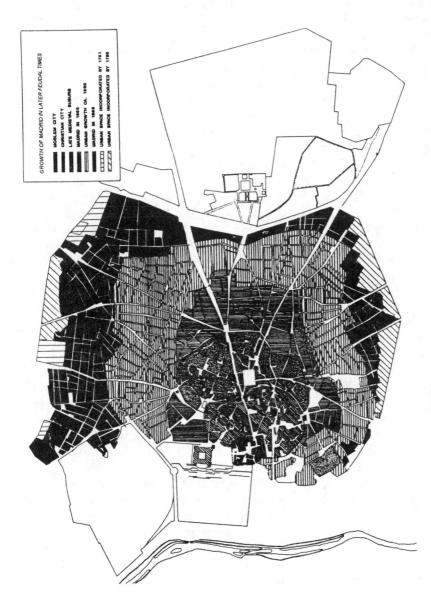

6.1   Growth of Madrid in later feudal times

by impoverished peasants seeking work in Madrid's growing manufac-turing, commercial and construction sectors.[13] Others sought employ-ment as servants to the Court, the bureaucracy, the nobility, or the clergy – these groups having expanded with the establishment of the absolutist state.

The expansion of the privileged class left a permanent mark on Madrid. In the mid-sixteenth century, the city had a small oligarchy and an even smaller ecclesiastical presence.[14] After the establishment of the Court in 1561, the numerous officials of the Royal Household and the state councils supplanted the local oligarchy and set off an exponential growth of the ruling class. There soon arose a housing problem: Madrid was ill-prepared for the arrival of so many distin-guished guests. In 1561, royal officials requisitioned 20 per cent of the 2500 existing dwellings, a number which still proved insufficient. The *Junta de Aposento*, or housing magistracy, thus decided to reserve half of the city's dwellings. Faced with the impossibility of requisitioning so many dwellings and the protests of privileged residents, the *Junta* transformed this demand into a tax called the 'Prerogative of Lodging', which would provide the funds needed to subsidize housing for the new bureaucracy. In 1621, 136 officials of the Royal Chapel, 607 members of the Royal Household, 551 officials of the Royal Guards and 308 bureaucrats received housing through this levy; in total 1602 members of the Court, a number that would soon grow with the building of the Buen Retiro palace and later when the Bourbons introduced new court offices.[15]

The establishment of the Court also transformed political power in Madrid, affecting the size and composition of the urban oligarchy. The crown usurped the functions of the municipal council, and directly supervised local politics through the Council of Castile and the *Sala de Alcaldes de Casa y Corte*, or Court Magistracy, responsible for supplies, justice and public order. Madrid remained subordinated to the political and fiscal interests of the Habsburg state.

At the same time, the sale of municipal offices, intended to reduce the royal treasury's chronic debt, increased the size of local government. By 1621 the 15 aldermen of the mid-sixteenth century had become 40. This growth favoured the expansion and renewal of Madrid's oligarchy, incorporating ennobled bureaucrats and certain distinguished creditors of the royal treasury who found in the acquisition of a government post a reliable route to upward social mobility. To avoid the risks of indiscriminate expansion, in 1603 the municipal council excluded from office those who had performed manual labour, engaged in petty commerce, or who had failed to prove their purity of blood. The hegemony of the feudal class within the council was thus secured while future expansion (always limited) assured its gradual renewal without altering its social composition. Analysis of the composition of the patrimonies of Madrid's aldermen during the seventeenth century reveals the character of this renovation. The aldermen's income derived from consolidated royal debt (*juros*) and from municipal bonds, a clear sign that their fortunes were made more in association with the feudal state than through more traditional sources of local wealth, which usually derived from exploitation of the municipal commons. When by the mid-seventeenth century both municipal and state treasuries began to threaten bankruptcy, many of the aldermen had moreover invested in agricultural property outside Madrid.[16]

The growth of the Court city increased the size of the bureaucracy as well. Around 1625, the number of officials in the Royal Household, the state councils and the city government was around 2000, some 1.5 per cent of the population. One hundred and thirty years later, these bureaucracies employed 5000 persons, or 3.3 per cent of the population. Madrid's bureaucracy had increased by 250 per cent while the rest of the population had grown by only 15.4 per cent.[17]

The links between these groups of the dominant class and the state apparatus affected the life of the lower classes, especially through food supply and fiscal policies. The growth of the nobility and the clergy was also felt in other spheres of life, including the real estate market. Since the late Middle Ages, the Castilian aristocracy had extracted its income through centralized feudal rent. At the beginning of the sixteenth century, two thirds of the income of Spain's grandees derived from the crown's alienated rents, particularly through the *alcabalas* and the *tercias reales*, levies that taxed commercial transactions and agrarian production respectively. At the same time, the last Trastámaras and the Catholic monarchs had assuaged the nobles by conceding them the right to entail estates in perpetuity and to withdraw them from the market. The majority of the nobility soon moved to Madrid, where the Court offered a potential source of privileges and additional income, particularly desirable during a period in which the aristocracy began to experience problems of liquidity.[18]

Beginning in the sixteenth century, the nobility sought to create networks of clients within the state apparatus in an attempt to defend and increase their patrimonies and incomes. This process culminated in the seventeenth century with the golden age of the *validos*, members of the aristocracy who gained control of the central state through their extensive system of clients. In the same period, the aristocracy expanded through the incorporation of bureaucrats and merchants who purchased titles, thus becoming a 'service nobility'. This process, intimately linked to the creation of patron/client networks, reached its zenith under the last Habsburgs and the early Bourbons.

The migration and expansion of the nobility left its mark on the urban fabric. After an initial phase in which most grandees rented rather than constructed palaces, from 1606 onward the nobility opted for a systematic policy of purchase. By 1658, 100 noble houses owned 6 per cent of Madrid's dwellings. This process reached its peak in the second half of the eighteenth century, when 202 members of the nobility owned 21 per cent of the buildings in Madrid: 745 houses and palaces that produced 23.5 per cent of total real estate income. Focusing on the aristocracy that owned dwellings and resided in Madrid confirms the chronology of feudalization: in contrast to the preeminence of the aristocracy of the blood in the early seventeenth century, of the 87 grandees and titled nobles who composed the resident *rentier* aristocracy in 1760, two thirds were from families that had acquired their titles during the reigns of Charles II and Philip V.[19]

Monastic institutions also partook of Madrid's growth. In 1550 there were a dozen convents in Madrid, while by the mid-eighteenth century there were close to 70, 42 of which (63 per cent) were founded between 1561 and 1650. In the century of Enlightenment, there was one friar for every 62 lay persons. The capital – as the nucleus of the collection and distribution of centralized feudal rent – became the scene of a struggle among the regular clergy and other social groups for control over the resources appropriated by the feudal system. The clergy lived in direct dependence on its rivals, thanks to the patronage of convents by the crown and powerful members of the ruling class.

The social composition of these religious communities reflected the ruling class's strategy of aiding the reproduction of the regular clergy by contributing its own offspring. The same conditions that led to the cloistering of this sector of the dominant class determined the peculiar economic structure of the monastic orders. Through donations and inheritances linked to masses and memorial services, the regular institutions formed a patrimony based on rents from private credit, government bonds and the municipal debt. Thus, the very existence of the regular clergy depended on densely woven networks of clients used to co-opt social agents directly implicated in the feudal state, with the goal of collecting the incomes earned from these patrimonies. Until the final decades of the seventeenth century, the friars managed to create the necessary networks, although a reduction of monastic clients and the parallel decrease in the collection of rents obliged the regulars to concentrate their income in the real estate market and rural estates. The effects of this shift were soon felt: while in 1658 the religious communities of both sexes possessed only 3.1 per cent of Madrid's buildings, in

1760 they owned 21.5 per cent. Clerics received three quarters of the interest collected on private capital within the Crown of Castile, along with 75 per cent of the municipal debt of Madrid.[20]

The expansion of these sectors of the dominant class, along with the demand created by the growth of the city, stimulated manufacturing, commerce, supply and construction. In 1622, there were 37 guilds within these sectors. Fourteen years later there were 58 corporations, 24 of which were connected to merchants, 29 to the artisan class and five to the professions. By 1731, the *Cinco Gremios Mayores*, or Five Major Guilds, had established their hegemony in Madrid by monopolizing the collection of provincial rents, part of the supply of the Royal Household, and by becoming one of the principal creditors to the city and the monarchy. In 1757, the secondary and tertiary sectors of the economy accounted for 46 per cent of occupations in Madrid, 80 per cent of which lived on salaries rather than on income from their own businesses.[21]

Even more significant than this mass of wage-earning workers was the number of servants, composing between 15.8 and 22 per cent of the population in the eighteenth century. Although it is impossible to calculate the incidence of paupers, the number of charitable institutions and contemporary reports indicate that the level was high, perhaps 15 per cent of the population if one includes the salaried workers without fixed residence who lived on the edge of subsistence.[22]

These social changes not only obliged the authorities to redouble their efforts to supply bread and other basic products.[23] They also influenced local fiscal policy. The needs of the crown and its treasury and the pressures to raise new resources to remedy the chronic municipal debt led to the levy of taxes upon consumer goods (*sisas*), which soon replaced rents from city estates as the chief source of municipal income. Thus, in the mid-eighteenth century, almost 97 per cent of municipal resources derived from the *sisas*, while rents from municipally owned properties accounted for only 3 per cent. The resulting sum, ten million reales, was barely enough to keep the city running, since 68 per cent of it was used to repay the debt contracted in the previous century, now in the hands of the privileged class and the larger guilds.[24]

In short, a late feudal Court city arose in the seventeenth and eighteenth centuries characterized by profound social disequilibria which in practice limited its long-term growth. A group of 300 privileged families, headed by the royal family itself, owned almost 69 per cent of Madrid's built-up area and received 36 per cent of the income from real estate. This group derived much of its wealth from the sale of primary products, participation in public and private credit, and through rents collected by the state. In its shadow was another group of rising classes composed of lawyers, merchants and guild masters. Competitors for the distribution of the surplus with the municipal and court oligarchies, this second group found itself in a less advantageous position, being excluded from key political bodies and possessing only 31 per cent of urban real property.

And the working classes? At least one quarter of them laboured as servants, becoming one more link in the endless networks of clients. Three quarters, between 94,000 and 112,000 people in the eighteenth century, owned no property and worked for wages in often miserable conditions. These workers paid 60 per cent of their salaries to rent and to state taxes, especially excises. Under such circumstances, a good portion of this population could not marry, while those who did so were forced to limit the size of their families. The concentration of ownership also explains the high cost of local housing. Privileged landlords, the only ones who could afford construction, refused to expand the housing market and risk lowering rents. Workers and their families were thus forced to live in expensive rooms, cellars or attics on leases that ranged from one month to a year. Catastrophes like the death of a family member or the loss of a job ended in indebtedness, often plunging the lowest segments of the popular classes into poverty. In just one century, 1580–1680, the popular classes lost 25 per cent of the city's housing and were pushed either to the fringe of the rental market or (literally) into the street.[25]

This brings us to the bottom of the social order: the utterly destitute, up to 15 per cent of the population. This group survived only with the aid of Madrid's expanding charitable institutions or, more frequently, by turning to begging or crime. The privileged class came to see Madrid's burgeoning population of paupers as a threat to life and property. This perception led to the creation of new disciplinary and repressive organs, like the *Sala de Alcaldes* in the seventeenth century, and the *Superintendencia General de Policía* in the eighteenth.[26] The threat was real, as demonstrated by two popular insurrections caused by profound subsistence and political crises: the so-called riots of Oropesa (1699) and Esquilache (1766).[27] The settlement of both conflicts consolidated the role of the military in the maintenance of public order and led to an effective food supply policy that combined the 'moral economy' of the early modern marketplace with sustained pressure on the surrounding countryside. In a Court city, food supply was moreover a lucrative business, particularly for those exempted from paying municipal customs. Not surprisingly, in the period under analysis, the roads leading to Madrid which brought the migrants needed to maintain the city's population, also witnessed the exit of the capital's ruling class to the countryside under its direct domination.

The impact on the hinterland

Madrid's growth produced profound effects on its hinterland. Following
Wrigley's model, one might guess that this growth would stimulate specialized agriculture geared towards the urban market.[28] The reality was
to the contrary. During the long seventeenth century, the process of
feudalization fragmented Madrid's hinterland while curtailing the forces
of production. These changes, linked to the expansion of the ruling class,
checked the long-term growth of the city, and made Madrid dependent
on ever more distant markets for wheat and other basic products.

To understand these changes one must go back to the early sixteenth
century. At that time, Madrid's hinterland was divided into three fiscal
territories (*sexmos*) that paid levies to Madrid's council (see Figure 6.2).
The *sexmos* encompassed 40 communities covering 1350 square kilometres. This area was comparable in size to the hinterlands of
Nuremburg, Zurich or Ulm, but was far smaller than those of the
powerful Italian *signorie* or Castilian-Leonese cities like Zamora or
Segovia.[29] The small size of Madrid's hinterland derived from the
peculiarities of the Christian resettlement of the territories north of the
Tagus in the eleventh century. The crown granted the right of settlement
to the urban seigneuries, setting off a fierce competition for territory.
Madrid was squeezed between the powerful Toledo and Segovia
councils, and contested Segovia's claim to control the territories situated
between the northern limit of its hinterland and the Sierra de
Guadarrama. The conflicts became so virulent in the thirteenth century
that the crown decided to reserve for itself the disputed territory which
was thereafter called the Real de Manzanares, although in 1383 it ceded
this zone to the powerful Infantado family.

During this lengthy period, the municipal oligarchy and Castilian
aristocracy consolidated their positions in Madrid's hinterland. While
the former strengthened its right of appropriation over the patrimony of
the surrounding area, the latter extended its seigneuries to the north east
and the south west. The result of this initial fracturing of city council
territory is shown in Figure 6.2: in the second half of the sixteenth
century, the aristocracy and lower nobility controlled 22.7 per cent of the
jurisdictions in Madrid's hinterland.[30]

The establishment of the Court in Madrid accelerated the fragmentation of this territory. At first, demographic growth stimulated agricultural production. As Figure 6.3 shows, the cultivation of new lands
increased the volume of cereals grown between 1561 and 1576 by

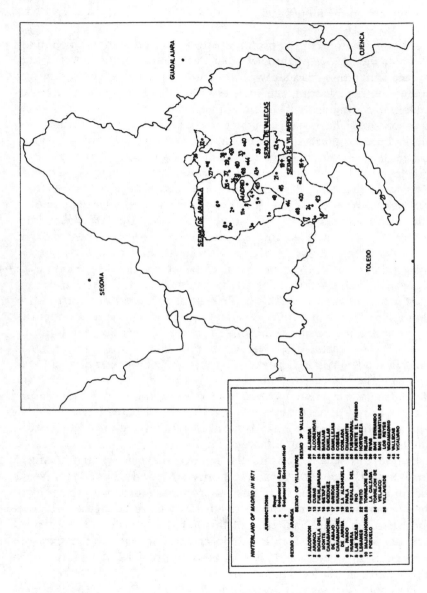

HINTERLAND OF MADRID IN 1571

JURISDICTIONS

● Royal
✦ Seigneurial (Lay)
✦ Seigneurial (Ecclesiastical)

SEXMO OF ARAVACA

1 ALCORCÓN
2 ARAVACA
3 BOADILLA DEL MONTE
4 CARABANCHEL DE ABAJO
5 CARABANCHEL DE ARRIBA
6 EL PARDO
7 HÚMERA
8 LEGANÉS
9 LIBARES
10 MAJADAHONDA
11 POZUELO

SEXMO OF VILLAVERDE

12 CASARRUBUELOS
13 CUBAS
14 FUENLABRADA
15 GETAFE
16 GRIÑÓN
17 GRIÑÓN
18 HUMANES
19 LA ALDEHUELA
20 PARLA
21 PERALES DEL RÍO
22 PINTO
23 TORREJÓN DE LA CALZADA
24 TORREJÓN DE VELASCO
25 VILLAVERDE

SEXMO OF VALLECAS

26 ALAMEDA
27 AMBROZ
28 AMBROZ
29 BARAJAS
30 CANILLAS
31 CANILLEJAS
32 COSLADA
33 CHAMARTÍN
34 CHAMARTÍN
35 FUENCARRAL
36 FUENTE EL FRESNO
37 HORTALEZA
38 REJAS
39 SAN FERNANDO DE
40 SAN SEBASTIÁN DE LOS REYES
41 LOS REYES
42 VACIAMADRID
43 VALLECAS
44 VICÁLVARO

6.2 Hinterland of Madrid in 1571

20 per cent.[31] Nevertheless, in the final quarter of the sixteenth century, wheat production – approximately 275,000 *fanegas* per year – satisfied less than half the demand of Madrid's population. In the 1580s the *Sala de Alcaldes* created the *pan de registro*, a policy obliging the villages around Madrid – whether under its direct jurisdiction or not – to supply the city with a specified amount of bread or wheat. Cereal production took a sharp downturn caused by over-cultivation. Thus, the area supplying the *pan de registro* was extended to a radius of over 100 kilometres from the capital.[32]

Difficulties in supplying the city sharpened the conflict between the urban oligarchy and the wealthy peasantry, who sought to reap maximum profit from this phase of agricultural expansion at the cost of the small producers. Both parties were well armed: the urban oligarchies dominated the political apparatus through which they benefited from the increasing surpluses generated by the municipal patrimony. On the other hand, their distance from the point of production made them dependent upon the rich peasants for collection of the rural surplus. This incipient rural bourgeoisie, which had begun to emerge in the Middle Ages, had little representation on Madrid's council but cultivated its own estates and those rented from other landlords, permitting it to control much of the rural surplus. Moreover, this class actively participated in local life, combining agriculture with livestock raising, small-scale transport, etc., and often held local offices. During the phase of growth – 1450–1560 – the urban oligarchs and wealthy peasants clashed repeatedly. To increase its income, the urban oligarchy had attempted to monopolize the rights to pasture, firewood, hunting and fishing which constituted the communal privileges of the *Villa y Tierra*. The representatives of the *sexmos* appealed to local courts to defend their rights. When the Court arrived in 1561, the issue was still pending.[33]

The establishment of the Court put an end to this precarious equilibrium. The state's financial troubles in the seventeenth century led to an expansion of the ruling class which came to control the majority of Madrid's land and property. The enlarged urban oligarchies consolidated their hegemony in the hinterland through the proliferation of estates. The outcome of this feudalization 'from above' was twofold. First, the newly established monarchy created an extensive royal patrimony around Madrid. After monopolizing the rights to firewood, pasture and cultivation, Ferdinand VI enclosed the property needed for the hunting grounds of El Pardo.[34]

Second, the royal treasury embarked on a policy of sales of privileges, patrimonies and incomes to reduce its deficit. Between 1610 and 1625 most of the *alcabala* and *tercia* taxes in Madrid's hinterland were alienated. Except for two municipalities in which the town government

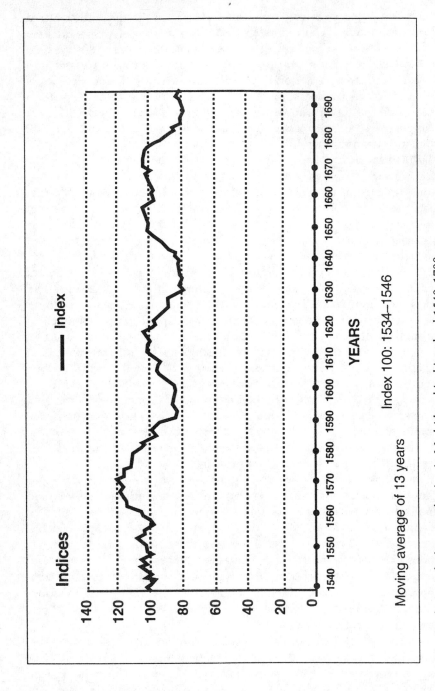

6.3 Evolution of wheat production in Madrid and its hinterland 1540–1700

controlled their collection, the majority of buyers belonged to the aristocracy and the service nobility. In 1625, jurisdictions comprising 20,000 royal vassals in the Crown of Castile were put up for sale, which led to the alienation of 13 localities from Madrid's hinterland. Again, the aristocracy and enobled bureaucrats were the principal buyers. By 1752, 59.1 per cent of the localities in Madrid's hinterland were under seigneurial jurisdiction, while royal jurisdiction was limited to 18 communities, many of which had earned this 'privilege' by expending large sums of money (see Figure 6.4).[35]

The next phase of sales took place between 1640 and 1652. The King decided to sell unused municipal lands (baldíos), the title to which the kingdom had granted to his grandfather. After parliament had authorized the alienation of baldíos to the sum of 150,000 ducats, Philip IV in 1644 sold a substantial portion situated in Madrid's hinterland. Excepting Vallecas, where wealthy farmers bought more than 1200 hectares, and Las Rozas and Majadahonda, where the buyers hailed from the local bourgeoisie, the bulk of the purchases were made by city dwellers, particularly members of the service nobility who had only recently joined the ruling class in the seventeenth century. Thanks to the persistent crises of the municipal and royal treasuries, the urban élite's invasion of Madrid's hinterland became a reality.[36]

During the second half of the seventeenth century and the first decades of the eighteenth, the uneven accumulation characteristic of the feudal system continued, although the leading role was now played by ecclesiastical institutions and the city government of Madrid itself. The former entered the market as part of a strategy to rebuild patrimonies after traditional sources of revenue had failed. Thus, between 1680 and 1740, the extensive rural properties of large monasteries like El Paular, Santo Domingo el Real or El Escorial were joined by the holdings of some 70 conventual foundations, including such important houses as San Felipe el Real, the Imperial College of the Jesuits and the Discalced Trinitarians. The means employed in this pooling of funds varied. In some cases, systematic purchases in nearby locations created reserves and farms to supply the monasteries; in others, the friars and nuns expropriated the lands of impoverished peasants through judicial foreclosures. Thus, by the mid-eighteenth century, the regular clergy had become some of the most important landholders in the area. At the same time, Madrid's council attempted to recoup the patrimony it had lost through the sale of baldíos. Thanks to the timidity of the crown during the mid-eighteenth century, practically all of the best pastures and communal lands had become the exclusive property of the municipal government.[37]

By 1760, the disentailment of communal property and the concentra-

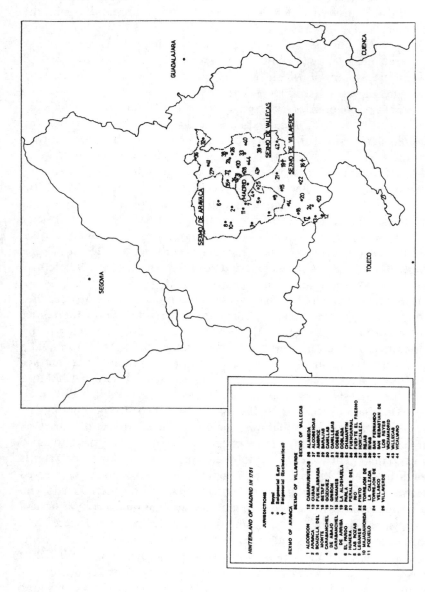

6.4 Hinterland of Madrid in 1751

tion of landownership had paradoxically caused an extreme fragmentation of property. Half of the 70,000 holdings around Madrid comprised barely two hectares, demonstrating the overwhelming prevalence of small-scale production. Sixty per cent of these small producers were not landowners but rural proletarians. This pattern of stratification could also be found among the landowners themselves, with a small group of absentee proprietors owning most of the land. This is particularly the case in the seigneuries where residents owned only 8 per cent of the land, while in royal territories residents owned 47 per cent.

Who were the seigneurial landowners? According to a mid-eighteenth-century census, 36 absentee proprietors owned 8 per cent of Madrid's hinterland. Of these, 13 were nobles, seven were monastic houses, eight local governments and eight rural and urban bourgeois, the latter demonstrating that some commoner families climbed socially despite resistance from the ruling class. But the distribution of the surplus makes clear the differences between local bourgeois and more exalted members of the ruling class: the thirteen feudal landlords and the seven religious houses extracted 69 per cent of the returns recorded in this category ('Larger Landowners') of the census. Furthermore, the noble *hacendados* owned jurisdictions and alienated incomes in their respective localities, while the ecclesiastical institutions were the principal beneficiaries of the incomes from private credit and collected, through the tithes, more than 20 per cent of the net product of the 'third estate'.[38]

The fragmentation of the hinterland had other effects. Between 1591 and 1752, the *Tierra de Madrid* lost some 22 per cent of its population, roughly the same as in other regions in the Kingdom of Castile during this period. This contraction checked migration from the country to Madrid and contributed to the process of de-urbanization.[39] To explain this phenomenon, some scholars have focused exclusively on the cities to the neglect of the hinterlands. J.E. Gelabert, for example, has argued that de-urbanization was caused by the crown's growing fiscal demands, which were logically greater in royal jurisdictions than in seigneuries. For this to be so, one would expect the urban (or potentially urban) population to migrate to the more 'benign' seigneurial zones subject to less fiscal pressure from the crown.[40]

Our analysis of the *Tierra de Madrid* proves the opposite: demographic contraction was greater in the seigneuries than in the royal domain. In three seigneurial communities of approximately 1800 inhabitants each (Leganés, Barajas and Torrejón de Velasco), the demographic contraction was 38.8 per cent, eleven points higher than that experienced within the royal jurisdictions (Getafe, Vallecas and Fuenlabrada). The unequal distribution of rural property in the mid-eighteenth century also confirms this trend: during the migration of the preceding period, the inhabitants of recently feudalized locations tended to move to royal territories. Peasants had good reason to fear the voraciousness of their new lords, as shown by the greater social polarization and inequality in the distribution of wealth within the seigneuries.[41]

A decline in agrarian production accompanied the loss in population. As Figure 6.3 shows, between 1585 and 1700 wheat production in the hinterland rarely reached the level of 1540. In the periods 1585-1615, 1620-50 and 1675-1700 there were extreme subsistence crises in which the level of production was 20 points below that of the first half of the sixteenth century. In such circumstances, aggravated by the privileged class withdrawing a growing percentage of the rural surplus from the market, the *Sala de Alcaldes'* food supply policy consisted of changing the area subject to *pan de registro*, at the same time strengthening the Court's regulatory function in fixing the price of wheat. Thus, between the end of the sixteenth century and the return of the Court from Valladolid in 1606, in the midst of a recuperation initiated by the cultivation of *baldíos*, the area subject to the *pan de registro* was bounded by a 55 kilometre radius of Madrid. After the phase of urban growth between 1606 and 1635, in which cereal production tended to decline, this area had increased to 110 kilometres, the size at which it remained until the end of the system. This intervention in local markets hurt small producers because they were never paid more than the rate fixed by the Council of Castile. In times of bad crops and intensified pressure on the hinterland, the villages subject to the *pan de registro* refused to satisfy their quotas. This situation was made worse by the decline of the system of granaries, established in outlying villages in order to house the surpluses the city exacted.[42]

The substantial increase in the fixed price of wheat in 1699 inaugurated a new phase in the supply of Madrid. Muleteers from Segovia contracted with cereal markets in Old Castile to transport supplies to Madrid. In order to offset the decline in the collection of the *pan de registro*, the city intensified its direct purchases in Segovia, Avila, Zamora, Salamanca and Valladolid. In 1746, the recently created *Junta de Abastos*, or Supply Council, built new granaries in Guadarrama and Navas de San Antonio which, together with the existing one in Arévalo, constituted the nuclei of traffic to Madrid. As a result, during the five year period 1761-65, the wheat and flour bought directly by the city or brought by the flourishing mule transport system measured 652,437 *fanegas* per year. This quantity satisfied 90 per cent of the city's needs. The rest was contributed by the seven nearby localities that specialized in that trade and by the privileged class itself. The trends are paradoxical, and diverge from David Ringrose's interpretations. Although the demographic contraction and the decline of agrarian production in the seventeenth century had set off another round of de-urbanization in Castile, the vast demands of the Court encouraged the gradual integration of Castilian markets in primary products. By the eighteenth century, the majority of wheat, wine and other products that arrived in Madrid came not from the hinterland but from the Meseta and the coastal regions, thanks in large part to a flourishing transportation system. Towards the end of the period, enterprising merchants and above all the great landowners also benefited from the abolition of customs duties and the introduction of a free trade in grains.[43]

Conclusion

By the end of the early modern period, then, the privileged class clearly dominated the *Tierra de Madrid*. Nevertheless, this triumph was not absolute, as shown by the presence of some rich peasants. Moreover, during the phase of expansion that began in 1740, tensions within the social order intensified. The new development provoked conflicts not only between nobles and clerics, but also between the privileged class and the bourgeoisie over the distribution of surpluses. Furthermore, the dynamic of growth, characterized by an increase in land rents, taxes and prices, accompanied by a reduction in salaries, intensified the process of proletarianization, threatening the position of dependent small producers and further limiting the mobility of the rural proletariat.

These trends set off new phases of social conflict. In seigneurial villages, the wealthy residents attempted to return to the jurisdiction of the crown; where ecclesiastical estates were powerful, the rural bourgeoisie and dependent small producers allied in resistance to clerical taxation. The most desperate segments of the rural proletariat joined the ranks of bandits that continuously menaced travellers and slowed the shipment of rural surpluses to the city.[44] The manner in which these disputes were resolved during the Liberal revolution and the specific class alliances that emerged from that period depended in large measure on changes in the structure of capital accumulation that occurred simultaneously in Madrid and its hinterland during the nineteenth century.

Notes

1. This work is part of the project 'Urbanization in Early Modern Spain: Country and City in the Crown of Castile, 16th-18th Centuries', funded by

the Subdirección General de Promoción de la Investigación (PB88-0182). We would like to thank the members of the Equipo Madrid, particularly Francisco Marín for the maps, José Luis Hernanz for information on jurisdictions and demography, and James Amelang and Chris Schmidt-Nowara for help with the translation.

2. J. de Vries, *European Urbanization, 1500-1800* (London, 1984); P.M. Hohenberg and L.H. Lees, *The Making of Urban Europe, 1000-1950* (Cambridge, Mass., 1985); P. Bairoch, J. Batou and P. Chevre, *La Population des Villes Européennes* (Geneva, 1988); H. van der Wee, 'Industrial dynamics and the process of urbanization and de-urbanization in the Low Countries from the late Middle Ages to the eighteenth century: a synthesis', in H. van der Wee, ed., *The Rise and Decline of Urban Industries in Italy and the Low Countries* (Leuven, 1988), pp.307-81.

3. For a more detailed criticism of the work of De Vries in particular, see J.M. López García, 'Las ciudades europeas en la transición al capitalismo: ¿urbanización o urbanizaciones?', *Historia Urbana*, vol.2 (1993), 71-83.

4. A pioneering effort at this sort of integrated explanation is J. Merrington, 'Town and country in the transition to capitalism', *New Left Review*, no.93 (1975), 71-92. This line of argument has been more extensively developed in R. Brenner, 'Agrarian Class Structure and Economic Development in Pre-Industrial Europe', *Past and Present*, no.70 (1976), 30-75; A. Mackay, 'Campo y ciudad en la Europa medieval', *Stvdia Historica*, vol.2.2 (1984), 27-53; R. Hilton, *English and French Towns in Feudal Society: A Comparative Study* (Cambridge, 1992).

5. L. Kuchenbuch and B. Michael, 'Zur Struktur und Dyamik der "feudalen" Produktionsweise im vorindustriellen Europa', in L. Kuchenbuch and B. Michael, eds, *Feudalismus-Materialen zur Theorie und Geschichte* (Frankfurt, 1977), 694-761; H. Frey, *La feudalidad europea y el régimen señorial español* (Mexico City, 1988); G. Bois, *La crisi del feudalisme a Europa a la fi de l'Edat Mitjana* (Barcelona, 1988), pp.65-79.

6. On the specific characteristics of Castilian feudalism and the special role of collective seigneuries, see J.M. Monsalvo Antón, 'Poder político y aparatos de estado en la Castilla bajomedieval: consideraciones sobre una problemática', *Stvdia Historica*, vol.4 (1986), 101-67, as well as the collective volumes *Concejos y ciudades en la Edad Media hispánica* (Madrid, 1990), and *En torno al feudalismo hispánico* (Madrid, 1991).

7. For the patrimonialization of municipal offices, see J.M. Monsalvo Antón, 'La sociedad política en los concejos castellanos de la Meseta durante la época del Regimiento medieval. La distribución social del poder', in *Concejos y ciudades*, 357-413. For the social bases of the absolutist state, see N. Elias, *Die höfische Gesellschaft* (Darmstadt, 1969); P. Anderson, *Lineages of the Absolutist State* (London, 1974); A. Torre, *Stato e società nell'ancien régime* (Turin, 1983), pp.18-35. The political role of sixteenth century Castilian cities is discussed in P. Fernández Albaladejo, 'Cortes y poder real: una perspectiva comparada', in *Las Cortes de Castilla y León en la Edad Moderna* (Valladolid, 1989), pp.479-99, and J.I. Fortea Pérez, *Monarquía y Cortes en la Corona de Castilla: las ciudades ante la política fiscal de Felipe II* (Salamanca, 1990).

8. Traditional explanations of Castilian de-urbanization can be found in V. Pérez Moreda, *Las crisis de mortalidad en la España interior (siglos XVI-XIX)* (Madrid, 1980); B. Bennassar, *Valladolid en el Siglo de Oro*

(Valladolid, 1983); D.R. Ringrose, *Madrid and the Spanish Economy, 1560-1850* (Berkeley, 1983); J.E. Gelabert, 'Urbanization and De-Urbanization in Castile, 1500-1800' (paper presented to the Ninth Economic History Conference, Berne, 1986); L.H. Lees and P.M. Hohenberg, 'Urban Decline and Regional Economies: Brabant, Castile and Lombardy, 1500-1800', *Comparative Studies in Society and History*, vol.31 (1989), 439-61.

9. Censuses of 1541 and 1591, in F. Ruiz Martín, 'Demografía eclesiástica hasta el siglo XIX', in *Diccionario de Historia Eclesiástica de España* (Madrid, 1972), vol.2, 682-733. Estimates of Madrid's population between these dates, 16,000 and 85,000 respectively, in A. Alvar Ezquerra, *El nacimiento de una capital europea: Madrid entre 1561 y 1606* (Madrid, 1989), ch.1. Growth was certainly uneven: the rural population multiplied 1.3 times, that of the city 5.3.

10. For population data, see M.F. Carbajo Isla, *La población de la villa de Madrid. Desde finales del siglo XVI hasta mediados del siglo XIX* (Madrid, 1987), pp.224-37. On the number of families per dwelling, C. Caro López, 'Casas y alquileres del Antiguo Madrid', *Anales del Instituto de Estudios Madrileños*, vol.20 (1983), 109-10.

11. F.J. Marín Perellón, 'Madrid: ¿una ciudad para un rey?', in Equipo Madrid, *Carlos III, Madrid y la Illustración* (Madrid, 1988), pp.125-51, and *idem*, 'Planimetría General de Madrid y Regalía de Aposento', in A. López Gomez, ed., *Estudios en torno a la Planimetría General de Madrid, 1749-70* (Madrid, 1989), pp.81-111. The number of dwellings in Madrid in the second half of the eighteenth century (7557) was smaller than that of Spanish cities with smaller populations, e.g. Valencia, Granada, Seville, Toledo; see Caro López, 'Casas y alquileres', 97-153.

12. Carbajo, *Población*, and J. Soubeyroux, 'Pauperismo y relaciones sociales en el Madrid del siglo XVIII', *Estudios de Historia Social*, vols 12-13 (1980), 20-6. For size of family units, see C. Larquié, 'Les familles madrilenes à l'époque moderne (aspects démographiques)', in S. Madrazo and V. Pinto, eds, *Madrid en la época moderna: Espacio, sociedad y cultura* (Madrid, 1991), pp.159-76.

13. This 'migration of misery' brought with it many beggars and vagabonds who formed an abundant pool of cheap labour. J. Soubeyroux, *Pauperisme et rapports sociaux à Madrid au XVIIIe siècle*, 2 vols (Lille, 1978); W.J. Callahan, *La Santa y Real Hermandad del Refugio y Piedad de Madrid, 1618-1832* (Madrid, 1980); J.L. Reyes Leoz, 'La cofradía de la Soledad. Religiosidad y beneficencia en Madrid (1567-1651)', *Hispania Sacra*, vol.39 (1987), 147-84.

14. M. Hernández, 'El cierre de las oligarquías urbanas en la Castilla Moderna: el estatuto del Concejo de Madrid (1603)', *Revista Internacional de Sociología*, vol.45 (1987), 179-98; J. Espinosa Romero, J.L. González Calvillo, J.L. Hernanz Elvira and J. González Pañero, 'La residencia nobiliaria en Madrid (siglos XVI-XVIII)', *Actas del I Congreso de Géografos e Historiadores* (Seville, 1995), pp.317-21; J. Pereira Pereira, 'La formación de los distritos parroquiales en el mundo urbano: San Martín de Madrid, siglos XII-XVII', (M.A. thesis, Universidad Autónoma de Madrid, 1990).

15. Marín, 'Planimetría', 81-6.

16. Hernández, 'El cierre', 190-3; *idem*, 'El poder difuso: estudio de la

oligarquía madrileña (1606-1808)', (Ph.D. dissertation, Universidad Autónoma de Madrid, 1991).

17. Estimates in Marín, 'Planimetría', 85-6, and Archivo de la Villa de Madrid/Secretaría, 1-109-1 (1625). For the eighteenth century, we have added the 2000 members of the Royal Household to the 3000 employees of municipal and royal governments counted by Ringrose: see his *Madrid* pp.89 and 416 of the Spanish edition. For Royal Household, see J. Jurado Sánchez, 'La financiación de la Casa Real en los siglos XVII y XVIII', (Ph.D. dissertation, Universidad Complutense de Madrid, 1996).

18. On the nobility, see A. Domínguez Ortíz, *Las clases privilegiadas en la España del Antiguo Régimen* (Madrid, 1973), pp.19-197; B. Clavero, *Mayorazgo. Propiedad feudal en Castilla, 1369-1836* (Madrid, 1979); B. Yun Casalilla, *Sobre la transición al capitalismo en Castilla. Economía y sociedad en Tierra de Campos (1500-1830)* (Salamanca, 1987), pp. 65-95, 219-64; I. Atienza Hernández, *Aristocracia, poder y riqueza en la España Moderna. La Casa de Osuna, siglos XV-XIX* (Madrid, 1987). On the crisis of liquidity during the sixteenth and seventeenth centuries, see C. Jago, 'The Influence of Debt on the Relations between Crown and Aristocracy in Seventeenth Century Castile', *Economic History Review*, 2nd Series, vol.26 (1973), 218-36, and his 'The Crisis of the Aristocracy in Seventeenth Century Castile', *Past and Present*, no.84 (1979), 60-90, although we disagree with the expression 'crisis of the aristocracy', given that the greater peerage remained the leading group of the dominant class until the end of the early modern period.

19. For the expansion of the aristocracy under the Habsburgs, see H. Kamen, *Spain in the Later Seventeenth Century, 1665-1700* (London, 1980), ch.9. For the buildings and rents of the aristocracy, and origins of the noble families resident in Madrid, see Espinosa et al., 'La residencia nobiliaria', and research in progress by Francisco J. Marín.

20. This last figure includes rents collected by the 1324 secular clerics then in the city, though the bulk of their income came from funeral ceremonies and other rituals. On the regular clergy, see J. Izquierdo Martín et al., 'Religiosidad barroca y oligarquías urbanas: la estrategia del clero regular madrileño (siglos XVI-XVIII)', in Madrazo and Pinto, *Madrid en la época moderna*, pp.265-301, and the same authors, 'Patronos y clientes. Relaciones de poder y parentesco en las comunidades conventuales madrileñas (siglos XVI-XVIII)' (paper presented to the II Congreso Italo-ibero di Demografia Storica, Savona, Italy, 1992). On municipal debt and the clergy, see C. de la Hoz García, 'Fiscalidad y Hacienda municipal en el Madrid del Antiguo Régimen. Las sisas (1680-1808)', (M.A. thesis, Universidad Autónoma de Madrid, 1985), p.141. For secular clergy, see V. Pinto Crespo, 'Una reforma desde arriba: Iglesia y religiosidad', in Equipo Madrid, *Carlos III*, pp.155-88.

21. M. Capella and A. Matilla, *Los Cinco Gremios Mayores. Estudio crítico-histórico* (Madrid, 1957); Ringrose, *Madrid*, table C-1. For guilds, see J.A. Nieto, 'La organización social del trabajo en Madrid durante los siglos XVII y XVIII' (M.A. thesis in progress).

22. See works cited in notes 13 and 21.

23. For bread supply, see C. de Castro, *El pan de Madrid. El abasto de las ciudades españolas del Antiguo Régimen* (Madrid, 1987); J.U. Bernardos Sanz, 'Madrid y la libertad de comercio de granos', in Equipo Madrid,

Carlos III, pp.103-24.

24. De la Hoz, 'Fiscalidad'; *idem,* 'El sistema fiscal de Madrid en el Antiguo Régimen: las sisas', *Anales del Instituto de Estudios Madrileños*, vol.25 (1988), 371-86, and 'Las reformas de la hacienda madrileña en la época de Carlos III', in Equipo Madrid, *Carlos III*, pp.77-101.

25. Soubeyroux, *Pauperisme*; Caro, 'Casas y alquileres', pp.110-15.

26. C. Martínez Soto, 'Delincuencia en Madrid. Siglo XVII', (M.A. thesis, Universidad Autónoma de Madrid, 1987); F. Hernández Sánchez, ' "La corte envidiable" (delincuencia y represión en el Madrid de Carlos III, 1759-88)', in Equipo Madrid, *Carlos III*, pp.331-53; P. Sánchez León and L. Moscoso Sarabia, 'La noción y la práctica de policía en la Ilustración española: la Superintendencia, sus fines y sus límites en el reinado de Carlos III (1782-92)', in *Actas del Congreso Internacional sobre 'Carlos III y la Ilustración'* (Madrid, 1989), vol.1, 495-502; A. Alloza Aparicio, 'Delincuencia y cambio social. Una aproximación al estudio de la criminalidad madrileña en el siglo XVIII', (M.A. thesis, Universidad Autónoma de Madrid, 1993).

27. T. Egido, 'El motín madrileño de 1699', *Investigaciones Históricas*, vol.2 (1980), 255-94; P. Vilar, 'El motín de Esquilache', *Revista de Occidente*, vol.107 (1971), 199-249; L. Rodríguez, 'El motín de Madrid de 1766', *ibid.*, vol.121 (1973), 24-49.

28. E.A. Wrigley, *People, Cities and Wealth: The Transformation of Traditional Society* (Oxford, 1987), Part II.

29. For hinterlands of other European cities, see M. Berengo, 'Città e "contado" in Italia dal XV al XVIII secolo', *Storia della Città*, vol.36 (1986), 107-11, 109. For hinterlands of Zamora and Segovia (2300 and 4000 square km respectively), see S. Moreta and A. Vaca, 'Los concejos urbanos, núcleos de señoríos corporativos conflictivos. Aproximación a las relaciones entre la oligarquía urbana y campesinos en Zamora y su tierra, siglo XV', *Agricultura y Sociedad*, vol.23 (1982), 343-85, 344; A. García Sanz, *Desarrollo y crisis del Antiguo Régimen en Castilla la Vieja. Economía y sociedad en tierras de Segovia de 1500 a 1814* (Madrid, 1977), p.19.

30. R. Gibert, *El concejo de Madrid. Su organización en los siglos XII a XV* (Madrid, 1949), p.147ff.; J. González, *Repoblación de Castilla la Nueva* (Madrid, 1977), vol.2, 7ff.; S. Madrazo et al., 'La Tierra de Madrid', in Madrazo and Pinto, *Madrid en la época moderna*, pp.27-68, esp. 33-50.

31. The graph is based on J. López-Salazar and M. Martín Galán, 'La producción cerealista en el arzobispado de Toledo, 1463-1699', *Cuadernos de Historia Moderna y Contemporánea*, vol.2 (1981), 21-103, esp. 71-87.

32. Castro, *El pan de Madrid*, p.192.

33. F.J. Hernando, 'El patrimonio municipal de Madrid: la tierra y función de la oligarquía urbana, 1450-1700', (paper presented to the IV Congreso de la Asociación de Historia Económica, Alicante, Spain, December 1989).

34. *Idem*, 'La lucha por el monte del Pardo. Rey, municipio y uso del espacio en el Madrid del Antiguo Régimen', *Cuadernos de Investigación Histórica*, vol.12 (1989), 169-96.

35. J.L. Hernanz Elvira, 'El proceso de señorializacion en la Europa meridional durante el siglo de Hierro (1560-1680)', (M.A. thesis, Universidad Autónoma de Madrid, 1994). Recently, Helen Nader, display-

ing a profound ignorance of the socio-economic reality of Castilian councils and their evolution from the late Middle Ages to the early modern period, has argued that the purchase of jurisdictions by municipal councils is proof of the development of democratic and semi-autonomous adminis trative organizations. This thesis completely ignores the councils' over- whelmingly noble composition. Moreover, many of the councils that purchased their liberty soon came under seigneurial control. See H. Nader, *Liberty in Absolutist Spain: The Habsburg Sale of Towns, 1516-1700* (Baltimore, 1990). For more extensive criticism of Nader's argument, see J. Izquierdo, '¿Libertad en la España absolutista?', *Historia Urbana*, vol.3 (1993, 131-4).

36. Hernando, 'El patrimonio municipal', and Hernanz, 'El proceso de señorializacion'.

37. Izquierdo Martín et al, 'Patrones y clientes', and J.F. Martín de las Mulas, 'La estructura del clero regular madrileño. Una aproximación al estudio de las economías monásticas en Madrid (1547-1844)', (M.A. thesis, Universidad Autónoma de Madrid, 1990). On the privatization of communal privileges by the municipal council, see Hernando, 'El patrimonio municipal'.

38. Madrazo et al., 'La Tierra de Madrid', 50-68.

39. J.M. López García et al., 'Urbanization and De-Urbanization in the Crown of Castile (16th-18th Centuries): A New Interpretation', (paper presented to the First Conference of the European Association of Urban Historians, Amsterdam, September 1992).

40. Gelabert, 'Urbanization'.

41. Hernanz, 'El proceso de señorializacion', ch.5; A. Molinié-Bertrand, *La population du royaume de Castille d'après de recensement de 1591*, 2 vols (Caen, 1976-80). For the differences in property and incomes between seigneurial and royal jurisdictions, see Madrazo et al., 'La Tierra de Madrid', 53-6.

42. Castro, *El pan de Madrid*, pp. 203-8.

43. J.U. Bernardos Sanz, 'Madrid y la libertad del comercio de granos', in Equipo Madrid, *Carlos III*, 108-22.

44. On jurisdictional conflicts between nobility and rural bourgeoisie, see Hernanz, 'El proceso de señorializacion'; on resistance to ecclesiastical taxation, see J.M. López García, 'El ocaso de los institutos de regulares castellanos en las postrimerías del Antiguo Régimen', *Hacienda Pública Española*, vol.108-9 (1987), 311—25; on banditry, see S. Madrazo, *La edad de oro de las diligencias. Madrid y el tráfico de viajeros en España antes del ferrocarril* (Madrid, 1991), ch.5.

CHAPTER SEVEN

Naples: Capital of the Enlightenment

Brigitte Marin

Throughout the eighteenth century, the Neapolitan economists and reformers engaged in lively debate about their city's functions and the implications of its growth for the rest of the kingdom.[1] This local debate was part of the broader current of urban thought that had developed in Europe since the Renaissance and whose focus shifted firmly in the eighteenth century towards economic analysis. The views and proposals of the Neapolitan *illuministi* concerning their capital were therefore unavoidably marked by the evolution in European economic thought from mercantilism to liberalism. It should be noted from the outset, however, that they did not simply reiterate the opposition between the metropolis as parasite and the capital city as motor for the rest of the economy. Neapolitan economic thought was in fact characterized less by reference to theoretical models than by observation, investigation and eclecticism. The partisans of reforms in the Kingdom of Naples were tireless in their efforts to measure the capital's economic weight within the kingdom, to assess the advantages and opportunities it represented and to limit the obstacle it posed to provincial development. With the sources of economic development thus identified, it was believed it would be possible to re-establish the kingdom among the great powers. More generally, it was in the broader context of the economy of the kingdom as a whole that an attempt was made to redefine the functions of the metropolis and find answers to the 'urban question'. The economic analysis of the city was thus always conducted in terms of reciprocity, interaction, interdependence and the circulation of wealth: the capital–provinces relationship and the economic organization of the territory[2] are central to the preoccupations of the Neapolitan *illuministi*. The theme of the interrelation and necessary complementarity between the city and its hinterland was not of course new,[3] nor specific to the Kingdom of Naples,[4] but the question assumed a special significance and urgency in the Mezzogiorno. In addition to the European intellectual context mentioned above, a number of local factors undoubtedly encouraged southern Italian urban thought to run in this direction.

The first point to note is the physical growth of Naples. By 1740, or thereabouts, the city had recovered its demographic level prior to the plague of 1656 in which it had lost approximately 60 per cent of its population. Naples, now the third city of Europe after London and Paris in terms of population, and the second city of the Mediterranean after Constantinople, experienced a strong demographic growth in the middle and final thirds of the eighteenth century, of which contemporary observers were highly aware.[5] To this awareness of the capital's considerable demographic expansion was added the trauma of famine in 1764, when thousands of peasants flocked to the city in the hope of finding bread, only to die in its streets. This crisis threw a harsh light on the imbalances caused by the economic privileges of the metropolis, exposing the kingdom's deep-seated structural ills and the fragility of its system of production and distribution; the debate over the growth of Naples, its ability to fulfil the role of capital and the reciprocal relations between the city and its provinces, acquired a new urgency.

Over and above the difficulties of the moment, there is no doubt that the development of urban thought in the Kingdom of Naples also owed much to political factors. In 1734, after two hundred years of foreign rule, Naples recovered its position as the capital of an independent kingdom and the home of an autonomous monarch, Charles of Bourbon. Contemporaries saw in this new-found independence a source of optimism for the future: now that the kingdom was no longer administered as a dependent province, it could quickly embark on economic and social progress, guided by the political will of the new dynasty. The departure of the Spanish in 1707 had been followed by bitter criticism of their political administration, and contemporaries now began to draw up an uncompromising appraisal of the kingdom based on detailed observations: 'at the start of the eighteenth century, the country began as it were to think about itself, to examine itself more closely ... and concluded that the urgent duty of the government was to implement a work of clearance and renewal'.[6] From the beginning of the eighteenth century, Paolo Mattia Doria in particular had denounced the economic imbalance produced in the kingdom by its overgrown capital; the bad government of the Spanish and the extensive privileges they had granted the city so as to secure its loyalty were blamed for creating a parasitic metropolis. Analyses of the kingdom's economic and social situation multiplied after 1734, as did projects for reform. The Kingdom of Naples in fact became the theatre of a reforming monarchy. This movement was particularly intense in the years 1736–44, before the Austrian War of Succession, and was again important in the 1750s; Charles of Bourbon's successor, Ferdinand IV, continued the work, notably in the 1780s.[7] Up to 1794, this reforming effort by the monarch had the backing and support of the enlightened Neapolitan élite, quick to respond to the initiatives of the new dynasty with ideas and projects of its own. In this context, then, it is especially interesting to study in parallel the thought of the Neapolitan *illuministi* on relations between Naples and the provinces, and the intentions of the royal administration regarding the redefinition of the capital's political and economic functions. At the head of an independent kingdom, the vocation of Naples was to become a great and magnificent metropolis contributing actively to the prosperity of the country, a symbol of the wealth of the kingdom and the power of its sovereign. The urban policy of the monarchs was thus directed: first, to exploiting the strength and wealth of the city while limiting any obstacle it might pose to economic development in the rest of the country; second, to regaining control over the development of the metropolis, that is the administration and authority of its territory and population, which were still largely in the hands of the old city administration.

From the standpoint of a study of the interactions and flows between Naples and its hinterland, the eighteenth century is rich both in terms of contemporary economic analyses and of official efforts to modify the long established balances – or imbalances – in the reciprocity of influences, with the aim of stimulating the economy of the country as a whole. By their close attention to conditions in the kingdom, the texts of the Neapolitan economists and *illuministi* provide historians with basic indications and even data whose pertinence must be explored using archive materials. Unfortunately, the quality and availability of sources for a detailed study of the Neapolitan economy in the eighteenth century are such that the historian is often forced to accept contemporary assertions at face value. The economic management of the city depended essentially on two sorts of institutions: first, the municipal administration, directed by the S. Lorenzo Tribunal, composed of six elected members from the *piazze* of the capital's nobility and one elected from the people; second, the organs of the central administration, the Secretary of State for Finances (*Azienda*) and *Real Camera della Sommaria*. However, the municipal archives of Naples were almost completely destroyed by fire in 1946, while the archives of the *Segretaria d'Azienda* are, for the most part, unusable. Since the 1950s, and under the impetus of P. Villani, the economic history of the Mezzogiorno has added much to our knowledge of the Kingdom of Naples in the eighteenth century (demography, property structures, market conditions, agriculture, economic organization of feudalism and so forth). Generally speaking, the study of the economy of the provinces overshadows that of the capital. Nonetheless, given the state of sources and historiography, the material advanced by Neapolitan economists in the eighteenth century can provide the basis for discussion and exploration of some of the mechanisms of economic exchange between Naples and its provinces, and to examine their reciprocal influences in the general development of the kingdom in the eighteenth century.

Naples, metropolis of the Enlightenment: the evidence of growth

A new source of concern for eighteenth century observers was the size and demographic growth of the capital. This phenomenon, typically viewed in a negative light, was reflected in Neapolitan works of political economy by the diffusion of the metaphor depicting the kingdom as a monster whose oversized head (the capital) rested on a slender, wasted body (the provinces).[8] The spectacular nature of the capital's demographic growth in the early decades of the eighteenth century was also reflected in the impression that contemporaries had of urban overcrowding, which led them to overestimate the size of the city's population. At the very beginning of the century, Paolo Mattia Doria recorded that Naples had more than 200,000 inhabitants 'even though the Neapolitans believe, mistakenly, that they number 500 and even 700 thousand'.[9] Travellers such as Montesquieu and Charles de Brosses, who visited the city in 1729 and 1739 respectively, also noted that it was currently reckoned to have half a million inhabitants. The excessive growth of Naples was contrasted with the sluggish demography of the provinces, linked to the belief that the kingdom had become steadily depopulated since ancient times and that it could sustain at least twice its present level of population.[10] In addition to the harmful consequences for the provinces of this growth of the capital, contemporary observers also drew attention to its negative implications in terms of food supplies, social control and politico-military risks.[11] That the growth of Naples was also a source of concern for politicians seeking to consolidate the authority of the new monarchy was clear from the 'Memoria per mandarsi alla corte di Spagna dal marchese Salas' prepared by the Minister, Bernardo Tanucci, on 24 October 1742.[12] According to the Minister, 'Naples has become an enormous and chaotic mass of houses, people, law courts ... It is into it that, with the connivance of the Spanish viceroys, through the persecutions of the barons, possessors of the greater part of the kingdom, through the political system which makes a single province of the entire kingdom, is drained as into a vast swamp, all the riches, all the evil-doing, and the greater part of the population of the kingdom itself.'[13] The threat to the monarchy was thus two-fold: from the Neapolitan nobility seeking to further its interests, and from the urban populace always ready to jeopardize the stability of the monarchy. In addition, the ease with which the English navy entered Naples harbour on 19 August 1742 and imposed on Charles of Bourbon an attitude of neutrality in the Austrian War of Succession, had exposed the military weakness of the capital and thus placed the kingdom at the mercy of aggression from a maritime power. The solution advocated by Tanucci was to abandon the old city for the town of Melfi, which was easier to defend.[14]

Were such views justified? Did the demographic growth of the capital really warrant new unease? From perhaps 215,000 inhabitants in the early years of the eighteenth century,[15] the population of Naples had risen to over 400,000 by the end of the century.[16] Growth in the early decades of the century was still making up the losses from the 1656 plague epidemic.[17] According to a manuscript of 1742,[18] the population of Naples stood at 315,000 inhabitants (monasteries and hospices included) and at approximately 450,000 if one included foreigners (100,000 individuals including the inhabitants of the kingdom and the members of other states not permanently resident in the city), soldiers (34,000) and the abandoned children of the Annunziata (600).[19] The minister Tanucci estimated the population of Naples at approximately 350,000 in 1764, the year in which the population growth was checked by famine and epidemic[20] – the crisis had no long-term effect on the total population,[21] and affected chiefly the peasants who had flocked to the capital at the first signs of famine in the countryside – though growth resumed in the final third of the eighteenth century. For this period, data are available from the *Calendari di Corte*, official statistics based on the parish registers and published annually from 1767. For 1798, this source gives a population of 435,930 inhabitants, suggesting that since 1765 the population had grown by 29 per cent. However, the figures from the *Calendari* have to be treated with caution since the mortality levels are probably underestimated, notably those concerning infant mortality and the hospitals.[22]

Contemporary observers stressed that the doubling of Naples' population over the century would not have been possible without a strong migratory current from the provinces to the capital. However, Claudia Petraccone has shown that this demographic growth also stemmed from a natural increase in the city's population: during the early eighteenth century, in the overall expansionary economic context, an increase in the number of marriages and births had the effect of rejuvenating the city's population. It was only once the demographic level prior to the 1656 plague had been reached again that signs of stagnation became apparent in the natural movement of the population.[23] Furthermore, the growth of Naples was not accompanied by a demographic shortfall in the provinces: on the contrary, the massive growth of the capital was 'one of the most significant indicators of the generalized increase in the population of the kingdom'.[24] This increase was greatest between the end of the seventeenth century and the 1750s.

Indeed, the recovery, coming after the difficult conditions of 1759–66, was made possible by the reserves built up in the years 1730–50. In 1767, the kingdom's total population exceeded 4 million inhabitants, though population growth slowed down after 1780, except in the Abruzzi, Capitanata and Molise provinces. The economy of the entire kingdom expanded at a regular rate until 1759; after the crisis of 1759–1766, there was a significant economic and demographic recovery, followed by another crisis in the 1790s, one exacerbated by the revolutionary upheavals. Naturally this overall growth masks regional contrasts. Whereas progress was extremely slow in the southernmost provinces, Calabria and Terra d'Otranto, the region centred on the capital experienced a remarkable development. Around the capital, which alone accounted for approximately 10 per cent of the population, an area within a radius of 50–60km was characterized by an exceptional concentration of population: 'if the inhabitants of the capital are included, 43 per cent of the population of the kingdom lived in the Neapolitan region'.[25] This region was also distinguished from the rest of the kingdom both by demographic behaviour that was similar to that of the capital, with relatively low birth and mortality rates, and by the presence of more than fifty agglomerations with over 5000 inhabitants and which together accounted for half the population of this zone.

Yet the eighteenth century was not the city's period of strongest demographic growth. The sharpest growth, in fact, occurred between the start of the sixteenth century and the first half of the seventeenth century and owed much to the policies implemented by the Spanish. The development of the centralized monarchy in the course of the sixteenth century resulted in the administrative and judicial functions becoming concentrated in Naples. Large numbers of feudal lords also moved to Naples, so as to demonstrate their loyalty and to be close to the Court and public affairs.[26] It was in fact through mastery of the capital, whose fidelity and support was secured by granting of privileges (fiscal, juridical, provisioning) which were in no small measure responsible for drawing the peasants to Naples, that the monarchy sought to consolidate its position against the provincial barons. The Spanish can be said to have developed an authentic 'strategy for the capital'.[27] Naples at this time still had the monopoly of university studies; as the kingdom's only large port, it was the point of convergence for the movements of large-scale and international trade; and it was here that the main religious institutions of the kingdom had their headquarters. The development of Naples in the eighteenth century in fact confirmed the orientations traced in the previous centuries. Recovering to and then exceeding the demographic level of the early seventeenth century, it once again assumed the role of a vast centre of consumption. By size, Naples was the third largest city in Europe but, in terms of its demographic weight relative to that of the kingdom as a whole, the city was closer to London than to Paris, which accounted for barely 2 per cent of the French population. An enormous gulf separated Naples from the other urban centres of the kingdom: at the end of the eighteenth century, the next largest city on the mainland, Bari, counted just 19,000 inhabitants, a twentieth the population of the capital. Contemporary commentators denounced a process of demographic growth that seemed to hinder development of the provinces. Yet even if the most striking phenomenon of the eighteenth century was the formation of an increasingly important zone of human concentration around Naples, the provinces, save those of the southern periphery, participated fully in this demographic growth, and sometimes, as in the Capitanata or on the Adriatic side of the Appennines, at faster rates than in Campania.

Viewed against this background, the fears expressed by the *illuministi* about the growth of Naples might appear excessive, the result less of observation of actual conditions in the kingdom than of commonplaces in the eighteenth century debate on towns and the expression of an anti-urban ideology. The question, in fact, requires exploration at another level. Contemporary demographic debate was indissociable from that over the production and circulation of wealth. The doubts expressed by administrators and economists in the eighteenth century regarding the growing demographic imbalance between Naples, its region and the rest of the kingdom were also related to judgments about the productive capacity of the metropolis.

Demographic growth and economic dynamism: the role of the capital in the debates of Neapolitan political economy

> All the dregs of humanity produced in the provinces make up the population of this city, and in this lies its greatness: not in fine buildings, and not in great merchants and thinkers and men of letters, as make Paris, London, Lisbon, and Amsterdam great cities; but in servants, in courtiers, for the most part of the lowest behaviour and dishonesty, in traders, barbers, whores, pimps, beggars, who, by intermarrying increase and multiply so that each generation is worse than the one before.[28]

Over and above this preoccupation with the size of the capital, this description of Neapolitan society made by Bernardo Tanucci in 1742 conveys his awareness of the quality of the urban population, a reflection of the economic and intellectual functions of the city. From the first half of the eighteenth century, political economists were aware of the disproportion between the capital's demographic size and its productive, commercial and financial structures. Naples was a great administrative and political capital, whose growth had been artificially stimulated by the policy of the Spanish rulers and by its privileged status *vis-à-vis* the rest of the kingdom; but it was far from being a great economic centre. In the 1750s, however, the Neapolitan economists had high hopes that the city's potential might induce economic development in the kingdom at large, pointing to the positive influence it had or could have on the provinces once a series of intelligent reforms had been undertaken.

Antonio Genovesi, for example, noting the country's demographic growth but also the inelastic supply of agricultural products due to the poor productivity of this sector, advocated development based on a solid agricultural base capable of supplying large quantities of low-cost food-stuffs. Trade could then develop, beginning with that in agricultural produce, and serving as the base for an industrial development which would reduce imports of manufactured products from abroad. Among the obstacles to implementation of this programme, Genovesi pointed to Naples, which concentrated the non-productive population of the kingdom, in particular the agricultural landlords, who were responsible for the accumulation in the city of wealth that was not reinvested in productive activities but spent on luxury consumption. He emphasized the indifference of urban society to the rural economy.[29] Wealth remained idle in Naples, and it was this that accounted for the financial inequality between the city and its provinces. In the latter, money was scarce and interest rates were high.[30] And precisely because Naples was where the country's wealth was concentrated, it was from here that the productive activities in the kingdom as a whole had to be financed. Genovesi was, in fact, seeking the means to redistribute wealth from the capital to the provinces. He also stressed the importance of Naples as a centre of consumption. He was aware of the city's role in changing patterns of consumption, and of the stimulatory impact of luxury consumption, providing it was satisfied by domestic output. Inspired by the example of London, he saw in Naples an opportunity for the kingdom to increase its wealth through trade. Finally, he stressed the 'civilizing' role played by a great capital and without which there can be no great power. Genovesi's view was very largely shared by Giovan Battista Maria Jannucci, who refused to dismiss the concentration of land and seigneurial rent in Naples as bad *per se*, since it formed the financial base necessary to make the capital a major pole of production able to channel as much back to the provinces as it drew from them. Jannucci was convinced that trade alone could enable the kingdom to catch up with the other European cities: in this perspective Naples con-stituted a major asset. Jannucci also noted how the countryside around the capital had enjoyed demographic, agricultural and commercial

development related to the Neapolitan consumer market, whereas the
distant rural areas, without the benefit of proximity to large urban
markets, had stagnated. The province of Terra di Lavoro and parts of the
Principato Citeriore e Ulteriore, regions with an important role in provisioning the capital, were in an excellent state of cultivation and enjoyed
a highly productive stability throughout the century.[31] Although the
wealth of Naples had as yet borne little fruit, with the money remaining
dormant in the banks of the capital,[32] at mid-century contemporary
observers were still hopeful of seeing it circulate throughout the kingdom
and of Naples becoming an economic metropolis comparable to London
and Paris.

In the last two decades of the century, by contrast, the political
economists no longer viewed Naples as the 'treasure' of the kingdom,
able to ensure its development: 'The flourishing state of a nation is not
measured by the size of its capital, but by the industry and wealth
diffused throughout the provinces.'[33] Genovesi had seen the social cost
of Naples' growth as a reflection of the real wealth of the city: far from
being evidence of urban misery, the beggars who teemed in the streets of
the city were a sign of its wealth; in this view, the poor were drawn to
Naples precisely because of its reputation for plenty.[34] By the end of the
century, in contrast, the metropolis' wealth was being denounced as
artificial, and it was the question of the provinces which received
priority treatment in the works of political economists like Giuseppe
Palmieri and Nicola Fiorentino. Given the international economic
context, hopes of transforming Naples into a centre of trade and production had evaporated, and the vocation of the capital was now judged
to be as an agrarian metropolis. This shift was reflected in cartography
for, whereas in the 1750s the map-makers had focused their efforts on
the capital,[35] in the 1780s, with priority given to unification of the
internal market and infrastructure provision, Giovanni Antonio Rizzi
Zannoni was charged with preparing a geographical atlas of the entire
kingdom.[36]

The economic analyses of the capital made by the Neapolitan
illuministi throughout the eighteenth century coincided with the aims
pursued by the monarchy. Up to the 1760s, for example, consistent with
the ideas of Genovesi and Jannucci, economic development along the
lines of the most advanced nations and an expansion of commercial and
manufacturing activity still seemed a real possibility for the Kingdom of
Naples. This was clear from the economic policy followed by Charles of
Bourbon, and, for example, from the creation in 1739 of the *Supremo
Magistrato di Commercio* with the task of fostering industry, trade and
shipping. This mercantilist policy was essentially geared to the needs of
the metropolis. It also drew inspiration from the enthusiasm that accom-

panied the new-found autonomy of the kingdom: observers took for granted that, thanks to the economic expansion experienced by the kingdom and to the end of the distorting effects of Spanish rule, the capital would become an important commercial and productive pole. But the growth that was experienced up to 1759, the result of the demographic increase and of successive good harvests, was not accompanied by a modification in economic structures. Naples shared what was becoming the status of the Mezzogiorno as a whole, namely a position of subordinance and dependence within the international economy. After the major crisis of 1764, one that was blamed in part on the waste and poor use of capital concentrated in the city in the hands of the nobility and a handful of merchants, another model of territorial development took shape, one in which Naples occupied a changed role. Under Charles of Bourbon, the authorities had taken little trouble to find out in detail conditions in the provinces and had formed a false view of the state of the kingdom. As Giuseppe Palmieri observed: 'those charged with its well-being have their eyes fixed on the flourishing state of the face, not seeing the misery and deformity of the limbs'.[37] The question of the development of the provinces thus became paramount in the final third of the eighteenth century; in future the priority was to limit the amount the city drew from the provinces (in the form of rents, taxes and commercial profits) and curb its domination over the countryside. Economic development was instead to depend on the regional centres responsible for organizing trade and commerce at the level of the provinces.

The Neapolitan economic pole and provincial development: some elements of economic exchange

The economic analysis of the urban question that evolved as eighteenth century economists sought to identify paths of development for their country contained an increasingly penetrating analysis of the economic exchanges between capital and provinces that is of considerable interest for the historian. Themes treated include: the heavy drain of wealth from the provinces to the capital (royal fiscality, feudal and ecclesiastical rent, land rents); the economic role of Naples as consumer market; the urban supply constraints; the financing of agriculture; the consumption and the investment of the city's capital; the role of Naples as a financial market and in international trade, and so on. In the current state of our knowledge about the economy of Naples, it is seldom possible to quantify these different parameters and measure their importance exactly. It is possible, however, to examine the nature of the role attributed to the city, which was not that of the parasitic capital *stricto sensu*, but nor was it that of Paris or London, the other cities in Europe comparable to Naples by their population size. In addition, the respective importance of the capital and the provinces in the economic development of the kingdom evolved in the course of the eighteenth century. As Giuseppe Galasso has pointed out, Naples under the Spanish experienced such growth and exercised such a hegemony over the provinces that the city was identified with the kingdom in its entirety,[38] to which, of course, it had given its name; the end of the eighteenth century, however, was marked by an 'awakening' of the provinces. To what extent was this development linked to changes in the functions of the capital?

Supply constraints: the *contratto alla voce*, a system for exploiting or helping the countryside?

When the reformers began to explore in detail the state of the kingdom's different provinces from the 1770s, they discovered with bitterness the weakness of the internal market, and blamed the absence of autonomous provincial development on the economic 'dictatorship' of Naples, on its monopolies and in particular on the constraints of its food supplies. According to Jannucci, in 1768 the city alone accounted for just over one twelfth of the kingdom's population (343,815 inhabitants out of a total of 4,017,694).[39] The author shows that even allowing for the number of inhabitants, the city's consumption was excessive. For example, according to Jannucci, the capital swallowed up 2,830,000 *tomoli*[40] of grain, equivalent to approximately 13 per cent of the kingdom's entire output, estimated at 22 million *tomoli*. The provisioning of Naples was organized in a way intended to guarantee low-cost supplies to the population of the capital and hence maintain social order. Giuseppe Maria Galanti denounced these *leggi annonarie* as a burden on the producing regions imposed by the city and in particular by a small group of privileged Neapolitan merchants. Under the capital's *annona* or provisioning privilege the municipal authorities, responsible for this key area of the city's economic administration, had to make purchases each year of wheat and other basic foodstuffs items such as olive oil in order to be able to sell them on the urban market at a 'just' price. But the authorities did not make the purchases themselves, instead subcontracted the provisioning out to merchants with whom a contract known as a *partito* was made. Each September, the authorities decided the amount of grain that was needed in the city and the merchants undertook to purchase that quantity in the countryside for resale to the city government at an agreed price, part of which was advanced by the city.

The merchants were able to earn handsome profits,[41] since they could purchase the produce much cheaper in the provinces thanks to the *contratto alla voce* system whereby agricultural produce was bought at a price (the *voce*) fixed immediately after the harvest, that is, when supply was greatest and prices lowest. In exchange, the purchasers advanced money to the farmers for the fieldwork, particularly at the time of sowing. In this way the producers were effectively excluded from the market and denied the profits of their productive activity, whereas the merchants, the exclusive owners of the foodstuffs and over which they had control, had lucrative outlets on city markets, their contract with the city government ensuring that they could sell the produce in favourable conditions. It may be noted that these merchants enjoyed fiscal privileges for the totality of their purchases; thus they bought more grain than was required by the city authorities, so that once their commitments to the city administration had been fulfilled they could deal directly with those who had obtained the privilege (*privativa*) to make and sell bread in the capital. These producers were committed to buying a certain amount of grain for breadmaking from the city administration, but they were free to use their own channels of supply for their supplementary needs. The merchants were thus in a position to sell all the grain purchased under the privileged conditions of the capital's *annona*, either to the city administration or to other outlets on the urban market.[42]

The privileges enjoyed by Naples in respect of food provisioning hampered free internal trade in basic items and were an obstacle to economic circulation in the provinces. The latter were also limited by the serious shortcomings in the road network, which was not only unusable for part of each year but had numerous turnpikes. The bulk of exchanges between the capital and the provinces were in fact handled by sea transport.

The privilege system allowed a small number of Neapolitan merchants linked to the city administration to make large profits at the expense of agrarian producers, whose contribution was poorly rewarded. In addition to the privileged conditions in which the Neapolitan merchants were able to obtain their supplies in the provinces, there were the profits they derived from the fact that Naples, as the single main port of the kingdom, had an important role as commercial intermediary: imports arrived at Naples, whence they were redistributed to the provinces. Yet the provisioning of the capital and *contratto alla voce* did include a form of reciprocity of economic exchange. The process described above was the consequence not just of the privileged status of the metropolis but also of the financial disequilibrium between Naples and the provinces. The Neapolitan merchants were favoured by interest rates (of the order of 3 per cent) far lower than those prevailing in the provinces (about 9 per cent). Financially, therefore, they easily dominated the provincial merchants, most of whom were forced to borrow from the monopolists of the capital and were thus reduced to the role of their commercial agents. This financial imbalance was also a consequence of the dearth of capital circulating in the provinces. The city's financial domination was in fact a monopoly; it is extraordinary, for example, that the *banchi* of Naples had no branches in the provinces. In these conditions, the funding for agriculture could only come from the capital, and doubtless it was only the great profits to be made by purchase of foodstuffs *alla voce* that incited the Neapolitan merchants to commit their money to agricultural production.[43] Given their economic state, the rural areas could not do without this credit, despite the high price that had to be paid to the metropolis. The result was clear: as Giuseppe Spiriti noted about Calabria, 'almost all the commerce of our native lands is in the hands of the aforementioned privileged'.[44] The redistribution of wealth produced by this concentration of financial resources in the capital, plus the supply needs of its large consumer market and theabuses fostered by the system, all tended to accentuate the imbalance between urban wealth and provincial poverty.

In a context where the political and social control of Naples remained the priority, the decision to free production in the provinces from the constraints of the *annona* presented the authorities with a difficult choice. The measures taken by the Bourbons towards restricting the monopoly of the great merchant middlemen between the countryside and the urban market were correspondingly timid and slow, as were those taken to liberalize the internal market in order to foster development of the agricultural sector.[45] It is noteworthy that exports of olive oil were once again prohibited for several years in the 1790s, despite the fact that provinces such as Terra d'Otranto, Terra di Bari and Calabria derived profits from direct exports of a large share of their output.[46] In the context of the revolutionary upheavals, the monarchy attached greater importance to preserving social order in the capital than to the autonomous economic development of the provinces. There is no doubt that the powerful economic interests which controlled the running of the capital's *annona* tended to limit the autonomous trade of the provinces. However, in the case of grain, for example, the scope for exporting was also limited by the productive capacity of southern agriculture: Jannucci, for example, estimated the kingdom's grain production at 22 million *tomoli*, domestic consumption at 18 million *tomoli*, and at 2.5 million *tomoli* the amount required for sowing. He thus sought the means, notably in terms of finance, to raise output to 30 million *tomoli* and thereby free completely the export trade in grain.[47] Despite the desire of the monarchy to encourage the kingdom's trade, the slenderness of agricultural surpluses and the concentration of the distribution system in the hands of a small group of powerful merchants, set clear limits to the granting of licenses to export (*tratte*).

The economic and financial submission of the provinces had its origin therefore in the massive concentration of capital in the city and its difficulties of finding funds for the productive activities of the countryside. It remains to be seen how this wealth concentrated in the metropolis, obtained in large part in the form of taxation and rent, was actually used in Naples, and how and in what proportion it was redistributed in the provinces.

Draining resources and redistribution: the question of public finances

From the first years of Charles of Bourbon's reign, special attention was given to the finances of the kingdom and to better control of receipts and expenditure, with in particular the setting up of a *Segretaria d'Azienda*, the supreme organ of control in the kingdom's financial affairs.[48] The economic recovery also had positive effects on fiscal revenue, since effective receipts now increased significantly, rising from 2,647,523 ducats in 1734 to 5,272,561 ducats in 1738; they subsequently fell but again exceeded the 5 million figure in 1753 and 1754.[49] There is no doubt that the provinces had to bear a greater fiscal burden than the capital did. Direct taxes represented nearly half of all fiscal receipts between 1734 and 1740. Yet the bulk of these direct taxes came from the provinces, in the form of the *fiscali*. Each year the *Università*, that is the communes of the provinces, paid the monarchy an amount that was in theory proportional to their number of households.[50] In contrast, by virtue of ancient privileges, the citizens of the capital were exempt from all direct taxation. However, the sums raised as *fiscali* did not all find their way into the royal coffers, since a proportion of them had in fact gradually been sold off to the state's creditors.[51] In all, the *fiscali* made up approximately one third of the fiscal receipts of the monarchy, though the total burden borne by the provinces was in fact significantly heavier. The peasantry paid the bulk of royal taxes and the cost of local administration, plus seigneurial and ecclesiastical dues.

The capital did contribute to public finances in the form of indirect taxation, of course, for the most part through taxes on consumption. Given the size of Naples, the city's salt tax was necessarily an important source of revenue and was moreover a favoured investment for Neapolitan capital. Not only had many of these indirect taxes been sold off, like the *fiscali*, by the state as settlement for debts, but their actual collection was not carried out directly by the state, the taxes having been farmed out, when they were known as *arrendamenti*. Taxes also had to be paid on the products consumed in the provinces. The preparation of the *onciario* cadaster and fiscal reform appear to have brought the *Università* little relief in the course of the century.[52]

These were two main sources of revenue, though an overall calculation has also to include customs duties, *donativi* and so forth. But if the respective proportions of the capital and the provinces in royal fiscality are hard to estimate with accuracy, it is nonetheless certain that the share paid by the provinces, in the light of the fiscal privileges enjoyed by the capital, was greater than that paid by the Neapolitans.

Conversely, when public expenditure is broken down according to where it was spent, Naples easily comes out top. It was thus the city that profited most from the economic spin-off from the redistribution of fiscal revenues in the country. The independence of the kingdom and the establishment of a splendid Court in the city meant a significant increase in expenditure linked to the royal household.[53] Also, following the political and administrative reorganization of the 1730s, increased expenditure was linked to government, administrative bodies and the stipends of functionaries. The strengthening of the central administration, with in particular the creation of four secretaries of state, was responsible for an increase in bureaucratic expenditure within the city. Furthermore, in the interests of better control over the metropolis, the crown appeared ready to undertake extra expenditure, as was shown by the creation of a new royal city police force in 1779. After its reform in 1798, this represented a force of 121 policemen, assisted by 28 *scrivani*, who received a salary for their work in the police administration, and by a police guard. From 1 January 1792, moreover the city police possessed a fund to which the Treasury paid 1220 ducats a month for the pay of the guards,[54] and from April of the same year it had its own secretariat, distinct from that of the Justice Ministry. The financial records of the kingdom cannot be used to compare the costs of the administration in the capital and in the provinces, since a large part of the funds necessary for local government came directly from the fiscal revenues raised by the administrators. In addition, since administrative posts in the provinces were often farmed out, the sum the state received from these administrators was independent of the money actually collected in the provinces by an officer and of the costs of the office in question.

Expenditure on education was wholly to the benefit of Naples. The running costs of the University (between 6000 and 10,000 ducats for the readers and officers in the 1730s), were added to in the course of the century by the creation of professional (naval, artillery) and learned academies. However, it was in the field of public works that the economic consequences of expenditure in the capital were most important.

The road-building operations conducted under Charles of Bourbon were revealing of the monarchy's metropolitan policy, since the three major arteries on which construction began all radiated out from the capital; they linked Naples to the Abruzzi, Puglia and Calabria. Above all, however, as the place of residence of an independent sovereign, Naples was turned into a vast building site. The monumental town-planning projects launched by Charles of Bourbon[55] had the aim of giving the city the aspect of a great European capital. Impressive public buildings now became the symbols of the new political reality. Whether for collective use (*Albergo dei Poveri*, *Granili*, port construction, etc.) or for the royal family and the Court (restructuring of the Royal Palace, suburban royal residences at Capodimonte, Portici, Caserta and so on), they all reflected the desire of the new dynasty to embellish and project the city's image. In the first six years of Charles of Bourbon's reign, the largest expenses in the field of public works were for the villas of Capodimonte and Portici (480,000 ducats),[56] and in the following years for the *Reggia* of Caserta. According to Giuseppe Maria Galanti, in 1789, the costs of purchasing the site and constructing the *Albergo dei Poveri*, intended to receive 8000 poor people, had risen to 900,000 ducats since 1751.[57] The public works policy of the monarchs thus generated considerable employment and helped to stimulate the Neapolitan economy, but had much less impact in the provinces, where the amounts devoted to improving agriculture or to remedying the serious shortcomings of the road network remained insignificant.

Land rent and urban investments

The capital received the largest share not only of fiscal receipts but also of land rents: 'In the seventeenth and eighteenth centuries, Naples lived and grew mainly on the rents that came to the barons from the provinces'.[58] This rent was generated within the framework of the seigneury by the sale of what was produced on the landholdings. Even approximate estimates are hard to make of the sums that were sent to Naples to support the lavish lifestyle of the barons who resided in the city. One example, however, concerns the Prince of Santobuono in the Abruzzi, who in 1789 drew from his lands a total annual rent of 3780 ducats, of which 2487 were sent to him in Naples.[59] This was not an exceptional case; for Aurelio Lepre the growth of Naples, as the point of convergence of feudal rent, was itself the very embodiment of the feudal system.[60] Still to be explored, of course, are the uses to which this rent was put.

Land was also the main source of rent to the religious orders. In 1769,

53 per cent of the total income of the Jesuits came from fiefs and agricultural properties, as against 12 per cent for example from the rent of houses in Naples. Economic expansion in the eighteenth century boosted the incomes of the barons, and to a lesser degree the religious houses, thanks to an increase in the value of agricultural output but also in ground rents. However, they appear not to have reinvested in agricultural production and improvement, or in any other productive activity. The need to persuade *rentiers* to reinvest in the productive sector of the kingdom's economy was a constant preoccupation for contemporary economists.[61]

The economy of Naples was in fact dominated by foreign capital. Having long since abandoned to foreigners international trade in favour of safer investments,[62] in land, in the *arrendamenti*[63] and in domestic trade, the Neapolitan merchants had a subordinate position in long-distance trade. In addition, the foreign powers had an interest in keeping the kingdom in a position of commercial dependence, with exports composed almost exclusively of raw materials and imports of manufactured products.[64] Antonio Genovesi demonstrated the degree to which the country was dependent on imported foreign goods.[65] Twenty years later, Giuseppe Palmieri noted that the situation had not changed: 'Several millions leave the kingdom to provide for the most vulgar and shoddy objects, while the most ordinary and basic crafts are either absent altogether or in short supply.'[66] But he also observed that developing and extending the industrial arts in a country was a difficult undertaking that required large investments.

According to the economists, however, what Naples lacked was not capital but entrepreneurs. The predominance of careers linked to the courts, the administration and the state apparatus was manifest from the seventeenth century onwards; whereas the primacy of the artisans in the political and administrative life of the city never recovered after the 1656 plague. Thus the *ceto medio* developed through the exercise of the so-called liberal professions, through the financial markets or from the role of commercial middlemen. This type of activity appeared to offer the surest path to social mobility, and to the accumulation and conservation of wealth that was more likely to be invested in the public debt than in manufacturing industry. The Neapolitan productive sector in fact experienced a certain decadence in the eighteenth century, notably with the decline of the *Arte della Seta*. The mercantile category was dominated by the great grain merchants involved in the *annona* of Naples, an activity which, as was seen earlier, had more affinities with usury than with trade. Attracted by the social model of the nobility, these merchants invested heavily in land, even in fiefs, and sought ennoblement: many Neapolitan *granisti* were ennobled in the second half of the eighteenth century. The urban bourgeoisie remained underdeveloped, investing mainly in properties that offered safe returns and eschewing the sector of manufacturing and long-distance trade, a sector in which, moreover, the opportunities diminished in the course of the century as the Mezzogiorno came to occupy an increasingly subordinate position in the European economy.

For the *illuministi*, the reluctance of the Neapolitan nobility to invest its revenues in the development of industry was one of the strongest relations between the backwardness of the southern economy and the urban question.[67] The nobility was not entirely absent from Neapolitan commerce, but its investments remained essentially usurious, linked to the business of the monopolists responsible for the capital's food supplies. Close ties in fact existed between the monopolistic merchants and the barons: not only was the provisioning of Naples controlled by the city administration, that is, by the elected members of the *piazze* of the Neapolitan nobility, but, by virtue of their feudal and other holdings, the barons had direct control over the countryside and thus shared actively in the profits that could be made through the *contratto alla voce*, for example, or the export licenses. In some cases, also, the nobility had joined forces with the great foreign merchants who ran Naples' international trade. Thus although the rent accumulated in the capital was by no means all wasted on splendour and luxury, the investments chosen were sterile in terms of developing the productive and commercial structure of the kingdom and its capital.[68]

The poor use made of the considerable quantities of capital that the economic expansion of the first half of the eighteenth century had concentrated in the hands of the Neapolitan monarchy, great noble families and a handful of important privileged merchants, was no doubt a factor exacerbating the crisis of 1764.

The 'awakening' of the provinces and the influence of the capital at the end of the eighteenth century

The end of the century, however, saw the increased autonomous development of the provinces, in the sense that their economies tended to be no longer geared wholly to the needs of the metropolis. The Abruzzi, for example, appeared to be oriented more towards Rome. The constitution of an agrarian and commercial bourgeoisie in the provinces, albeit on a modest scale, often on the margins of or even within the feudal system, was accompanied by the emergence of 'new curiosities, needs, interests, movements in cultural life, present nearly everywhere in the life of the provinces'.[69]

The Neapolitan merchants, whose profits were made from the

difference in price between Naples and the provinces, notably for grain provisioning, had no interest in seeing any lessening of the metropolis' domination over the rest of the country. Nonetheless, by the end of the century the existence of a provincial bourgeoisie was increasingly evident. In part this was a rural bourgeoisie of peasant origins (tenant farmers of Puglia, agents of the nobles and so forth), who had profited from the rising prices in the second half of the eighteenth century and bought land. No doubt more numerous, however, was the urban provincial bourgeoisie. It would appear, then, that independently of the capital, some provinces were able to benefit from the economic situation.

Yet the role of Naples, as a consumer market and as centre of financial concentration, was not wholly alien to the development of some regions and should not be underestimated: the regions immediately around the capital such as Caserta, Salerno, Avellino, Aversa, experienced strong demographic growth associated with a productive and commercial development which made it one of the most prosperous territories in the kingdom. The close links that the capital had with the neighbouring zones had a stimulating effect on agriculture: 'the cost of land and the yields obtained were among the highest in the Mezzogiorno'.[70] Trade in these regions also benefited from the infrastructures built for the capital by the Bourbons: the roads that converged on Naples from the provinces all necessarily went through those zones close to the metropolis, which as a result were a good deal less isolated than many other rural parts of the kingdom. In addition to the large-volume trade between Naples and the provinces of Terra di Lavoro, Principato Ulteriore and Principato Citeriore, which was linked especially to the provisioning of the city, there was also a small-scale trade such as could only exist in a great centre of consumption like Naples. In this way came into being a network of small peasant holdings producing for the urban market. Cultivation of fruit and vegetables, for example, experienced spectacular development, and the *ortolani* (market-gardeners) figured among the wealthiest categories of peasants. The commercial activity available to the peasants of the surroundings of Naples, because of proximity to the city's market, early on distinguished them from their counterparts of the interior of the kingdom, remote from any large centre of population. Thus in spite of the controls and constraints that Naples imposed on the regions from which it drew its supplies, the city did contribute significantly to the development of surrounding territories within a radius of 50 kilometres.

Turning to the provinces further from the metropolis, the regions most closely linked to Naples also experienced a relative economic dynamism. The iniquities of the system of the *contratto alla voce* notwithstanding, the injection of capital from the Neapolitan *granisti* into the city's supply zones such as the Capitanata had a positive impact on the development of agriculture, by encouraging the use of hitherto unculti-vated land. In this way the Neapolitan monopolists financed not only the commercialization of agricultural output but also the increase in the area of land under cultivation. This was important, since in the southern provinces the development of trade, crafts and services all depended on the agrarian sector. The example of the Capitanata allows us to modify the image of the exploitation of the provinces by the Neapolitan finan-cial élite; towards the end of the eighteenth century the action of the monopolists appears to have had appreciable economic benefits even in the provinces.[71]

Another region of the Puglia, Terra di Bari, presents a different type of development, one that seems to have been encouraged by its weaker ties of dependence with the capital, notably when compared with the nearby Terra d'Otranto. The most dynamic economic sector in these regions was the olive oil trade: 60–70 per cent of all the oil exported from the kingdom was handled by the ports of Puglia. Terra d'Otranto[72] was more closely linked to the provisioning of Naples, and its export trade was entirely financed by foreign merchants, with the English, in particu-lar, dominating the market. Yet it was Naples that acted as intermediary between provincial and foreign merchants, and the fact of commerce being in the hands of foreigners appears to have exacerbated the finan-cial dependence of the local merchants *vis-à-vis* the metropolis. Furthermore, the internal market was reduced to the capital and its region. In Terra di Bari, by contrast, the Neapolitan monopolists were less present, and the commercial centres were able to develop their Adriatic commerce untrammelled by foreign control, and thus without being forced to use the capital as intermediary.[73] In this case the trade in oil was more under the control of the provincials themselves, and a solid class of local merchants and shippers grew up in the second half of the eighteenth century. Bari developed significantly between then and the nineteenth century, and the city increasingly occupied the role of second urban pole of the mainland Mezzogiorno.[74]

Compared with the hegemony that Naples had exercised over its provinces in the previous century, new territorial balances, within which the position of the metropolis was modified, gradually emerged at the end of the 1700s and were consolidated in the nineteenth century.

Conclusion

The image that the eighteenth-century economists transmit is one of a rapidly growing capital, absorbing the resources and vitality of the provinces yet without, despite the hopes of the years 1730-60, succeeding in establishing itself as an economic centre capable of giving an impetus to the development of the Mezzogiorno. It is true that a large part of the fiscal revenues of the kingdom was employed exclusively to the advantage of the metropolis, which acquired a new dimension in the eighteenth century, one visible even in its physical form; true also that the land rents that flowed into the city failed to be invested usefully for the development of the country's productive activities. For all this, however, the model of the parasitic city draining the resources of its hinterland and generating luxury and misery is inadequate. Within its region, in a zone of influence of little more than 50 kilometres in radius, Naples did manage to induce a degree of growth; beyond this limit, the relations of influence were less intense and seem to have been limited essentially to extraction of rent and royal taxes. But Naples was not solely responsible for the economic weakness of provinces which were to a large degree still under the control of the feudal barons. As was the case throughout the modern period, the growth of the city in the eighteenth century owed more to its political function and to its role as instrument of the monarchy against feudalism, than to the real economic forces present in the kingdom. The economic price paid by the provinces for the growth of Naples did nonetheless enable the Mezzogiorno to retain a place in Europe's most advanced cultural networks and to participate fully in the Enlightenment. And the cultural and intellectual functions of the city that enabled it to play a role in international cultural life were not without a positive influence on the provinces: large numbers of provincials were educated and trained in Naples, where they had the opportunity to participate in the networks of cultural and intellectual sociability that extended far beyond the boundaries of the kingdom. Thus if Naples seems to have had little economic influence in the 'awakening' of the provinces at the end of the eighteenth century, its cultural influence should not be underestimated: this was also part of the exchange between the capital and its provinces.

Notes

1. Cf. F. Venturi, 'Napoli capitale nel pensiero dei riformatori illuministi', in *Storia d'Italia*, vol.8 (1971), 1-73.
2. Cf. P. Mascilli Migliorini, 'La politica territoriale dell'Illuminismo moderato nel regno di Napoli', *Prospettive Settanta* (1983), pp.183-94.
3. See for example A. Lemaître, *La Métropolitée* (Amsterdam, 1682). From the outset the author insists on the importance that the capital gives to economic exchange: 'Capital cities draw their life and their glory from all the parts of the State, and in turn give it back to all the Provinces ... Thus

the Metropolitan City showers the members of the Provinces with its money, its industry and the fruits of its trade, and draws from them the materials for their production ... In a word, the Capital City protects the country and the people, reveals and fructifies their assets, which in turn make the Capital prosper ... the purpose of the Capital City is utility, its own and that of the Provinces; in such a way that while it receives so it gives, having as immediate justification the just proportion and the right balance between itself and the country, and as ultimate justification the prosperity and well-being of itself and the State,' (pp.5-10).

4.　To consider just the Italian states, the importance accorded to this theme in the eighteenth century is reflected in the question posed by the Academy of Sciences, Letters and Beaux Arts of Mantua: 'What should the balance be of population and trade between a city and its hinterland, describing its disorders and their practical remedies, and the most obvious sources of mutual support and need?' For one notable reply see Giovanni Battista Gherardo d'Arco, *Dell'armonia politico-economica tra la città e il suo territorio* (1771).

5.　As noted by D. Demarco, 'Il dibattito settecentesco sulla popolazione in Italia', in *La popolazione italiana nel Settecento* (Bologna, 1980), pp.539-90; the most important Italian eighteenth century theorists on population were Neapolitans (or Milanais).

6.　M. Schipa, 'Problemi napoletani al principio del secolo XVIII. Notizie storiche (1701-1713)', *Atti della Accademia Pontaniana*, vol.28 (1898), memoir 13.

7.　On the reforms of the Bourbons in the eighteenth century, see E. Chiosi, 'Il Regno dal 1734 al 1799' in G. Galasso and R. Romeo, eds, *Storia del Mezzogiorno*, vol.4.2 (Rome, 1986), 371-467; A.M. Rao, *Il Regno di Napoli nel Settecento* (Naples, 1984); and in particular the recent essay by A.M. Rao, 'Il riformismo borbonico a Napoli', in *Il secolo dei Lumi e delle riforme* (*Storia della società italiana*, vol.12) (Milan, 1989), 215-90.

8.　'It can be said that the kingdom is like a monstrous figure which has a huge head, that is, the capital, Naples, and a tiny body, which is all the rest of the inhabitants of the kingdom,' in *Alcune riflessioni intorno al presente Governo del Regno di Napoli sotto l'Augusto Imperatore Carlo VI* (1733), Library of the Società Napoletana di Storia Patria, Ms XXI. A. 7., f.16. This image quickly became a commonplace and was still current at the end of the century: e.g. 'there can be no doubt that our capital is out of all proportion to the rest of the kingdom, and can truthfully be described as a giant's head on the body of a pygmy, a state of affairs which does great harm to both,' Salvatore Pignatelli, *Ragionamenti economici, politici e militari* (Naples, 1782), p.136.

9.　P.M. Doria, *Relazione dello Stato Politico, Economico e Civile del Regno di Napoli, prima dell'Entrata dell'Armi Tedesche in detto Regno*, National Library of Naples, Ms branc. V. D. 2., ff.61-2.

10.　See for example the observations of Giovan Battista Maria Jannucci (president of the *Supremo Magistrato di Commercio* in 1763), *Economia del commercio del Regno di Napoli (1767-1768)* ed. F. Assante (Naples, 1981), vol.1, 36.

11.　See esp. P.M. Doria, *Del Commercio del Regno di Napoli con l'aggiunta di un'appendice. Lettera diretta al signor don Francesco Ventura, degnissimo presidente del Magistrato del commercio*, National Library of Naples, Ms branc. V. D. 2., extract published in R. Ajello, ed., *Dal Muratori al Cesarotti*, vol.5 (Milan, 1978), 909-16.

12. B. Tanucci, *Epistolario*, ed. R.P. Coppini, L. Del Bianco and R. Nieri, vol.1 (Rome, 1980), 635-8.

13. *Ibid.*, p.635.

14. Chiosi, 'Il Regno dal 1734 al 1799', pp.380-1.

15. 215,608 in the *Nota del numero delle anime di ciascheduna delle parrocchie della Città e Borghi di Napoli, giusta lo stato di esse nell'anno 1707, incluendo anche i luoghi pii*, Library of the Società Napoletana di Storia Patria, Ms XXXI. C. 8. f.61.

16. On the population of the city of Naples, see B. Capasso, 'Sulla circoscrizione civile e ecclesiastica e sulla popolazione della città di Napoli dalla fine del secolo XIII al 1809. Ricerche e documenti', *Atti della Accademia Pontaniana* (Naples, 1883), pp.99-180; C. Petraccone, *Napoli dal '500 all '800. Problemi di storia demografica e sociale* (Naples, 1974).

17. Cf. G. Botti, 'La peste del 1656 a Napoli e dintorni nei registri parrocchiali del tempo', in *Atti dell' Accademia di Scienze Morali e Politiche*, vol.82 (1980), pp.1-26.

18. *Ristretto Generale della numerazione di tutte le parrocchie, Monasterij, ed Ospedali, suoi Borghi, e Casali di questa Città di Napoli fatta nell' anno 1742*, Library of the Società Napoletana di Storia Patria, Ms XXII. E. 29.

19. Discounting the figure – no doubt exaggerated – for foreigners, the population of Naples, according to Petraccone, *Napoli*, p.135, had grown by 64 per cent since 1688.

20. Cf. F. Venturi, '1764: Napoli nell' anno della fame', *Rivista Storica Italiana* vol.85(2) (1973), 394-472.

21. Cf. Petraccone, *Napoli*, p.168 et seq.

22. See R. Pilati, 'Il problema della redazione dei calendari e notiziari di corte a Napoli tra la fine del Settecento e l'inizio dell' Ottocento', in *La demografia storica delle città italiane* (Bolognà, 1982), pp.371-7.

23. Cf. Petraccone, *Napoli*, pp.141-61.

24. P. Villani, *Mezzogiorno tra riforme e rivoluzione* (Bari, 1977), p.4.

25. *Ibid.*, p.95.

26. On the consequences of the settling of the nobility in the capital for architecture and urban development, see G. Labrot, *Baroni in Città. Residenze e comportamenti dell' aristocrazia napoletana. 1530-1734* (Naples, 1979), and more recently, *idem, Palazzi napoletani. Storie di nobili e cortigiani 1520-1750* (Naples, 1993).

27. Cf. G. Galasso, *Napoli spagnola dopo Masaniello. Politica. Cultura. Società* (Naples, 1972).

28. Tanucci, *Epistolario*, vol.1, 635.

29. A. Genovesi, *L'agricoltore sperimentato di Cosimo Trinci con alcune aggiunte dell' abate Genovesi* (Naples, 1769, 1st edn, Naples, 1764), preface.

30. A. Genovesi, *Lettere familiari* (Naples, 1788), vol.2, 22, letter of 10 August 1764.

31. Cf. Jannucci, *Economia*, vol.4, 777.

32. On the establishment of what were essentially deposit banks, see E. De Simone, 'I banchi pubblici nel XVII secolo', in G. D'Agostino, *La vita economica a Napoli nel '600* (Naples, 1987), pp. 37-52.

33. G.M. Galanti, *Della descrizione geografica e politica delle Sicilie*, (Naples,

1793), vol.1, p.xi.

34.   A. Genovesi, *Lettere accademiche su la question se sieno più felici gl'ignoranti, che gli scienziati* (Naples, 1764), p.104.

35.   See G. Carafa, *Lettera ad un amico contenente alcune considerazioni sull' utilità e gloria che si trarebbe di una esatta carta topografica della città di Napoli e del suo contorno* (Naples, 1750).

36.   Cf. G. Brancaccio, 'La cartografia napoletana dal riformismo illuminato all' Unità', in G. Alisio and V. Valerio, eds, *Cartografia napoletana dal 1781 al 1889. Il Regno, Napoli, la Terra di Bari* (Naples, 1983).

37.   G. Palmieri, *Riflessioni sulla pubblica felicità relativamente al Regno di Napoli* (Naples, 1787), p.206.

38.   G. Galasso, 'Tradizione, metamorfosi e identità di un'antica capitale', in G. Galasso, ed., *Napoli* (Rome/Bari, 1987), pp.11-45.

39.   Jannucci, *Economia*, vol.1, 64-5.

40.   The *tomolo* is roughly equal to 0.55 hectolitre. According to the calculations of R. Romano, *Prezzi, salari e servizzi a Napoli nel secolo XVIII (1734-1806)* (Milan, 1965), p.71, the capital consumed between 2 and 2.6 million *tomoli* of grain.

41.   Cf. G. Civile, 'Granisti e annona a Napoli nel XVIII secolo', in *Studi sulla società meridionale* (Naples, 1978), pp.47-99.

42.   Cf. P. Macry, 'Ceto mercantile e azienda agricola nel regno di Napoli: il contratto alla voce nel XVIII secolo', *Quaderni Storici*, (1972), 851-909. On the grain market, see *idem, Mercato e società nel Regno di Napoli. Commercio del grano e politica economica del '700* (Naples, 1974).

43.   On the vital role of the Neapolitan merchants in financing the agriculture of the provinces and the consequent need to maintain the *contratto alla voce*, see in particular the views of Ferdinando Galiani in the exposé he addressed to the King on 22 October 1787, in F. Diaz and L. Guerci, eds, *Illuministi italiani, VI, Opere di Ferdinando Galiani* (Milan/Naples, 1975), p.742 *et seq.*

44.   G. Spiriti, *Riflessioni economico-politiche* (Naples, 1793), p.150.

45.   Cf. Macry, *Mercato e società*, ch.6.

46.   On the production and sale of olive oil, see P. Chorley, *Oil, Silk and Enlightenment. Economic problems of XVIIIth century Naples* (Naples, 1965), and A. Lepre, *Contadini, borghesi ed operai nel tramonto del feudalismo napoletano* (Milan, 1963), pp.241-68.

47.   Cf. Jannucci, *Economia*, vol.3, 705 *et seq.*

48.   For an analysis of finances under Charles of Bourbon, see in particular I. Zilli, *Carlo di Borbone e la rinascita del Regno di Napoli. Le finanze pubbliche, 1734-42* (Naples, 1990), on which most of what follows is based. For the second half of the century, see L. Bianchini, *Le finanze delle Due Sicilie* (Naples, 1859), and G. Masi, *L'azienda pubblica del Regno di Napoli dal 1771 al 1782* (Bari, 1948).

49.   Cf. R. Romano, 'La situazione finanziaria del Regno di Napoli attraverso il bilancio generale dell'anno 1734', *Archivio Storico per le Provincie Napoletane* (1947), 151-68.

50.   The fiscal households were fixed definitively in 1669, and by the eighteenth century no longer corresponded to demographic households. A new enumeration was conducted under Charles of Bourbon and the new fiscal base came into effect on 1 January 1737.

51.   According to Zilli, *Carlo di Borbone*, p.83, two thirds of *fiscali* were in the

hands of private individuals.

52. Cf. Villani, *Mezzogiorno tra riforme e rivoluzione*, p.105 *et seq.*

53. According to Zilli, *Carlo di Borbone*, p.133, in 1738 this expenditure had reached 1,562,389 ducats, equal to 29 per cent of revenue: this large sum is explained in part by work under way on the royal palace. On the other hand, the costs of the other royal residences, borne directly by the General Treasury, are not included in the Royal Household. According to Masi, *L'azienda*, p.124, the expenditure of the latter represented 18 per cent of the budget of the state in 1780.

54. Archivio di Stato di Napoli, Segretaria di Stato di Polizia, Dispacci, 1, ff.2-4.

55. For details of the construction programmes of the Bourbons, see C. De Seta, *Napoli* (Rome/Bari, 1981), pp.165-208, and G. Alisio, *Urbanistica napoletana del Settecento* (Naples, 1979).

56. Zilli, *Carlo di Borbone*, pp.172-3.

57. Galanti, *Della descrizione*, vol.3, 167.

58. A. Lepre, *Feudi e masserie. Problemi della società meridionale nel '600 e nel '700* (Naples, 1973), p.10.

59. *Ibid.*

60. A. Lepre, *Terra di Lavoro nell' età moderna* (Naples, 1978), p.12.

61. Villani, *Mezzogiorno tra riforme e rivoluzione*, p.19.

62. On the role of the English in the trade of the Mezzogiorno, see G. Pagano De Divitis, *Mercanti inglesi nell'Italia del Seicento. Navi, traffici, egemonie* (Venice, 1990).

63. On this type of investment, see L. De Rosa, *Studi sugli Arrendamenti del Regno di Napoli* (Naples, 1963).

64. See in particular E. Lo Sardo, *Napoli e Londra nel XVIII secolo. Le relazioni economiche* (Naples, 1991).

65. A. Genovesi, *Delle lezioni di commercio o sia d'economia civile* (Naples, 1765-67), especially part 1, ch.22, para. XXI.

66. G. Palmieri, *Della richezza nazionale* (Naples, 1792), ch.5.

67. See esp. Jannucci, *Economia*, vol.1, ch.5.

68. Cf. A. Lepre, *Il Mezzogiorno dal feudalismo al capitalismo* (Naples, 1979), p.175 *et seq.*

69. Galasso, 'Tradizione, metamorfosi e identità', p.19.

70. P. Macry, 'Vecchio e nuovo nel secolo dei Lumi', in F. Barbagallo, ed., *Storia della Campania* (Naples, 1978), p.284.

71. Cf. E. Cerrito, 'Strutture economiche e distribuzione del reddito in Capitanata nel Decennio francese', in A. Massafra, ed., *Produzione, mercato e classi sociali nella Capitanata moderne e contemporanea* (Foggia, 1984), pp.133-265.

72. On this province, see M.A. Visceglia, *Territorio feudo e potere locale. Terra d'Otranto tra Medioevo ed Età moderna* (Naples, 1988).

73. See M.A. Visceglia, 'Il commercio dei porti pugliesi nel Settecento. Ipotesi di ricerca', in P. Villani, ed., *Economia e classi sociali nella Puglia moderna* (Naples, 1974), pp.187-220.

74. For the development of the city of Bari, see F. Tateo, ed., *Storia di Bari nell' antico regime*, vol.1 (Rome/Bari, 1991).

CHAPTER EIGHT

The Metropolis in the Sand-pit – Berlin and Brandenburg

Helga Schultz

The metropolis and its ambivalent role

Amid the sandy plains of the Brandenburg Marches – the 'sand-pit of the Holy Roman Empire' as it was once mockingly called – Berlin is rising above the surrounding countryside, a front rank commercial centre once again, with almost four million inhabitants; in former times a European centre of culture and science, the old and new capital of Germany. The modern city contrasts sharply with its agrarian hinterland of small and medium sized towns and sleepy, backward villages and hamlets. It seems to be a commonplace that a metropolis is prone to create a dreary and barren environment, that it fast absorbs all the urban functions of the hinterland and does not permit any other urban centre of importance to develop more than modest dimensions.[1] This effect seems to be less in those places where, since the Middle Ages, cities have grown out of flourishing landscapes, such as Paris in the Ile-de-France, London at the centre of the rich southern counties, Vienna in Lower Austria or Prague in Bohemia.

Berlin, however, emerged from solitary bleakness. Of course it was a bleakness moderated by central European conditions but, nevertheless, the city developed in a region marked by soils of low fertility, sparsely developed crafts and trades and thin settlement. These features were destined to create the specific superiority that characterized Berlin *vis-à-vis* its hinterland. But it is doubtful if this superior position was wholly beneficial for the metropolis.

Early developments

Late in the Middle Ages, Berlin, at that time named Berlin/Cölln, a twin town, had emerged as one of the innumerable German trade and commercial centres, with a certain regional significance and enjoying considerable autonomy for its citizens. The town was linked to the Hanseatic League. Roughly a dozen overseas merchants maintained trading relations with Hamburg and the Netherlands, and via Pomeranian and Mecklenburgian seaports on the Baltic Sea.[2] Its wide spectrum of trade commodities included imported fish, and grain exported from the Brandenburg hinterland.

The foundation of Berlin's economic prosperity was provided by a specialized system of trades and crafts organized in several dozen guilds. Their needs and their products determined a system of barter trading with the peasants and burghers living in the surrounding villages and small towns. In addition to foodstuffs from the countryside, the Berliners obtained raw materials like wool, flax and leather, and drank beer from Bernau and Neuruppin rather than their own brew.

Berlin could not claim its own surrounding territory, as was the case for the cities of Ulm and Lübeck or even the Hanseatic town of Rostock. However, the bourgeois families of Berlin possessed feudal estates in 94 surrounding villages which, within a range of 20 kilometres, exceeded even the property of aristocratic and princely owners.[3] Berlin was not a centre of the church, for the episcopal seat was the town of Brandenburg. And even up to 1811 Berlin had no university; the first university in the Brandenburg Marches was founded in Frankfurt-an-der-Oder in 1506.

In the late Middle Ages, among the towns of the Brandenburg Marches the position of Berlin/Cölln could be best described as first among equals. In 1377 Berlin/Cölln contributed 500 Marks in silver to the feudal property tax of Emperor Karl IV, a sum equal to those contributed by the Fair city of Frankfurt-an-der-Oder, Prenzlau in the Uckermark or Stendal in the Altmark.[4] Berlin was foremost among those regional centres only because it was the place of assembly for the Estates of the Marches. Thus, the picture of medieval Berlin was marked by a modest petty-bourgeois style, an urban averageness in striking contrast to the splendours of the early histories of Paris, London or Prague. Historians of Berlin have paid little attention to its medieval past but it was this early history which rooted Berlin more deeply in the hinterland of Brandenburg than the new foundation of St Petersburg in the swamps at the mouth of the Neva.

The period of expansion

After 1451, with their castle built on the Cölln-side banks of the Spree river, the Hohenzollerns made the dual town of Berlin/Cölln into their permanent residence. This was the moment when, indisputably, the town was elevated to first place among its Brandenburg rivals (see Figure 8.1). But trade, guilds, population and the extent of the town long remained within the old framework. It was only after the Thirty Years' War, following reconstruction and consolidation, that the rapid growth of

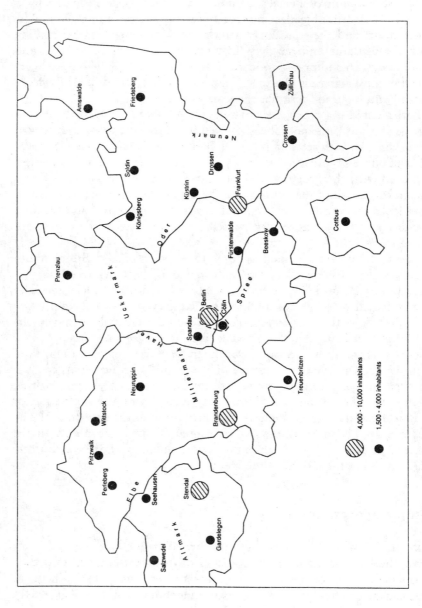

8.1 Towns in Brandenburg about 1650

Berlin began to change fundamentally its relations with the surrounding region of the Brandenburg Marches.

By the start of the eighteenth century Berlin had experienced something like a second foundation, with the transition to a new type of very dynamic urban growth and the leap to a new level in the hierarchy of towns. With annual growth rates of 3 and 4 per cent, Berlin experienced a quadrupling of its population between 1670 and 1720. By the end of the eighteenth century it was the second biggest German city behind the imperial metropolis of Vienna, and only a short time later it had overtaken even that.

During the heyday of industrialization, between 1840 and 1890, Berlin once again achieved the fabulous growth rates of the early pioneering period around 1700, with the population doubling twice within this fifty year period. The dynamism of Berlin in the nineteenth century exceeded even that of the old European metropolises of Paris and London, yet without attaining their size. While these cities were able to increase the number of inhabitants by five- or even six-fold, the population of Berlin, in only one century, increased by fourteen-fold.[5] In contrast, the development of the population in the hinterland (in the Kurmark and the Neumark which at the beginning of the nineteenth century were merged to form the province of Brandenburg) proceeded at a more modest rate. Here annual growth rates were always below 1 per cent.[6] Even today Brandenburg is one of the most sparsely populated German states.

The reasons for Berlin's rise appear to be simple and obvious. Its role as the royal seat and capital of the absolutist state of Brandenburg-Prussia seems to provide an adequate and complete explanation for the history of the city in the eighteenth century, just as its position as the German capital explains the nineteenth century boom. Non-economic factors have proved to be important for the history of cities during the early modern period. The capitals and royal seats of absolutism were usually established at junctures in the European network of cities in this epoch. This network was already noted then. It continued during the urbanization of the nineteenth century and almost until the present.[7] The ascendancy of Berlin was coupled with the rise of the state of Brandenburg-Prussia, advancing to become the youngest great power in Europe.

However, rapid urban growth cannot be taken as a general characteristic of absolutist capital cities. As a rule, they expanded only for relatively short periods during the extension of state power. Such 'promotion fever' was experienced by St Petersburg, *ad extremis*, under Peter the Great, by Stockholm under Gustavus Adolphus, and by Copenhagen under Christian IV. After this burst of growth the size of the city stabilized. This is also evident in the case of other capitals in the

Empire. Munich and Hanover contented themselves with annual growth rates of about half a per cent, while Dresden and Vienna had, on average, growth rates of 1 per cent per annum in the eighteenth century.[8]

Berlin was quite different. The development of Berlin gained extra-ordinary momentum from the special economic policy pursued by the state. This policy, inaccurately described as 'mercantilist', served to allocate the economic potential of the state to its capital. The major pillars were provided by the expansion of population and the promotion of manufacturing.[9] If the Hohenzollerns wanted to expand their state through military action they were forced initially to increase the financial resources of the country through domestic manufactures.

The efforts of the Hohenzollerns were not directed only towards Berlin. The Prussian kings took great pains to help support the country towns of the Brandenburg Marches by, for example, the introduction of mirror manufacture to Neustadt-Dosse, the manufacture of steel cutlery in Neustadt-Eberswalde, and cloth manufactures in the area between Neuruppin and Strausberg.

Nor was the concern with population growth confined to Berlin. Originally, the Elector, in his 1685 edict, wanted to distribute the Huguenots over the smaller towns of the Brandenburg Marches which had been devastated by the Thirty Years' War. But, overwhelmingly, they continued to settle in Berlin, in the vicinity of the Court.[10] A similar trend can be observed with the Bohemian weavers.

The poverty of the country, the prevailing feudal ties of the population, the conservative trade and industrial constitution of the towns and the complete lack of a market for more sophisticated and specialist products were severe obstacles to the policy of mercantilism in the Brandenburg hinterland. The greater splendour and expanding size of the capital city led to a growing contrast between the townships in Brandenburg and the attractive power of the royal residence, which sucked in the economic potential, the entrepreneurial initiative and the innovative forces of the country.

The peculiarity of Berlin lies in its rise as an economic centre that provided not only luxury goods and services, but also turned out products for mass consumption and military needs. This course was set by King Friedrich Wilhelm I, the Soldier King, who, after taking power in 1713, tried to change the structure of Berlin. He converted a centre of sophisticated courtly culture into a huge garrison in which soldiers and civilians alike were engaged in the manufacture of cheap cloth for uniforms as well as fine woollen suits for officers.[11] The frugality of life in the surrounding countryside also provides a key to this aspect of metropolitan policy. In view of the concentration of labour, manufacturing facilities and infrastructure, it was only Berlin that could develop in this direction. These royal policies paradoxically laid the foundation-stone for the importance of Berlin as an industrial centre independent of the Court and its function as capital. This concentration of economic potential developed a particular dynamic. Berlin's economic development gained more and more independence from state subsidies after the abolition of the guilds and the introduction of freedom of trade by the Stein-Hardenberg reforms in 1808. Entrepreneurs such as August Borsig and Werner Siemens, who founded the metal and electrical industries, became key figures of the age of industrial revolution in Berlin. But these developments do not alter fundamentally the importance of government policy in the rise of the metropolis. The economic power of Berlin can be explained fully only in the context of its function as both the political and military centre of the Prussian state. Only this specific conjunction led to Berlin's exceptional economic development, which surpassed all other central European cities during the course of the industrial revolution.

The scale and nature of government intervention becomes strikingly apparent when we look at the industrial regions of the central European area from the end of the Middle Ages up to our own century. Despite all the sweeping changes brought about by the shift in trade routes, the de-industrialization after the collapse of the original industries and the industrial revolution of the nineteenth century, the big industrial regions have generally enjoyed a large measure of stability. This is true for the belt of the Hanseatic seaports on the Baltic and North Sea, the region along the Lower Rhine and Westphalia, the small-trade regions around the low mountain range, the Saxony-Bohemia-Silesia region and the Upper-German-Swiss area, which are all highly congested regions with changing industrial orientations. Amid the still mainly agrarian German north east there is only one newly emerging region, the economic region of Berlin.

The relationship between the capital and its surrounding countryside appears ambiguous. Did the city really attract and absorb all the potential of the hinterland or did it have a more positive influence on the development of its surrounding area?

Changes in the economic region: food supply

It became increasingly difficult for the surrounding countryside to supply an ever-expanding Berlin with foodstuffs, raw materials and fuel. From an early date the grain surpluses of the entire Brandenburg Marches were found inadequate to supply the city with bread, and from the close of the seventeenth century rulers had repeatedly prohibited the export of grain from the Brandenburg Marches. When prices rose in 1718 the King ordered the opening of the wartime reserves in order to distribute subsidized grain to Berliners, a measure much applauded in Europe.[12] Grain remained the staple food of the capital till the beginning of the nineteenth century when it was replaced by the potato. In 1793 the excise register shows a per-capita consumption of 214 kilograms of bread compared with little more than 7 kilograms of potatoes.[13] It was necessary to transport grain to Berlin from the Neumark (beyond the Oder river), from East and West Prussia and from the fertile area around Magdeburg.[14] Berlin butchers even toured the countryside far into Silesia or the Prussian part of Poland in a search for suppliers of meat for the metropolitan market.

The problem of food supply can be viewed as an outcome of the contradiction between the manufacturing-capitalist agglomeration of Berlin and the feudal system of agriculture in the surrounding country-side. Taxes and services turned out to be such a burden on peasants that there was no scope nor incentive left to them to raise production. Although several tenants introduced the innovations of English agricul-ture to the sandy soil of the Brandenburg Marches,[15] crop rotation remained exceptional and the extensive three-field system of soil cultiva-tion continued predominant. In 1801 the yield from wheat cultivation in Brandenburg reached only four to one of seed; for the other staple grains the yield was even lower.[16]

Harnisch has impressively outlined the great rise of agriculture in the Marches after the liberation of the peasants in 1810–11 as a result of the Stein-Hardenberg reforms. It was only from that time that the surrounding countryside could exploit the metropolitan market. Even so, the example of a peasant who had taken up dairy farming for the Berlin market and supplied 600 litres of milk and 20 kilograms of butter daily from his 200 head of cattle was still worthy of special note by officials in 1842. And this farm enterprise was favoured in that it was situated on the road to Hamburg, only some eight miles away from Berlin, and was a rural estate rather than a farmstead.[17]

After the abolition of feudal restrictions the peasants of Branden-burg were able to respond in a limited way to the opportunities of the metropolitan market. The smallness of their holdings, the burden of taxes, the lack of credit for modernization and, not least, the poor infra-structure, prevented them from fully exploiting the market. Only the horticultural region around Werder, south west of Berlin, with its intensive cultivation developed into an integral part of the Berlin economic region.

Changes in the economic region: industrial settlement

In the beginning the growth of Berlin's industry was constrained by feudal state policies. These policies consisted mainly of a strict separation between the manufacturing and trading towns on the one hand and the agrarian countryside on the other. This concept was mostly aimed at enforcing strictly the payment of the excise at town gates. Rural industry within the Electoral County of Brandenburg subsisted at such a low level that there were hardly any skilled artisans who could move to work in the manufactures of the city.[18] Berlin's textile industry relied for the time being on expanding into the small or medium sized towns of the Brandenburg Marches, such as Neuruppin or Strausberg, where much of the weaving of cheaper cloth for Berlin's manufacturers took place.[19]

By the middle of the eighteenth century the Berlin manufacturers, because of a persistent lack of spun yarn, had induced the King to make an exception to the strict separation of town from countryside by constructing a ring of spinning and weaving villages around the capital. This could be achieved only with the help of 'colonists'. Foreign skilled labourers, mainly Saxon weavers, settled in the valley of the river Spree south east of Berlin, in the villages of Friedrichshagen, Gosen and Neu-Zittau, named after the Saxon town of Zittau. Bohemian exiles established rural weaving mills in Rixdorf (today Neukölln) and in Nowawes (Potsdam-Babelsberg).[20] Thus developed the beginnings of a rural industrial area around Berlin, though it did not reach the density of true proto-industrial regions.[21]

The introduction of free trade created opportunities for industries in the towns of Brandenburg as well as in the rural countryside. Industry in the Brandenburg hinterland developed much more rapidly than in the capital during the first half of the nineteenth century. Berlin's share of all Brandenburgians and Berliners carrying on trade or business fell from 36 per cent in 1800 to only 22 per cent in 1849 (see Figure 8.2).[22] Textiles, metal industries and, increasingly, mechanical engineering represented the main production in the hinterland as well as in the capital. The old medium sized towns of Neustadt-Eberswalde, Brandenburg, Potsdam, Neuruppin and Frankfurt-an-der-Oder represented the centres of this industrial region. All these towns were directly connected with Berlin by waterways and highways and later on by railways.[23] These industrial subcentres did not, however, develop into independent industrial agglomerations. The economic expansion which had been enjoyed by the hinterland during the early era of industrialization faded during the era of high industrialization. The crisis of the 1870s, the so-called 'founders' crash' *Gründerkrach*, destroyed many businesses in small and medium sized towns, whereas Berlin's economy soon experienced a new boom. The reason for this lies in all probability in the now overwhelming economic competition of the metropolis.

Thus every independent economic development which was not symbiotically connected with metropolitan industry was increasingly doomed. Once again all dynamic growth focused on the city of Berlin. Berlin as an economic centre was no longer based on the textile industry but on mechanical engineering and finally on the electrical industry.[24]

A fire ring of factories developed around the city, reaching from Rummelsburg to Moabit and Spandau. Rising property prices and the density of the inner city led to a shift of the industrial belt to the outskirts. Simultaneously, former rural suburbs developed into overcrowded working-class residential districts. Old suburbs such as Moabit, an agrarian Huguenot settlement, or Rixdorf, a Bohemian weaving colony, lost their specific characteristics during the great wave of industrialization. The uniformity of the working-class districts also extended to their demographic composition.[25] The villages surrounding Berlin became de facto, and eventually in 1920, with the creation of 'Groß-Berlin', de jure administrative districts of the capital.[26] The towns of Charlottenburg, Spandau and Köpenick in Berlin's surrounding area grew to meet the expanding metropolis.[27]

After 1871 the old nucleus of what was by now the capital of the German Empire was transformed into the City of Berlin, where government offices, banks, department stores and publishing houses displaced residents. The borders between metropolis and the surrounding area became increasingly blurred. Berlin made use of its outer environs for siting production plants, for storage and disposal, for its transport system and even for recreation. From 1890 an urban region with a radius of about 50 kilometres came into being, within which all economic and social structures depended on Berlin.[28] These surrounding areas formed the Berlin Umland in the strict sense of economic geographers. Beyond this, the Brandenburg hinterland was pervaded by a weakly developed mixture of agriculture and industry, where the influence of the metropolis was perceived more as a burden than a stimulus.

Berliners and Brandenburgians: immigration

The residential and capital city not only developed its own economic region, it also created its own demographic habitat. The sparseness of the population and the industrial underdevelopment of the hinterland induced a higher level of immigration into Berlin than into any other European capital. Berlin constituted a melting pot of people seeking employment, with adventurers from various European territories and empires, especially during the period of construction after 1700. Only the inhabitants of the Catholic territories remained largely excluded; the Prussian kings tolerated Roman Catholics within their residential city only after the conquest of Silesia, when prudence dictated their acceptance. Every seventh Berliner was a Huguenot at the beginning of the eighteenth century.[29] Bohemians,[30] Swiss, people from the Palatinate (Pfälzer), and Swabians eagerly sought the benefits of colonists' privileges.[31] The Jewish middle class stimulated through its international connections not only the economic but even more the intellectual life of the city.[32] Attention should also be drawn to the neglected influence of Saxon artisans, merchants and innkeepers. A sixth of the artisans registered as new citizens came from Saxony during the eighteenth century (see Figure 8.2).[33] These immigrants came from urbanized regions with flourishing industries. A distinctively urban, mobile and openminded society developed from such origins. Berliner wit and the keen political alertness of the Berliners was already proverbial by the close of the eighteenth century. Immigration also influenced language. The Berlin dialect developed during the eighteenth century and replaced lower German (*niederdeutsch*) as the colloquial language. The Upper Saxon bias of this urban slang was already noticeable by the sixteenth century, but it became dominant only under the influence of the strong Saxon immigration.[34] Naturally the French population of Berlin also left its linguistic imprint. The linguistic difference between the high German (*hochdeutsch*) language of the city and the lower German of the hinterland of Brandenburg indicates the marked cleavage between the Berliners and the country people of the Brandenburg Marches. The Berlin dialect invaded the whole region of the Marches during the nineteenth century and provided an indicator of the hegemony of the metropolis over the hinterland. Thus the unity of language of the city and the hinterland was re-established.

But what contribution did the people of Brandenburg make to the rise of the capital? Their influence ought to have been the greatest if numbers are any guide. The majority of immigrants to Berlin during the entire eighteenth century consisted of people from Brandenburg.[35] But these immigrants from close by faced many handicaps compared to more distant migrants. People from Brandenburg came from the agricultural sector or from the underdeveloped trade and commerce of the country towns. A very high proportion of these immigrants were day labourers' sons or peasants' daughters without specialized professional skills. They were therefore forced to seek employment as unskilled workers in the building trade, in firms of carriers, as housemaids or servants. Brandenburgers also provided most of the common soldiers in the military garrison. In addition many of them had to cope with the

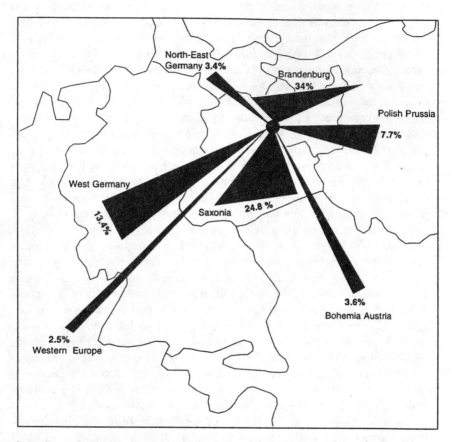

8.2   Regional origins of Berlin artisans in the eighteenth century

handicap of illiteracy. Their chances of marriage were diminished because of their inferior social status.[36] All these factors explain the dominance of foreigners in the culture of the city of Berlin.

But these pessimistic remarks should not be overstated. Almost half of Berlin's bakers and butchers migrated from the Brandenburg Marches during the eighteenth century. Among them were self-consciously successful and educated men such as the master baker Johann Friedrich Heyde, who was the only master craftsman at that time to serve as first churchwarden and who left behind a very interesting chronicle.[37]

Only in the course of industrialization were these demographic proportions reversed as long-distance immigration began to surpass immigration from nearby. Only 30 per cent of newly registered Berlin citizens came from Brandenburg by the year 1900. The stream of immigrants from Eastern Prussia continued to rise until it constituted – at a third of all newcomers – the largest overall contingent of all immigrants. The great internal migration from Germany's agrarian East to the prospering industrial West began to get under way. A similar phenomenon regarding the structure of immigration into Vienna during the nineteenth century has been noted by Ehmer and Fassmann: Bohemians and Moravians pushed people from Lower Austria into the background during the middle of the century.[38]

The proverbial Berlin saying that almost every real Berliner comes from Silesia ought to be regarded as one of the many delusions concerning demographic issues in everyday life. Only one eighth of the immigrants came from Silesia, even during the period of industrialization, but a third from Prussia and Pomerania. Nevertheless, the Silesians succeeded in replacing the Saxons in the role they had performed in Berlin's industry in the age of manufacture. This fact seems to be valid not only in a numerical sense, but also with regard to professional qualifications and industrial activity.[39] Many Silesians could be found amongst the upper strata of Berlin's proletariat, amongst the skilled labourers with an artisan background.

Immigration ceased to be a concern of the government's after the Stein-Hardenberg reforms in 1808-11. Privileges for colonists were already being gradually abolished during the eighteenth century. At the beginning of the nineteenth century Berlin's middle classes associated immigration with growing pauperism.[40] The reforms simultaneously inaugurated liberty of settlement in the towns and transferred the duty of poor relief from the state to municipal authorities. This was often regarded as too high a burden for the purses of the citizens. Thus magistrates could only complain about the 'easiness of establishing oneself here, especially ... for all ...

indigent persons'.[41]

Berlin opposed the extension of the city limits, due to the same anxieties, until the close of the nineteenth century. The suburbs with their dense working-class population and accompanying social problems and costs ought to remain outside in the surrounding areas of Brandenburg. Only after the settlement of a substantial taxpaying middle class in the western suburbs at the beginning of the twentieth century did the city government change its mind regarding the incorporation of outer areas.[42]

Taking an overall view of the history of the relationship between Berlin and its hinterland, the conclusions seem to point in a rather negative direction. The existence of a metropolis evidently provided only marginal stimuli for economic growth in the hinterland. The big city only transformed the surrounding area into a urban region. Small and medium sized towns in the hinterland could only develop through the intervention of the state attempting to transform them into regional cultural and political centres. The dominance of the metropolis was most overwhelming during periods of unrestrained capitalism, when it created a regional wasteland, a veritable 'sand-pit'.

Notes

1. P.M. Hohenberg and L. Hollen Lees, *The Making of Urban Europe 1000-1950* (Cambridge, Mass., 1985), pp.215–47. D.R. Ringrose, 'Metropolitan Cities as Parasites', in E. Aerts and P. Clark, eds, *Metropolitan Cities and their Hinterlands in Early Modern Europe* (Leuven, 1990), pp.21–38.
2. E. Müller-Mertens, *Geschichte Berlins von den Anfängen bis 1945* (Berlin, 1987), pp.89–103.
3. Müller-Mertens, *Geschichte Berlins*, p.115; E.-M. Engel and B. Zientara, *Feudalstruktur, Lehnbürgertum und Fernhandel im spät-mittelalterlichen Brandenburg* (Weimar, 1967).
4. Müller-Mertens, *Geschichte Berlins*, p.126.
5. H. Schultz, *Berlin 1650-1800, Sozialgeschichte einer Residenz*, (Berlin, 1987), pp.321–5; H. Thümmler, 'Berlins Stadtgebiet und Einwohner im 19. und Anfang des 20. Jahrhunderts', in *Jahrbuch für Wirtschaftsgeschichte 1987* (Berlin, 1987), p.22.
6. H.-H. Müller, *Märkische Landwirtschaft vor den Agrarreformen von 1807* (Potsdam, 1967), pp.23–4; H. Harnisch, 'Bevölkerung und Wirtschaft. Über die Zusammenhange zwischen sozialökonomischer Struktur und demographischer Entwicklung im Spatfeudalismus', in *Jahrbuch für Wirtschaftsgeschichte 1975* (Berlin, 1975).
7. J. de Vries, *European Urbanization 1500-1800* (London, 1984); E.A. Wrigley, 'Metropolitan Cities and their Hinterlands: Stimulus and Constraints to Growth', in Aerts and Clark, *Metropolitan Cities*, pp.12–20; Hohenberg and Lees, *Making*, pp.137–71.
8. Schultz, *Berlin*, p.323.

9. I. Mittenzwei and E. Herzfeld, *Brandenburg-Preussen 1648-1789. Das Zeitalter des Absolutismus in Wort und Bild* (Berlin, 1988); I. Mittenzwei, *Preussen nach dem Siebenjährigen Krieg. Auseinandersetzungen zwischen Bürgertum und Staat um die Wirtschaftspolitik* (Berlin, 1979).

10. K. Hinze, *Die Arbeiterfrage zu Beginn des modernen Kapitalismus in Brandenburg-Preussen 1685-1806* (Berlin, 1963); S. Jersch-Wenzel, *Juden und 'Franzosen' in der Wirtschaft des Raumes Berlin-Brandenburg zur Zeit des Merkantilismus* (Berlin, 1978); J. Wilke, 'Die Französische Kolonie', in Schultz, *Berlin*, pp.353-430.

11. H. Schultz, 'Capital policies of the Hohenzollerns in Berlin (1650-1800)', in H. Diederiks, P. Hohenberg and M. Waganaar, eds, *Economic Policy in Europe Since the Late Middle Ages. The Visible Hand and the Fortune of Cities* (Leicester, 1992), pp.67-77; C. Hinrichs, 'Die Wollindustrie in Preussen unter Friedrich Wilhelm I', *Acta Borussica. Denkmäler der preussischen Staatsverwaltung im 18. Jahrhundert*, Part II(5) (Berlin, 1933).

12. W. Naude, *Die Getreidehandelspolitik und Kriegsmagazinverwaltung Brandenburg-Preussens bis 1740* (Berlin, 1901), pp.305-6.

13. Schultz, *Berlin*, p.237.

14. H. Harnisch, *Kapitalistische Agrarreform und industrielle Revolution. Agrarhistorische Untersuchungen über das ostelbische Preussen zwischen Spätfeudalismus und bürgerlich-demokratischer Revolution von 1848/49 unter besonderer Berücksichtigung der Provinz Brandenburg* (Weimar, 1984), pp.44, 45.

15. H.-H. Müller, 'Domänen und Domänenpächter in Brandenburg-Preussen im 18. Jahrhundert', in *Jahrbuch für Wirtschaftsgeschichte 1965* (Berlin, 1965), pp.152-60.

16. Harnisch, *Kapitalistische Agrarreform*, p.45.

17. *Ibid.*, p.248.

18. H. Schultz, *Landhandwerk im Übergang vom Feudalismus zum Kapitalismus. Vergleichender Überblick und Fallstudie Mecklenburg-Schwerin* (Berlin, 1983), pp.165-6; K.H. Kaufhold, *Das Gewerbe in Preussen um 1800* (Göttingen, 1978), pp.44-50.

19. H. Krüger, *Zur Geschichte der Manufakturen und der Manufakturarbeiter in Preussen. Die mittleren Provinzen in der zweiten Hälfte des 18. Jahrhunderts* (Berlin, 1958).

20. G. Vogler, *Zur Geschichte der Weber und Spinner von Nowawes 1751-1785* (Potsdam, 1965).

21. F. Escher, *Berlin und sein Umland. Zur Genese der Berliner Stadtlandschaft bis zum Beginn des 20. Jahrhunderts* (Berlin, 1985), pp.108-19.

22. Kaufhold, *Gewerbe*, pp.491-3; O. Busch, *Industrialisierung und Gewerbe im Raum Berlin/Brandenburg 1800-1850* (Berlin, 1971), p.141.

23. Busch, *ibid.*, pp.139-50.

24. L. Baar, 'Berlin in der industriellen Revolution. Zu Anstoss und Anlauf, Durchsetzung und Abschluss', in *Jahrbuch für Wirtschaftsgeschichte 1987* (Berlin, 1987), pp.67-84; W. Fischer, 'Die preussiche Residenz auf dem Wege zur Industriestadt', in *Berlin und seine Wirtschaft. Ein Weg aus der Geschichte in die Zukunft* (Berlin, 1987), pp.59-78.

25. I. Thienel, *Städtewachstum im Industrialisierungsprozess des 19. Jahrhunderts. Das Berliner Beispiel* (Berlin, 1973).

26. H.-J. Rach, *Die Dörfer in Berlin. Handbuch der ehemaligen*

Landgemeinden im Stadtgebiet von Berlin (Berlin, 1988).
27. Thümmler, 'Berlins Stadtgebiet', pp.9–30.
28. A. Zimm, ed., *Berlin und sein Umland. Eine geographische Monographie* (Gotha, 1988), pp.210–17.
29. J. Wilke in G. Bregulla, ed., *Hugenotten in Berlin* (Berlin, 1988), pp.13–87.
30. E. Winter, *Die tschechische und slowakische Emigration in Deutschland im 17. und 18. Jahrhundert. Beiträge zur Geschichte der hussitischen Tradition* (Berlin, 1955).
31. E. Kaeber, ed., *Die Bürgerbücher und Bürgerprotokollbücher Berlins von 1701-1750* (Berlin, 1934), pp.80–4.
32. Jersch-Wenzel, *Juden*.
33. H. Schultz, 'Die Herkunft der Berliner Handwerker im 18. Jahrhundert', in *International Symposium of Handicraft History*, vol.1 (Veszprem, 1983), 49–62.
34. J. Schildt and H. Schmidt, eds, *Berlinisch. Geschichtliche Einführung in die Sprache einer Stadt* (Berlin, 1986), pp.100–72, 214–98.
35. H. Schultz, 'Bewegung und Entwicklung – demographische Prozesse in Städten des Spätfeudalismus', in *Jahrbuch für Wirtschaftsgeschichte 1988* (Berlin, 1988), pp.91–133.
36. *Idem*, 'Land – Stadt – Wanderung im Manufakturzeitalter. Das Beispiel Berlin', in *Jahrbuch für Geschichte des Feudalismus*, vol.6 (Berlin, 1987), 277–92.
37. *Idem*, 'The Chronicle of the Berlin Master Baker Johann Friedrich Heyde', in Georg Iggers, ed., *Marxist Historiography in Transformation. East German Social History in the 1980s* (New York, 1991), pp.188–203.
38. J. Ehmer and H. Fassmann, 'Zur Sozialstruktur von Zuwanderern nach Wien im 19. Jahrhundert', in E. François, ed., *Immigration et Societé Urbaine en Europe Occidentale, XVIe-XXe Siècle* (Paris, 1985), pp.31–45.
39. Thienel, *Städte wachstum*, pp.399–430.
40. J. Reulecke, *Geschichte der Urbanisierung in Deutschland* (Frankfurt-am-Main, 1985), pp.14–40.
41. A. Pokiser, 'Funktion der städtischen Armendirektion des Berliner Magistrats in der ersten Hälfte des 19. Jahrhunderts', (Ph.D. thesis, Humboldt-Universität, Berlin, 1987), p.32.
42. Thümmler, 'Berlins Stadtgebiet', pp.9–30.

CHAPTER NINE

Budapest and its Hinterland: the Development of Twin Cities 1720–1850[1]

Vera Bácskai

Antecedents

The factors determining the development of Budapest in the eighteenth and early nineteenth centuries were substantially different from those influencing the growth of the majority of capitals in Europe. As a result of its advantageous geographical location – the city is situated in the middle of the country, alongside the Danube and at the intersection of several important overland routes – it was the economic factor, trade, that played a fundamental role in its rise. At the same time, the reinforcement of central state administration tended to inhibit the city's progress. After the expulsion of the Turks in 1686 the country became part of the Habsburg Empire. Vienna, the capital of the empire, was the residence of the royal Court and the main state institutions; so that it was Vienna that enjoyed all the benefits of being the administrative centre and the fruits of royal attention, which tended to give European capitals and ducal residences a splendid and decorative face. Moreover, in origin Buda and Pest were twin cities, divided administratively and geographically – Buda on the hilly west bank of the Danube and Pest on the low-lying plain to the east – with before 1849 only a pontoon bridge to link them. With the triumph of the Habsburgs, Buda was deprived not only of its leading role as the old capital but, along with Pest, of its urban existence as well. Depopulated and ruined in the onerous siege of 1686 (which lasted nearly three months) and devastated by the pillage and arson of the conquering armies, the two cities had to be rebuilt completely and settled with new inhabitants. Neither did they regain automatically their earlier urban status. The military government of the first years of Habsburg rule was followed by submission to the Austrian Treasury and so both Buda and Pest sank to the legal status of seigneurial towns. It was only after a tenacious struggle and great financial sacrifices over some twenty years that, in 1705, the two cities succeeded in regaining the charter which once again gave them the rights of royal free cities. And another six years were to pass before they were able to translate these paper rights into urban reality.

The rise of the twin cities

Though the charter re-established the metropolitan status of Buda, the title of capital remained an empty label, since the town did not fulfil even the role of a provincial centre. Hungarian governmental agencies worked in Pozsony (close to the Austrian border) and the Diet was also held there. Therefore, the functions of Buda hardly differed from those of other Hungarian urban settlements. As it was a handicraft and commercial centre of a rather limited area, it was only its urbanized character and relatively high population in the Hungarian context (10–13,000 inhabitants in the early eighteenth century and about 24,000 in the 1780s)[2] which raised it to the top stratum of the settlement hierarchy.

Nevertheless, the commercial activity of Pest – the city lying on the east bank of the Danube, which kept its administrative independence until 1873 – grew significantly beyond the boundaries of a mere regional market. The high turnover of its markets attracted many domestic and foreign merchants. The market incomes of the city quadrupled from the 1730s to the 1790s, through the growth of taxes paid upon products and manufactures at the expense of those paid upon animals.[3] At the end of the century some 30,000 visitors (exceeding the number of permanent inhabitants) indicated European-wide respect for its market and the scale of its wholesale business, making the city the leading centre for internal trade. The university professor of statistics, M. Schwartner, designated Pest in 1798 'the emergent London of Hungary'.[4]

The increasing importance of the city was manifested in the unprecedented rise of its population: from 3500 at the beginning of the eighteenth century to 20,000 by the end. The number of inhabitants in Pest increased five-fold (climbing thereby from eighteenth to fifth place in the hierarchy of towns in terms of population). Meanwhile the population of Buda grew relatively more slowly, multiplying by a factor of 1.5 between 1700 and 1800. Nonetheless, it was still Hungary's third largest city in 1800.

As the population grew, both cities expanded. By the middle of the eighteenth century, Pest had overflowed beyond its medieval walls. The developing suburbs took up an ever-growing area of arable land and gardens surrounding the town. At the end of the eighteenth century, about two thirds of the 1800 houses in Pest were located in the three suburbs, and the foundation of a new suburb was in progress.[5] As Buda had possessed suburbs as early as the Middle Ages, the territorial expansion of that city was less significant, and only one new suburb was created in the eighteenth century.

By 1800, the national economic importance of Pest had become so evident that the Emperor Joseph II, when taking measures to strengthen administrative centralization, decided to remove the governmental agencies from Pozsony to the neighbourhood of this busy centre, which already since 1724 had housed the superior law courts. However, it was Buda that was chosen for the seat of these agencies. That decision was taken partly in deference to Buda's status as the former capital, and partly for its more sedate urban manner compared to that of its busy sister city. Futhermore, Buda's overwhelmingly German population gave it preference in the eyes of the Viennese Court as more suitable for housing central government departments. It possessed craftsmen and shop-keepers capable of providing luxury goods and services for royal officials, as well as enough elegant and commodious houses to suit their style of life. As a result, the principal administrative and finance departments, the Council of the Governor General and the Hungarian Royal Treasury were all transferred from Pozsony to Buda in 1784. Consequently, the Castle of Buda became the residence of the King's Governor, the Palatine. Thus, Buda once more became a capital in the administrative sense of the word. Moreover, the university, which was formerly located at Nagyszombat (a city near to Pozsony) was moved in 1777 to Buda, and then in 1783 transferred to Pest. That went a long way towards increasing the latter's cultural influence.

Thus the functions of capital city were carried out by two neighbouring towns with independent administrative status, separated only by the Danube. Buda served as the centre of state administration and Pest as the economic and cultural centre. At the same time, Pozsony remained the seat of the Hungarian Parliament or Diet and it was not until the political agitation of the 1830s that Budapest became the real centre of Hungary's political life.

The impetus for growth: the capital's role as commercial centre

Economic activity continued to be the essential factor in the development of the twin capitals. Between 1804 and 1851 the population of Buda grew by one and a half times and that of Pest by four and a half times. While at the beginning of the nineteenth century, Pest was the fifth largest town in terms of population, by the middle of the century it housed more than 100,000 inhabitants. It had thereby emerged as the largest town and, one can say, the only large city in the country. (Buda had at this time a population of about 40,000.)[6]

The Napoleonic wars encouraged the growth of trade and brought a great but transitory prosperity. After that, there followed a recession, but innovations in transport, especially with the steamships on the Danube in the 1830s, gave a new impetus to trade. The economic role of Pest was fundamental, and not purely from a national point of view. It was considered by contemporaries to be one of the most important commercial centres of Europe in the early nineteenth century. The number of business contracts and the scale of turnover approached those of the Leipzig and Frankfurt fairs. According to contemporary estimates, four Pest fairs in the 1820s each had a gross turnover of some 15–16 million forints and half of that involved raw materials.[7] After Vienna, Pest was the most significant trading town on the Danube. Though Pest was inferior to Vienna in handicraft products and manufactures, the scale of its trade in raw materials, particularly wool and tobacco, and the size of its markets for livestock were unequalled in Europe. The city also functioned as the main distribution point for imported industrial goods, not only via its great open fairs, but as a consequence of the stability of supply through the city's specialist trade and warehousing businesses. A commercial directory in 1827 registered in all 103 warehouses, among them 11 for hardware, 26 for textiles and clothing, 8 for chemicals, 11 for furniture and a further 11 for stoneware, pottery, porcelain and glassware.[8] The activity of these warehouses strongly influenced the development of trade in Hungary, both in the wholesale and retail sectors. As they offered purchasing possibilities for rural merchants, they enhanced the importance of the commercial role of Pest at the same time. The extensive size of the hinterland of Pest mirrored the role of the city in internal trade. Nevertheless, visitors came to its markets from a far wider area, almost the whole country. Wholesale merchants of Pest had branch shops and regular clients in distant towns, and so kept in direct touch with all the larger centres.[9] The function of the capital in the economic life of the country as a whole was clearly positive. But how did it influence economic conditions in its hinterland?

The hinterland of the capital

A census completed in 1828, which recorded the names of regularly visited market places, provides the basis for an analysis of the market areas of towns, among them the capital of Hungary.[10] The population of Budapest (i.e. of Buda and Pest together) amounted to 86,000 at that time.[11] Its hinterland, where people traded with no other town, covered 110 settlements and 227,000 people; and 372,000 inhabitants of another 124 settlements declared the capital to be one of the places where they traded.

Agriculture and food supply

Food demand by inhabitants of the capital provided an important stimulus to agricultural production in the hinterland. In contrast to the majority of Hungarian towns, arable cultivation was unimportant within the boundaries of the urban settlement. Wine production alone had strong traditions in both cities, but mainly in Buda. While in Pest in the first half of the nineteenth century viticulture was driven into the background by the expansion of commerce, in Buda, on the contrary, both the scope of vineyards and the number of wine-growers increased, followed by a decrease of the average size of vineyards. Thus viticulture remained an important factor in the city's economy.[12] This was reflected in the growing proportion of wine-growers among the citizens (cives).

City dwellers constituted a significant body of consumers, since the yearly demand for flour amounted to 60,000–700,000 quintals and the demand for meat was met by about 18,000 animals.[13] Such great demand made sales, even in small quantities, profitable for the surrounding settlements and this helped to increase grain production. Several settlements in the area specialized in different branches of agricultural production – for example vegetables and fruit, grapes and tobacco – mainly in order to meet the demand of the capital. The progress of horticulture was particularly rapid in Soroksár and Fót, two villages in the immediate vicinity of the capital (the inhabitants of the former benefited from meat and milk supply as well), but fruit and vegetables were brought to the market from more distant places too, for instance from the town of Kecskemét, 70 kilometres from Pest. Women brought milk and dairy products, poultry and eggs to the weekly market from the neighbouring settlements. Some of the main commodities in the trade of Pest, wool and tobacco, originated in part from the latifundia and peasant farms of the hinterland. Though the scale of the grain trade in the capital should not be exaggerated, its merchants were clearly engaged in purchasing grain surpluses.[14]

Increasing demand in the capital, followed by a gradual specialization of agricultural production, meant that the peasantry became more and more dependent on the market. Because of the advantageous opportunities for selling, they had enough money to buy products offered in the town; that is to say, they created a consumer force for the capital via their purchasing power.

Handicraft activity in the hinterland

Early demand by inhabitants of the hinterland for industrial goods had been met by the numerous artisans of the capital. The number of masters increased in the eighteenth century from about 400 in 1720 to 1039 in 1774 and to 4100 in 1828; the growth was in line with that of the population as a whole. Supply became more variegated: in contrast to the 55 occupations registered in 1720, 153 different kinds of trade were carried on in 1828.[15] But in the first half of the nineteenth century the role of crafts declined because of a reduction in demand. This was due, firstly, to the growing importation of foreign industrial products and, secondly, to the development of the rural handicraft industry. The numerical growth of craftsmen no longer kept pace with the growth of the population and, as a more important sign of decline, the average number of journeymen per workshop decreased significantly.

As for the situation in the hinterland, handicraft activity showed greater progress in the environs of the capital than in the market areas of other towns. According to the census of 1828, 2844 artisans with 471 journeymen practised 66 different occupations in the region around Budapest. Here there were 15 artisans per 1000 inhabitants, while the ratio was six to 1000 in the vicinity of other towns. Eighty-six per cent of rural artisans worked in the 19 market towns (oppida) within the market area, more than a quarter of them in the three oppida that carried on some functions of an urban centre.

The neighbourhood of Pest, which offered big markets, promoted the development of rural handicrafts from the end of the eighteenth century. We have comparative data from 1760[16] concerning the settlements of Pest County, which covered almost the whole market area of the capital. Among the 93 registered settlements, 61 belonged in 1828 to the immediate environs of Pest, a further 11 were tied both to Pest and to other towns and 19 of them sold their products solely in other towns. The growth of population followed more or less the same path in the different zones that surrounded the central area of attraction. In the close vicinity of Pest the number of artisans rose from 638 in 1760 to 1452 in 1828, that is to say, by two and a half times; the number of occupations practised here grew from 38 to 47. In the second, outer zone, the former figure increased from 76 to 110, the latter from 14 to 28. Finally, the number of artisans fell from 101 to 64 in settlements belonging to the market areas of other, more distant towns. In the middle of the eighteenth century only one third of rural artisans worked in market towns; in 1828, 74 per cent of those working in settlements attached only to Pest and 58 per cent of those living in settlements in the intermediate zones of Pest's market area resided in market towns. Thus the development of the capital clearly stimulated the development of settlements with urban characteristics.

As one indication of the growing demand from the rural population, we find not only well-known trades providing products for mass consumption – including millers, smiths, bootmakers, tailors, weavers and butchers (often involved in cattle-dealing) – but also some rare, previously unknown crafts also appeared sporadically in the countryside – carpenters, bricklayers, locksmiths. Expansion can be observed in the clothing industry as well. We lack precise data on this development but it can be conjectured that many rural artisans may have learnt a trade in the capital, and then, lacking the chance to open their own workshops there, settled in the countryside. All this proves that, contrary to former views, neither the large-scale inflow of foreign products, nor the developed urban handicraft sector, could stop the growth of rural handicrafts. Quite the reverse: the growing purchasing power of the rural population promoted the development of smaller regional centres of handicrafts.

Competition from artisans in the hinterland affected the artisans of the capital in different ways. Some traders like tailors and bootmakers lost part of their network of rural consumers. But other crafts obtained more customers than before, as a result of demand from rural artisans for tools, raw materials and other products. Overall, however, there can be no doubt that the economic relationship between the capital and itshinterland remained in a traditional framework. Co-operation in the production process, with the utilization of raw materials or products coming from the hinterland, did not develop. While a great part of the raw materials and semi-finished articles produced in the hinterland were prepared or refined in Vienna (for instance, dyeing of yarn and different materials), the textile mills of Budapest had to procure supplies from the distant northeastern regions of Hungary or from abroad.

The commercial network of the hinterland

In the first half of the nineteenth century merchants became more and more important in the relationships between the capital and its environs, by means of the regular connections between city merchants and rural shopkeepers and dealers. Nine hundred and fifty-three traders ran businesses in Budapest's hinterland in 1828, that is to say, the ratio of traders was 1.6 per 1000 inhabitants, while this ratio was 0.5:1000 in the market areas of other towns. In the case of the market towns, the degree of concentration of merchants was lower than that of artisans: that is, merchants were distributed half in villages and half in market towns. In settlements for which we have comparable data from the middle of the eighteenth century, 46 traders were registered in 1760, and 258 in 1828; that is to say, the number of traders had increased five-fold. There was a certain change in their composition as well: partly a slight growth of specialist traders, partly the replacement of Greek Orthodox merchants by Jews. However, the majority of rural tradesmen were small traders, itinerant vendors and pedlars. Some of them, mainly the Jewish ones, purchased grain, wool, feathers, wine, potash, animals and leather. They also collected rags, in most cases in small quantities, and sold manufactures purchased from Viennese workshops, or from the merchants and warehouses in Pest. Shopkeepers such as chandlers and grocers appeared only sporadically in villages, but more frequently in market towns, where a few specialized shops were opened as well.

Most traders in the countryside sold in retail and had a modest capital: only 5 per cent of them in 1828 had an income exceeding 100 forints, which was necessary for a more extended trade. The majority of those were resident in Óbuda (now a district of Budapest) which was a small market town in the close vicinity of Buda, and they specialized in wool or other commodities. No exact information survives for the business relations of the rural traders but fragmentary data imply that the overwhelming majority of them – at least in terms of credit – were tied to the merchants of Pest, and some may have been subordinated directly to them, or commissioned by them.

The pull of the city: the pattern of immigration

The great capital city undoubtedly encouraged the economic development of its hinterland and contributed to the progess of rural commercial life. That contributed to a growth of income differentials, which in turn worked to eradicate the old feudal structures. The population of the immediate hinterland increased some one and a half times, exceeding the national average, between 1786 and 1828, despite the fact that the capital and its labour market attracted many rural migrants. Above all, the flow of unskilled workers into Budapest grew significantly. They earned their living, for example, as labourers and vine dressers, building workers, loaders, servants and so forth. The number of immigrants from other towns remained low; a considerable number of immigrants came only from the perimeters of the hinterland.[17] But the capital offered a chance for earning a livelihood not only for the immigrants: the transport and viticulture sectors at Buda also provided temporary jobs and sources of income for the inhabitants of several neighbouring settlements.

Furthermore, the attraction exercised by the capital over the nobility and the intellectuals through its increasing administrative, cultural and political functions stretched far beyond the boundaries of the hinterland. Besides landowners living in the vicinity, aristocrats and landed gentry from the whole of the country spent more and more time at Budapest, making more frequent and longer visits. Though the great aristocrats preferred the more eventful social life of Vienna to the modest sociability of Pest, nonetheless a growing number purchased a mansion or had one built in the city. Moreover, many of them erected mansions for the purpose of acquiring rental revenue. Some noble families owned several houses in the capital: 19 of them had two or more houses rented out in Pest, altogether 66 houses with a total annual rent of 122,645 forints, 13 per cent of all rental income recorded in 1828.[18] So aristocratic expenditure contributed to urban development and to some extent it also promoted financial and industrial development as well, as some of the liberal-minded aristocrats and gentry invested capital in industrial and financial enterprises (for instance the Commercial Bank), which were established as share companies.

Obviously, the interrelationships between the capital city and its environs was not limited to the exchange of goods and economic cooperation. The links were far more diverse than that. Above all, it is crucial to discuss the complex cultural, political and administrative influence of the capital - which affected far more than the immediate hinterland of Budapest.

The capital and other towns

The capital of Hungary has often been accused by political and social commentators of undermining the urbanization of other towns through its exceptional development. It is true that this charge was made mainly after World War I, with regard to the effect of the capital on the reduced territory of the country. Nevertheless, how do we explain the situation before the period of industrialization, in the first half of the nineteenth century?

Population growth in comparison to other European capitals

The growth of the population of the twin cities of Budapest exceeded not only that of other Hungarian towns, but that of all other European capitals as well. Between 1804 and 1850 the number of inhabitants rose three times (i.e. 300 per cent - compared with Paris which grew by 36 per cent, or London by 60 per cent. The population doubled in the case of Vienna during the period 1781-1850, and increased by 66 per cent in Prague between 1791 and 1850.[19] Of course, we must acknowledge that the number of inhabitants in the Hungarian capital was much lower than that of other European capitals at the start of our investigation. With the exception of Prague, the number of inhabitants in each European capital city exceeded 100,000 in the first years of the nineteenth century, while Budapest had achieved only some 50,000. Its subsequent growth, however, exceeded that of other cities. Problems in the development of the urban settlement pattern in Hungary played some part in the expansion of the capital. In the first half of the nineteenth century the population of other Hungarian towns inhabited by more than 10,000 people and enjoying legal status (including episcopal sees regarded as towns by contemporary statisticians) increased by 77 per cent. But the rate of growth of similar medium sized towns in other European countries at this time exceeded that of their capitals. (The population of towns inhabited by more than 20,000 people increased two and a half times; towns with populations of between 10,000 and 20,000 grew by one third.) The most rapid development was produced by the largest cities in Hungary, as it was in England and France. But in those countries the number of cities also increased considerably. For example, in France the number of towns with populations of over 20,000 grew from 30 to 55. In England the respective figures expanded even more notably, from 45 to 122 for towns of above 20,000, and from 15 to 63 in the case of towns with populations between 10,000 and 20,000. In Hungary, meanwhile, the number of larger towns remained almost unchanged. (See Table 9.1.)

Low numbers of major cities, which reflected the early phase of urbanization, were characteristic of almost all the provinces of the Habsburg Monarchy. Indeed, in comparison with other regions Hungary enjoyed a broader pattern of large cities. The number of towns inhabited by more than 10,000 people (excluding those in the Italian provinces) in Austria amounted to seven in 1830 and eight in 1851; for Bohemia, the comparable figures were one and four, whereas there were

Table 9.1   Number of Hungarian towns by size category, 1828–51

Size category	1828	1851
Under 2000	5	5
2000 to 4999	18	18
5000 to 9999	14	12
10,000 to 19,999	17	17
20,000 to 49,999	6	7
50,000 to 99,999	1	1
100,000 or over	–	1

21 and 22 in Hungary during the same years (in addition, in Hungary 34 market towns belonged to this size of settlement). But while the population of the larger cities increased five-fold in Bohemia, accompanied by the modest advance of Prague, and by one and a half times in the Austrian provinces, exceeding the rate of growth of Vienna, in Hungary the 17 per cent expansion of the larger cities fell far behind the 56 per cent growth of the capital.[20]

The pattern of urban growth in Hungary

The extremely rapid development of Budapest can be observed from the 1820s onwards. Between 1787 and 1804 the rate of increase of towns with more than 10,000 inhabitants still exceeded that of the capital (i.e. 190 and 178 per cent). Between 1827 and 1851, however, the population of the capital doubled, whereas that of other towns – except small towns under 5000 inhabitants – decreased or stagnated. (See Table 9.2.)

Thus the dominant role of the capital in the course of urbanization had already appeared at the first stage of the bourgeois transformation. If only the chartered towns are considered, it may appear that Budapest increased at the cost of all the other large towns in the country. But, as was indicated above, as well as the towns enjoying legal status there was also a relatively large number of market towns or agrarian towns, situated mostly on the Great Plain, each with a population exceeding 10,000 inhabitants. Of the 56 settlements inhabited by more than 10,000 people, including the capital, only 22 had the legal status of town in 1851; another 11 fulfilled urban functions without this title, while a further 23 were market towns and villages with no important central role. Thus only half of the 1,110,000 people living in settlements with more than 10,000 inhabitants belonged to the circle of real town dwellers; 14 per cent of them lived in towns with urban functions but without the official title, and the remaining one third were inhabitants of agrarian towns and villages lacking central functions. While in

Table 9.2 Hungarian population growth by size category, 1830–51

Category	Percentage growth
Capital	155.9
Over 10,000	116.8
5000 to 9999	129.5
2000 to 4999	90.8

the second quarter of the nineteenth century the chartered large towns decreased or stagnated, the population of market towns with more than 10,000 inhabitants increased by 9 per cent. Meanwhile, contrary to all expectations, the total population of settlements with central place functions decreased by 6 per cent while that of the others, lacking central functions, increased by 13 per cent.

This well-known and long-established feature of Hungarian urbanization has not yet stimulated detailed investigation, so we can only guess at the reasons for it. In my opinion the phenomenon was strongly connected to changes in the Hungarian settlement pattern, which were developing in the first part of the nineteenth century, and which were comparable to those which had taken place in the seventeenth and eighteenth centuries in the developed countries of Europe. The importance in former local centres – towns and market towns – of handicrafts and trade declined. Economic progress promoted the development of some new and old centres of large-scale internal and foreign trade, in which the capital had a unique advantage. In consequence, urban status and urban functions gradually diverged from each other but, due to the survival of feudal conditions, contemporary law did not recognize these changes. Insignificant declining small centres preserved their urban title, while populous settlements with urban functions were not able to obtain urban status. Since modern industrial factories did not become a massive factor of development for a long time, and the influence of railway construction appeared only in the second half of the century, the principal incentives for modern urbanization were missing. The stimulus for urban development and an urban concentration of population remained trade and commercial dealings in the main export articles of the country, which were agricultural products. Hence the characteristic feature of Hungarian urbanization in the second quarter of the nineteenth century: on the one hand, the very rapid growth of the capital, concentrating more and more on the turnover of foreign trade; on the other hand, stagnation of most of the chartered large towns and a modest rise of the large market towns, whose economy was based mainly on agriculture. However, there was not a self-sufficient production of foodstuffs, typical of rural and semi-urban settlements, but rather a specialized, market-oriented agrarian economy. The large agrarian towns, which were supported initially by extensive cattle breeding on their vast pasture-lands and later, particularly from the time of the Napoleonic wars, by corn production, created a peculiar settlement pattern of the *tanya* type: an urban core surrounded by a huge semi-rural zone and scattered homesteads in the midst of arable lands. The high concentration of people promoted the development of crafts and commerce, which served above all the local population and triggered the growth of urban-type commercial, administrative and educational institutions. Thus despite the agrarian character of the economy some features of urbanity were undoubtedly acquired.

The process of transformation of the urban network continued in the second half of the nineteenth century, by that time influenced by railway construction and industrialization, but following partly the pattern of the first half of the century. Recognition of the consequences of the transformation of the urban network and changes in urban hierarchy was completed only by legislation of the 1870s and 1880s, which reorganized the legal status of towns. In consequence, of the 81 royal free towns (including those of Croatia and Transylvania), 73 were legally qualified as towns, while of the 800 market towns another 58 were similarly elevated. The population of these 131 towns amounted to 1.4 million in 1850 and 2.4 million in 1890: in other words it increased by 73 per cent while that of the whole country increased only by 30 per cent. The dominance of the capital in the urbanization process continued. Here the number of inhabitants grew by one and a half times, that of the other towns by one third. Budapest with its almost 500,000 inhabitants in 1890 was the only large town in Hungary, both by virtue of its large population and by the urbanity of its way of life. The number of towns with more than 10,000 inhabitants rose from 57 to 73 in 1890, but with another 34 non-town settlements of the same size.[21]

To sum up it can be stated that urbanization in nineteenth century Hungary was rather unbalanced. The rapid growth of the capital was not followed by the development of an adequate network of large and middle sized towns. A second notable feature was the great number and continuous growth of the very populous agrarian towns, indicating the unusually powerful role of agriculture in concentrating population into urban settlements. We must therefore be careful in evaluating the process of urbanization in this region by reference to population data alone.

Towns everywhere have their own specific qualities. Budapest may have been the 'emergent London of Hungary' but it remained also a city at the crossroads between the West European and Hungarian economies.

Conclusion

The precondition for the metropolitan upsurge of Budapest differed from the conditions determining the rise of most European capitals in the early modern period. The impetus for the growth of the latter was the residence of the royal Court and the centralization and bureaucratization of state administration. Their urban development was determined mainly by the needs and consumption of the growing number of state officials and of landed classes attracted by the Court and later on by the pleasures and sociability offered by urban life. Budapest lacked all these favourable conditions and in the early eighteenth century it seemed to share the fate of many other decayed medieval royal residences.

The spectacular growth of Buda and Pest during the eighteenth century was based on economic activity, above all on the nationwide commercial activity of Pest. At the end of the eighteenth century it became the undoubted economic centre of the whole country and that was the reason it was favoured by Joseph II as the new seat of governmental agencies destined to carry out the unification of state administration. Thenceforward the town gradually acquired other functions of capital cities as well; however, it remained a subordinate provincial/national capital in the shadow of Vienna. As a consequence the growth and economic impact of other élites in the capital was limited. This may help to explain the strengthening of economic relations with the hinterland and Pest's increasing influence on the adjoining countryside.

Up to the second quarter of the nineteenth century the growth of Budapest was the result of market-driven urban development rather than of state-initiated political urbanization.[22] It was the emerging national market which reshaped the urban hierarchy and raised the capital to the top. However, the growing gap between the capital and other towns suggests that the primacy of Budapest was a growing factor in the subsequent retardation of Hungarian urban development.

Notes

1. My thanks to Peter Clark and Penelope Corfield for advice on translating this paper into English.
2. *Budapest története III*, ed. D. Kosáry (Budapest, 1975), p.127.
3. *Ibid.*, pp.118, 124. For a detailed report on the fair held in 1756 written by the Count Otto Haugwitz and Ferdinand Procop, see A. Fournier, *Handel und Verkehr in Ungarn und Polen um die Mitte des 18. Jahrhunderts* (Vienna, 1887), pp.73–5.
4. M. Schwartner, *Statistik des Königreichs Ungarn* (Pest, 1798), p.77; *Budapest története III*, p.124.
5. V. Bácskai, *Pest város topográfiai mutatója*, 2 vols, (Budapest, 1975–82).
6. J. Kovacsics, ed., *A történeti statisztika forrásai* (Budapest, 1957), p.416.
7. P. Magda, *Magyar Országnak és a határ örzö katonaság vidékinek legujabb statisztikai és geographiai leirása* (Pest, 1819); J. Csaplovics, *Gemälde von Ungarn* (Pest, 1829), vol.2, 81–4.
8. J.A. von Dorffinger, *Wegweiser für Fremde und Einheimische durch die königl. ung. Freystadt Pesth* (Pest, 1827).
9. V. Bácskai and L. Nagy, *Piackörzetek, piacközpontok és városok*

Magyarországon 1828-ban (Budapest, 1984), pp.223-8.

10. Hungarian National Archives, N 26. Conscriptio regnicolaris art.VII. 1827 ordinata, 1828-32; Bácskai and Nagy, *Piackörzetek.*

11. L. Nagy, *Notitiae politico-geographico-statisticae Inclyti Regni Hungariae Partiumque eidem adnexarum* (Buda, 1828).

12. F. Schams, *Ungarns Weinbau* (Pest, 1833), pp.17-35; *Budapest története III*, pp.361-4.

13. F. Schams, *Vollständige Beschreibung der Königlichen Freystadt in Ungarn Pest* (Pest, 1821), p.487.

14. V. Bácskai, 'Adalékok az 1840-es évek gabonakereskedelmének történetéhez', Agrártörténeti Szemle, vol.18 (1986), 262-72.

15. *Budapest története III*, pp.100, 330-1.

16. I. Wellmann, *A parasztnép sorsa Pest megyében kétszáz évvel ezelött tulajdon vallomásainak tükrében* (Budapest, 1967).

17. Z. Fallenbüchel, 'Pest város népességének származáshelyei a statisztika és a kartográfia tükrében (1687-1770)', in *Történeti Statisztikai Közlemények* (1958), pp.1-2, 65-72; V. Bácskai, 'Pest társadalomtörténetének vizsgálata a házasságkötések alapján (1735-1830)', *Tanulmányok Budapest Multjából XXI* (Budapest, 1979), pp.49-104.

18. V. Bácskai, *Towns and Urban Society in Early Nineteenth-Century Hungary* (Budapest, 1989), p.126.

19. A.F. Weber, *The Growth of Cities in the Nineteenth Century* (New York, 1899).

20. *Tafeln zur Statistik der Oesterreichischen Monarchie.*

21. G. Thirring, 'Városaink népességének alakulása 1787-töl 1910-ig', *Városi Szemle*, vol.4 (1911), 465-92; E. Kovács and L. Katus, eds, *Magyarország története 1848-1890* (Budapest, 1979), pp.1137-9.

22. Cf. D.R. Ringrose, 'Metropolitan Cities as Parasites', in E. Aerts and P. Clark, eds, *Metropolitan Cities and their Hinterlands in Early Modern Europe* (Leuven, 1990), pp.34-5.

CHAPTER TEN

Between Capital, Residential Town and Metropolis: the Development of Warsaw in the Sixteenth to Eighteenth Centuries

Maria Bogucka

Introduction

At the outset we are confronted by the problem of the definition of the typology of towns, a subject which has been much discussed recently.[1] We are going to use the simplest criteria for defining the urban community on the basis of size (number of inhabitants) and of functions – the political, cultural and economic role of the city in the development of the country. We also need to make a distinction between a capital, the centre of political life, whether practical or symbolic, and a metropolis, a city dominating a country because of its demographic dimensions and economic or cultural significance. Such a distinction is very important, especially in the case of Polish urbanization. To explain this better we have to begin with some general statements concerning Polish urban history.

Between 1500 and 1800 Poland was a rural nation; at least 80 per cent of its population lived in the countryside and more than 50 per cent of the town dwellers were partly employed in agriculture. The number of towns ranged from 600 at the end of the fifteenth century to about 900 from the end of the sixteenth to the close of the eighteenth century; but only eight of these exceeded 10,000 inhabitants. The most numerous group were small boroughs with anything between 500 and 2000 residents.[2]

A specific feature of urbanization in Poland was that as many as three towns were competing for the status of capital. Cracow, the old medieval centre of the country, lost its real significance at the end of the fifteenth century, yet until the end of the eighteenth century it was the place where Polish kings were crowned and buried; the sacral role of Cracow was thus maintained till the end of the period. But the political and cultural leadership of Cracow was eclipsed, even though its demographic importance (about 28,000 inhabitants) remained considerable. There was also an economic decline. In the Middle Ages Cracow's merchants were active in the large transit trade and foreign exchange as well as in home commerce. In the sixteenth to eighteenth centuries the foreign trade of the city became less active, while in home trade Cracow declined into being the market centre of a region with a radius of no more than 25–30 kilometres.[3]

The real economic capital of the Polish Commonwealth from the end of the fifteenth century was the city of Gdańsk. At least 80 per cent of Polish grain exported by sea passed through Gdańsk's harbour. The exports via Gdańsk of timber, ash and pitch were of similar proportions. Since agricultural and forest products constituted the majority of Poland's exports, it is likely that Gdańsk's merchants controlled about three-quarters of Poland's total exports. Imports via Gdańsk should be estimated at about two-thirds of total Polish imports in the early modern period.[4] Gdańsk's hinterland was very large and covered almost the whole of the Polish territories: Great and Little Poland, Masovia, Red Ruthenia and even Podolia and Ukraine.[5] Gdańsk was also the biggest centre of banking[6] and industry with about 7000 workshops in the middle of the seventeenth century,[7] as well as the richest and most populous city in the Polish state. By the end of the sixteenth century it had 40,000 inhabitants, by the middle of the seventeenth century 100,000 and by the end of the eighteenth century 50,000.[8] It was also an important centre of culture, with its Academic School equal to the best European universities; students came to attend it from Poland, Lithuania, Scandinavia, Germany and the Czech lands. The city was famous for its distinguished scholars, its printing houses and artists, who worked for the rich local burghers as well as for the Royal Court and the Polish magnates.[9] Cultural influences from Gdańsk extended throughout the Polish Commonwealth. By the first half of the seventeenth century Gdańsk had already surpassed the status of a provincial town and had become a sort of metropolis. As the focus of extensive economic activity, Gdańsk corresponds exactly to the definition of a metropolis propounded by an English scholar many decades ago but still very useful: 'The metropolitan market may be described as a large district having one centre in which is focused a considerable trade. Trade between outlying parts of course may take place, but it is that between the metropolitan town and the rest of the area that dominates all. This is chiefly the exchange of the raw products of the country for the manu-factured or imported goods of the town. The prices of all goods sent to the metropolitan centre are 'made' there, or, in other words, prices diminish as the distance from the centre is increased.'[10] It should be added that Gdańsk was an economic metropolis with a clear parasitic character, feeding upon the unfavourable structure of the Polish economy and society including the weakness of other Polish towns, the growth of the manorial economy and the 'second enserfment' of the peasantry, which had begun in the sixteenth century.[11] It was a metropolis which, however, could not become a capital, because of its ethnic character, its separatist tendencies and its constant struggle against the central power.

The onset of Warsaw's development

Warsaw, the second or perhaps the third capital of Poland, could by no means be regarded as a metropolis, at least not until the second half of the eighteenth century. At the beginning of the sixteenth century it was a modest provincial town, newly incorporated in 1526 into the Polish state. Formerly the capital of the duchy of Masovia, it was a rather small city (6000–10,000 inhabitants) having an underdeveloped industrial sector and a limited share in the Vistula trade, with the shipment of grain and timber down the river to Gdańsk.[12] The beginning of its great career was the result of political events, not of internal development. The Polish-Lithuanian Union, established at Lublin on 1 July 1569, had to bind two large countries into one state. It happened that Warsaw was situated exactly in the middle of this state. The city was located much closer to Lithuania than the old traditional capital, Cracow, which lay in the distant southwestern corner of the country. One of Warsaw's major advantages was its central situation astride the main internal lines of communication; another was its position as a port, located on the largest Polish river, the Vistula, and having close ties with Gdańsk, Cracow and other important towns as well as with different parts of the country. It was easy for magnates and the gentry from Poland, as well as from Lithuania, to reach Warsaw at any time. This resulted in the agreement that the sessions of the Polish-Lithuanian Seym should be held in future at Warsaw. Thus its favourable geographical location offered Warsaw the first glimpse of the glory, as well as the misery, of its future as a capital.

The role of the Royal Court

The process of transformation from a provincial town into a city with the functions of a capital took several decades (see Figures 10.1, 10.2). The general policy of the Polish gentry was unfavourable to the idea of creating a single strong centre in the state: thus the supreme courts of justice for the gentry (*Trybunały*) were located in 1578 not in Warsaw but in the cities of Piotrków (for Poland) and Lublin (for Lithuania). A special treasury to maintain a small regular army was established in

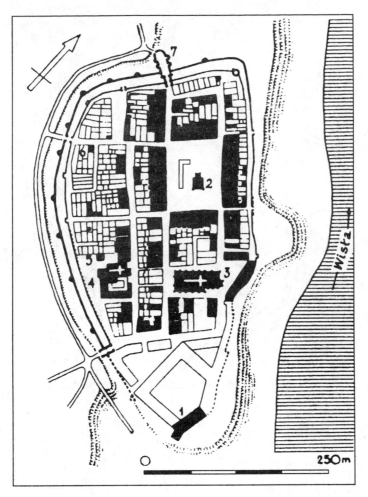

10.1 Old Warsaw in the sixteenth to seventeenth centuries

Reconstructed plan of the old city's centre. Scale 1:10 000. After S. Zaryn, *Kamienica Warzawska w XV i XVI wieku*, 'Kwartalnik Architektury i Urbanistyki', no. 2, 1963. Key: 1. Residential part of Gothic castle; 2. Town hall; 3. Collegiate Church of St John; 4. Augustinian church and monastery; 5. Hospital of the Holy Spirit; 6. Synagogue; 7. Barbican leading into the New Town. Remnants of Gothic buildings are marked in black.

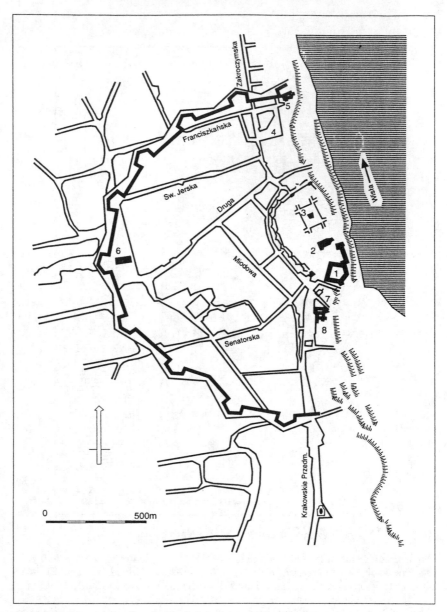

10.2   Warsaw in the first half of the seventeenth century

Line of bastion fortifications built in 1621. Scale 1: 25 000. Reconstructed by the author. Key: 1. Royal Castle; 2. Parish Church of St John; 3. Old Town market square; 4. New Town market square; 5. Church of the Virgin Mary; 6. Almshouse for old soldiers (later arsenal); 7. St Clare's (Bernardine nuns') Church (torn down in first half of 19th century); 8. St Anne's (Bernardine) Church.

1563 in a small town in Masovia - Rawa Mazowiecka. However, important steps for the future of Warsaw occurred between 1569 and 1611, when the Royal Court of the Vasas settled permanently in Warsaw Castle, which was enlarged and luxuriously remodelled in Baroque style by the Italian architects Jacobo Rodondo, Santi Gucci and Giovanni Trevano. Before the castle a large square was laid out and adorned with the magnificent monument, the so-called Sigismund Column, which was soon to become a symbol of Warsaw. In close proximity to the city, at Ujazdów, a new summer palace for the King and his family was constructed in similar style, with large Italian gardens and even a zoo. In the Warsaw suburb of Krakowskie Przedmieście the splendid Villa Regia - later called Casimir Palace - was founded; it was surrounded by beautiful gardens full of exotic plants and animals. The Royal Court of the Vasas was an important centre of political, social and cultural activities. Here foreign envoys and legates of the Holy See came in huge processions, to be received in official audience by the King and his dignitaries; here banquets, balls and receptions were held. Important political events were also concentrated in Warsaw: military triumphs were celebrated there, for example in 1612, when Hetman S. Żółkiewski brought to the city the captured Russian Czar, Vasyli Szujski, with his brothers. Here homage was paid to the King by the vassals of the Commonwealth, as in 1633 and 1641 by Prussian rulers.

An important part in Court ceremonies and festivities was played by theatrical and operatic performances. In 1638 a permanent auditorium with the latest technical stage facilities was set up at the royal Castle in Warsaw. It was of great significance that Sigismund III Vasa, as well as his sons and successors Ladislaus IV and John Casimir, were active patrons of the arts and sciences. On their personal initiative many famous artists - architects, painters, sculptors, musicians - came to Warsaw to work. Sigismund III Vasa established an extensive royal art gallery at the Castle, buying numerous works in Italy, the Netherlands and Germany. One of the Rubens' pupils, Pieter Claes Soutman, came to Warsaw to paint the King and his wife Constance Habsburg in their splendid coronation robes; Joseph Heintz and Martin Kober also acted as royal portrait artists. Thomas Dolabella, a Polish-nationalized Italian, worked for the Vasas too, while subsequent Court artists included Christian Melich, Pieter Dancker de Rij, Adolf Boy, Bartholomeus Strobel, as well as many local painters. The royal collection was constantly enlarged with paintings, bronzes and marbles purchased by the King in Poland and abroad. Under the Vasas, Warsaw for the first time established its cultural significance as the leading city of the Commonwealth.[13]

As the network of Polish bishoprics had been erected in the Middle

Ages, Warsaw did not have the chance to become an episcopal see. But the great concentration of clergy and religious houses – Jesuits, Dominicans, Capuchins, Franciscans, Carmelites, Teatins, Piarists, Bernardins, Bridgetins, Nuns of the Visitation, Sisters of Charity, Sisters of the Blessed Sacrament – made the city an important centre of religious life, especially in the seventeenth and eighteenth centuries, when several religious brotherhoods were founded and the structure of parishes improved.

Residential town

It was natural for Warsaw to become, step by step, a focus for those magnates and wealthy nobles who wanted to take an active part in the political and cultural life of the country. They had to maintain a residence close to the Court and to the seats of the high offices of state. They wished in this way to display their prestige and riches as well as to make themselves comfortable when taking part in public affairs. Near the royal residences settled the powerful magnates Kazanowski, Koniecpolski, Ossoliński, the bishops of Cracow and of Gniezno, the last primate of Poland. Competing with the king and among themselves, they built in Warsaw monumental palaces, filled with galleries of paintings and sculptures, collections of books, arms and tapestries and surrounded by beautifully designed gardens.

Warsaw was growing very quickly. In the years 1621 to 1623 the newly built area within the city walls already covered about 125 hectares compared with only 25 at the beginning of the sixteenth century, but the real extension of the town was much more impressive. Suburbs were mushrooming around the city, encircling it with a belt of small townships, which were in fact parts of the same urban entity. The process was connected with massive purchases of suburban property by the nobles and the development of their possessions, the so-called *iurisdictiones*, such as Leszno, Grzybów, Praga, Skaryszew, Nowy Swiat, Tłomackie, Aleksandria and Wielopole. They were exempt from the town's jurisdiction and free of any urban taxes.

By the middle of the seventeenth century more than half the property in Warsaw's suburbs belonged to the clergy, magnates and gentry. The old town's centre (the so-called Old and New Warsaw), still mostly in the hands of the burghers, was marginalized by the quickly expanding new sections of the city, which were being filled with palaces, mansions, monasteries and churches. A poem written in the 1640s, portraying the splendid growth of Warsaw, enumerates eight substantial palaces, 20 churches and more than 60 magnificent mansions of the nobility newly constructed on the left bank of the Vistula.[14] The burghers' tenements grew in number more slowly. Their number, however, rose from 706 in 1564 to 861 in 1655 in the city's central area.[15] They were built, and existing gothic examples rebuilt, in the new Renaissance and Baroque styles. Often as high as three or four storeys, adorned with splendid façades and attics, covered with paintings and sculpted decorations, they were nonetheless much more modest than the residences of the magnates or the religious buildings. The city walls were rebuilt and enlarged; a Renaissance barbican was completed in 1548 and several gates erected: the White Gate in 1560, the Bridge's Gate in 1582 and the Side Gate in 1603. The town hall was rebuilt in the Renaissance style in the 1580s and later in the Baroque style (1620–21).

The architectural boom was accompanied by rapid demographic growth. In the 1630s and 1640s Warsaw's population may be estimated at 20–30,000 inhabitants; only Gdańsk exceeded it with its 100,000 inhabitants. The proportion of noblemen and their servants, as well as clergy, was very high – more than 25 per cent of the total population of the city in ordinary times. At the time of General Seyms (parliaments), and especially during royal elections, the number of people dwelling in Warsaw could rise to 50,000 or even 100,000 persons.[16] Thus during Seyms and elections the gatherings of the gentry with their retinues greatly exceeded the city population, which often caused serious difficulties. Housing and feeding such large numbers was not an easy task even for a town with many inns and shops. On top of this the nobles and their servants were disorderly and inclined to violence. It was not uncommon during Seyms for burgher property to be damaged or even destroyed. Problems of this type were the price which Warsaw had to pay for its growing role as the capital of a large country – the Polish-Lithuanian Commonwealth.

As a large residential centre, Warsaw's trade developed mainly in response to the demands of the Royal Court as well as the needs of magnates and rich gentry settled in the city. There was above all a large import trade of luxury goods from Italy, France, Germany and England via the seaports of Gdańsk and Elblag as well as via the land routes through such cities as Poznań and Cracow. Oriental textiles, rugs and arms came by way of Lublin, Lwow and Zamość. Hence the extensive commercial links of Warsaw's merchants with other cities and other countries. The Warsaw burghers' share in exports of Polish grain and timber was considerable in spite of competition from the gentry's own trade and shipping.[17] In the years 1573–76 between 50 and 70 per cent of grain going through the Włocławek customs office down the Vistula river belonged to Warsaw tradesmen.[18] Warsaw also became a major centre of credit operations, connected especially with Gdańsk.[19]

The manufacturing sector of the city's economy was less dynamic, because of the high levels of imports of industrial goods from abroad. Some crafts however were prospering: building industries linked to the architectural boom, dressmaking and jewelmaking and all kinds of services from catering to shoemending. The most typical economic unit for the sixteenth and seventeenth centuries was the small workshop where only a master and one or two journeymen worked; but one also notes the emergence of some large mills, brickyards and foundries.[20]

Warsaw and its hinterland

The economic and social impact of Warsaw on its hinterland was grow-ing visibly. The demographic expansion of the city was based mostly on the influx of newcomers from small Masovian towns and villages; they were petty nobles as well as town dwellers and peasants. 61.5 per cent of new citizens of Warsaw in the years 1551–75 came from Masovia, 51.1 per cent in the years 1610–25.[21] Masovia was also the region which supplied the city with much of its daily provisions, such as meat, fish, poultry, butter, milk, fruit and vegetables. Grain was brought partly from some more distant parts of the country, while spices, lemons, figs and other exotic fruits as well as foreign wines and delicacies came from Gdańsk. Access to Warsaw's large market, the possibility of buying there various industrial goods as well as borrowing money, greatly stimulated the Masovian economy. Petty nobles, inhabitants of small townships, and peasants came swarming to the big city to exploit every kind of opportunity: to sell, to buy, to get a job, to make money, to form good connections and to find influential patrons. Warsaw's hinterland in those years might be said to cover the whole of Masovia's territory, that is about 33,493 square kilometres. Demographically the city had already begun to recruit far outside this immediate hinterland. The number of newcomers to Warsaw from Masovia dropped from over 50 per cent to 32.6 per cent in the years 1626–50; 49.6 per cent of new citizens were now from other parts of the Commonwealth, with 17.8 per cent coming from abroad.[22]

Mid-seventeenth century wars: destruction and reconstruction

The devastating wars of the mid-seventeenth century caused tremendous destruction in all Polish cities. Warsaw was terribly affected. The Swedish occupation from September 1655 resulted in the ruin of many of its inhabitants. Besides fiscal levies - Warsaw had to pay during six months the enormous sum of 240,000 Polish zlotys to the occupying authorities – the city was obliged to provide accommodation and daily subsistence to the Swedish army. Swedish soldiers plundered houses in search of hidden food, alcohol, clothes, jewels and money. The situation was aggravated by the virtual collapse of any commercial or industrial activities. The poor lost the roofs over their heads because the Swedish authorities ordered the destruction of all small houses and sheds encircling the city walls in preparation for a Polish counter-attack. The siege of Warsaw in the spring of 1656 and the great Polish-Swedish battle (June 1656) on Warsaw's outskirts ended in the destruction of the town. In August 1656 the Swedish army again seized Warsaw, this second occupation once more accompanied by the plundering and killing of the inhabitants. It is true that Swedish soldiers very soon left the city, but in June 1657 it came under renewed occupation, this time by the troops of the Transylvanian Duke Georg Rakoczy, a Swedish ally. The town dwellers had yet again to suffer levies, plundering and violence.

The war resulted in the ruination of the city; about 60 per cent of its buildings were destroyed; the burghers became very poor. The number of inhabitants declined drastically to 5000-6000.[23]

The disaster, however, was a shortlived phenomenon. Urban reconstruction in the second half of the seventeenth century was everywhere a very slow and painful process, but Warsaw was able to recover relatively quickly and effectively, thus increasing the distinction between itself and other Polish towns. However, Warsaw's revival was due not to its impoverished town dwellers, but to the magnates and noblemen who returned to the city as soon as the Swedish invaders had left the country. This élite influx resulted in the final shaping of Warsaw as a large agglomeration of magnates' palaces and gentlemen's mansions, a residential town dominated by feudal elements. Among the biggest and most beautiful residences built in the last quarter of the seventeenth century in Warsaw were the monumental Krasiński's palace (1681-99), the two residences of the Kotowskis (1683 and 1688), Radziwiłł's palace (1673), Gniński's palace (1681-85), Potocki's palace (after 1683) and the rebuilding of Ossoliński's palace (after 1689). These splendid buildings were the work of a number of famous architects including Tylman van Gameren (Gamerski), Murano Bellotti and Isidor Affaita.[24]

Limited functions of the capital

It should be stressed that Warsaw in the second half of the seventeenth century and at the beginning of the eighteenth century was much more a residential city than a real capital. This was the result (as well as the symbol) of the general political and social evolution of the Polish Commonwealth at this time, above all the transformation of its power structure. Because of the decay of the highest central institutions as well as the lack of a central bureaucracy, power shifted in the second half of the seventeenth century away from the centre of the Polish state, from the General Seym, to the provincial gatherings of the local gentry (the local diets called *sejmiki*), from the Royal Court to the courts of the provincial magnates. Since the political and cultural role of the Royal Court and central institutions based in Warsaw was declining drastically, the city was not able to perform in Polish life the role played by the big capitals of Western Europe, such as London or Paris. In addition, Polish magnates and gentry did not enjoy living in cities.[25] Their ideal was the idyllic countryside with space and free air for everybody. The same love of the countryside appeared in the attitude of the Polish King John III Sobieski, a former magnate, who ruled the country in the second half of the seventeenth century. He would flee Warsaw and its palaces for his country residences at every opportunity. Sobieski built three residences on Warsaw's outskirts - at Marymont, Mokotów and Wilanów - for this purpose.

The city's cultural role also suffered at this time because of the lack of a university or academic schools as well as from the weakness of the burgher class. A broad range of imports of foreign industrial and luxury goods slowed the development of Warsaw's industrial production. Only a few crafts working for the royal and magnate courts flourished: for instance, the goldsmiths' trade, pottery, dressmaking, the building industry and several service activities.[26] The big handicap for burghers was the fact that noble residents of Warsaw brought in craftsmen and workers from their own manors in the countryside and let them work in the city, in order to avoid paying townsmen for their services.

Warsaw's commerce in grain and forest products, the main trade of the Polish countryside, as well as the city's share in foreign and transit trade both remained on a modest scale because of competition from rich Gdańsk merchants and the growing commercial activities of the Polish gentry. About 70 per cent of the grain sent down the Vistula to Gdańsk was transported by the aristocracy, who travelled to that port to sell their produce and to make purchases of manufactured goods and colonial wares, bypassing the merchants of the cities in the interior of Poland, including Warsaw.[27] Thus Warsaw in the second half of the seventeenth century constituted the centre of regional commerce in Masovia rather than the focus of nationwide Polish trade. The trade in some luxury goods however was still concentrated in Warsaw because of the need to supply the royal as well as magnate courts.[28] The largest credit and banking operations were concentrated in Gdańsk as well as in those towns where big annual fairs were held, such as Lublin or Lwow; Warsaw in this respect played only a complementary role.[29]

Politically, the city was losing its meaning. The disintegration of the Polish parliamentary system dealt a heavy blow to Warsaw's role as a capital. Out of forty-four Seyms convened during the second half of the seventeenth century, fifteen were dissolved and two ended without passing any laws. In the first half of the eighteenth century 90 per cent of Seyms ended in failure. From 1678 several Seyms were held not at Warsaw but at Grodno. At the same time, the most important decisions were taken at local diets held in small provincial towns. The situation was aggravated especially under the rule of the Saxon Kings (1696–1763) who were incapable of creating a strong centre of government. On the other hand, it should be stressed that under Saxon rule Warsaw became once again an important centre of culture with the construction of new royal residences and the development of the Royal Court as the focus of an advanced and civilized social life.[30]

The centre of the Enlightenment

The new phase in Warsaw's development came only in the second half of the eighteenth century. It was closely linked to the general change in the political, social and cultural life of Poland. The Enlightenment brought a fierce struggle for the fundamental reform of the state. It resulted in the rapid transformation of the power structure of the Commonwealth and the revival of the Polish economy and culture. These processes introduced a basic change in Warsaw's position: the city became a centre of the Enlightenment movement which illumined the whole country.

The late eighteenth century was characterized by an enormous demographic expansion of Warsaw. Its population was 24,000 in 1754, but reached 63,000 in 1764 and more than 100,000 in 1792, far exceeding the biggest Polish towns (Gdańsk 50,000, Cracow 25,000, Poznań 21,000).[31] This increase was not due to internal demographic factors, but resulted from the heavy influx of migrants from the whole country as well as from abroad. The capital's population, however, as a proportion of the country's total was not very impressive: at the end of the eighteenth century it represented only 1.1 per cent of Poland's population, a proportion similar to that in the Habsburg Empire but inferior to those of England (London represented 5.8 per cent of the total English population), Prussia (Berlin, 2.5 per cent) or France (Paris, 2.3 per cent).[32] Immigration to Warsaw seems therefore to have had a relatively slight impact on the national demographic pattern. However, its catchment area in the second half of the eighteenth century covered the whole vast territory of the Polish Commonwealth; thus the growth of the capital had a limited effect on its direct hinterland – on Masovia. At the same time, the economic and social disintegration of the Polish lands meant that developments in distant corners of the country were influenced more by local factors than by central stimuli coming from Warsaw.

Growth of a modern city

The impact of Warsaw's rapidly expanding trade and industry on its hinterland was of limited and ambiguous significance in this context. In internal trade Warsaw still played a rather small role; big fairs were not held in the capital. The growing demands of the city's food market stimulated to some extent the agricultural production in the south-eastern regions of the country (southern Masovia, Little Poland, Ukraine), though northern parts of Masovia, Great Poland, Kujavien and Royal Prussia were still linked to Gdańsk and the Baltic coast, as in previous centuries. On the other hand, Warsaw's role in Polish foreign trade through the import of textiles, luxury goods and the like, was growing markedly. In both cases, however, these were old traditional trades, underlining the unhealthy economic structure of the country, with the export of agricultural products and raw materials offset by the import of industrial goods, leading to a negative balance of trade. Of course, the city's successes in foreign trade made it an important source of capital formation and led to the enormous enrichment of Warsaw merchants and businessmen in the second half of the eighteenth century.[33] But they did not invest in provincial trade or provincial industry, nor did they try to improve agricultural production. Their profits were mostly used for luxury consumption. It could be argued that the growth of the capital's activities, instead of stimulating the provincial economy, caused difficulties for other towns and their inhabitants. Competition between the capital and provincial towns resulted in anti-Warsaw feeling among provincial burghers as well as among the gentry.[34]

Closely related to the growth of trade was the development of industry. In the 1780s Warsaw became a major centre for textiles as well as of several other industries (production of stockings, hats, belts, carriages, paper, chinaware, leatherware, service activities and building). Many production units were built on a large scale; big factory-type workshops manufactured goods not only for the city market but to meet the demand of magnates and rich gentry from the whole country. At the end of the eighteenth century Warsaw grew to be a serious competitor to Gdańsk in supplying Polish nobles with different consumer goods.[35]

At the same time, the city became an important centre of banking, dictating types of credit and rates of interest to the whole country. The activities of the Warsaw bankers covered large areas of the Polish-Lithuanian state. They also maintained close contacts with the biggest European credit centres, especially with bankers and money dealers in the Netherlands.[36]

Of great importance for trade and banking was the emergence of a centralized postal system and regular postal services. In the 1770s Warsaw became the headquarters of this system, which encompassed the whole territory of the Polish-Lithuanian Commonwealth. It linked the centre of the state with its periphery not only in a political sense. Creating a web of regular communications, it enabled the circulation of economic news, orders and messages, giving Warsaw merchants a great advantage over the inhabitants of other cities.

Assuming the role of a metropolis

The transformation of Warsaw and its growth into a modern city during the last decades of the eighteenth century is reflected in many contemporary sources – in travellers' descriptions, pamphlets, poems, letters. Recent research on Warsaw, however, has tended to play down the effect of the city's rise on the provincial economy. The phenomenon was too short-lived to make a real impact on the general state of the Polish territories. Growing within the framework of an agricultural, backward economy, Warsaw served mainly the needs of distant magnate estates and gentry manors rather than its own immediate hinterland – the region of Masovia. The disproportion in size between the capital and the enormously large territory of the Polish state, as well as the disintegration of this state, made the success of the capital an isolated phenomenon without great consequence. It was Witold Kula who once said that on the sea of the Polish economy there were formed at the end of the eighteenth century a few islands of development and innovation, linked to Warsaw, but too dispersed and weak to change the general structure of the country.[37]

Warsaw's impact on Polish society seems to have been more extensive and definitely positive. The cultural as well as political role of the city was increased by the activities of the last Polish King, Stanislaus Augustus Poniatowski. His aim was to introduce reforms which would remove the most obvious disadvantages of the system of magnate oligarchy and help Poland out of its economic and cultural backwardness. The Royal Court became a focus of new political thinking, with politicians and writers fighting obscurantism and the underdevelopment of Polish society. The patronage of Stanislaus Augustus, whose enthusiasm and inspiration decisively influenced Polish art of the period, resulted in the emergence of a new architectural style named after him. The leading architects in these years were royal collaborators – Domenico Merlini, John Kamsetzer and Stanislaus Zawadzki. The building activity of the king, with the renovation and transformation of Warsaw Royal Castle and the construction of a charming complex of summer residences called Łazienki on Warsaw's outskirts (with the magnificent Palace on the Water), as well as royal patronage of painters (including such artists as M. Bacciarelli and B. Canaletto) and of belles-lettres and science, made Warsaw again the leading centre of Polish culture. It is remarkable that at a time of deep economic and political crisis an architectural boom was spreading over the Polish territories. The palaces, town houses and churches which were built in this epoch, even in the distant parts of the country, followed the patterns and style elaborated in Warsaw. Many courts of enlightened magnates tried to follow the models of social behaviour and patronage set by the Royal Court of Warsaw.[38] The city in those years could rightly be called a cultural metropolis.

The foundation in Warsaw of two excellent high schools – the Collegium Nobilium (Gentry College, 1740) and Szkoła Rycerska (Knights' School, 1765) initiated the modernization of the whole Polish educational system. Here young Poles became acquainted with the new ideas of the European Enlightenment and prepared to take an active part in public and political life. The graduates of those schools were leading politicians and reformers in the years to come, including T. Kościuszko, K. Kniaziewicz and J.U. Niemcewicz. In 1747 the first public library was founded in Warsaw by the brothers Josef and Andrew Załuskis. It was one of the first and largest public libraries in the world and played a major role in Warsaw's cultural development.

The economic progress of the capital resulted in many fundamental social changes. The germs of a modern bourgeoisie and modern intelligentsia, as well as of modern working class, were evolving in Warsaw, stimulating the development of the whole country. The emergence of a group of modern businesses was of great importance for the transition from old social patterns. Wealthy businessmen in the city quickly developed new political and cultural aspirations. They wanted to become real partners of the gentry in more than an economic sense, striving to emulate them in building luxurious palaces and spending newly accumulated wealth on the patronage of arts and luxury consumption on an unprecedented scale. The prominence achieved by burghers in the intellectual life of the country was likewise a new phenomenon, leading to the reconstruction of social mentalities. As the middle class became more learned and enlightened, it became more active in Polish society. It provided not only scholars, jurists and learned priests as in the past, but also leading political thinkers. By the end of the eighteenth century Warsaw was developing a real revolutionary potential. The city saw a great concentration of people, of both noble and burgher origin, striving for radical social and political reform in the country, with important consequences for Poland's development as a modern nation and state.[39]

Thus the significance of Warsaw in the second half of the eighteenth century stemmed mainly from the city's leading role in the powerful movement for social and political reform. It was in Warsaw that the first political journalist groups began to work. Newspapers and periodicals of all kinds were some of the exciting manifestations of Warsaw's cultural effervescence in this period; the city had a virtual monopoly of the mass media. The Polish National Theatre was founded in Warsaw, its performances supporting the patriotic movement. Many clubs, formed on the model of the French Jacobins, influenced not only Warsaw's inhabitants, but also provincial gentry and town dwellers visiting the capital. Warsaw was the cradle of the ferment of ideas which affected the population of the whole country.[40] In October 1788 there met in Warsaw the General Diet, which came to be known as the Great Seym: for four years its activities, including the passing of the famous Constitution of 3rd May 1791, were assisted and fiercely supported by the city's population. In 1793 Warsaw was to play a leading role in Kościuszko's Insurrection. Thus, in the tragic last years of the Polish-Lithuanian Commonwealth the city at last assumed the full political role of a capital and at the same time functioned as a cultural metropolis. The further development of Warsaw, however, was interrupted and blocked for many decades because of the partition of Polish territories and the abolition of the Polish state (1793–95). Yet its symbolic role continued to exist during the nineteenth century.

Conclusion

The development of Warsaw in the early modern period can thus be divided into three phases. Firstly, the late sixteenth and early seventeenth centuries, when Warsaw was performing several functions of a capital; a time when its economic as well as its cultural role was important but limited. Secondly, the second half of the seventeenth and the first half of the eighteenth centuries, when it lost its leading political role as a capital and was essentially a residential city. Finally, the second half of the eighteenth century, when Warsaw resumed its role as a capital and became a metropolis. It was, however, a metropolis more in a cultural and political than economic or social sense. It is true that Warsaw's role in Polish foreign trade as well as its industry were growing rapidly in the second half of the eighteenth century. But the demand for luxury goods – the base of Warsaw's economic activities – could have only a limited influence on the large population of a very big country. The economic ties between Warsaw and the provinces of the Polish-Lithuanian state were weak, in spite of the development of some trade and credit links as well as the emergence of postal services. The emerging information network on a national scale served cultural and political activities rather than economic ones. Growing within the framework of an agricultural, backward economy, Warsaw was an isolated island of progress in the huge sea of a rural, still feudal society. It might be said that at the end of the eighteenth century Warsaw became a cultural and political metropolis because of the lack of competition: its old rivals, Cracow and Gdańsk, like other Polish cities much reduced in demographic and economic significance, had lost their ability to compete. The enormous concentration of ideas and activities of the Enlightened period in one place – in Warsaw – resulted from the weakness and backwardness of the whole country. The divergence between Warsaw, political and cultural metropolis, and the rest of the Polish-Lithuanian Commonwealth was too great at the end of the eighteenth century for the capital to take a leading role in the successful creation of a modern society and a modern Polish state.

Notes

1. See E. Ennen and F. Irsigler, eds, 'Die frühneuzeitliche Stadt. Referate und Aussprachen auf der achten Arbeitstagung des Arbeitskreises für landschaftliche deutsche Städteforschung in Erlangen von 30. Sept. bis 3. Oct. 1970', *Westfäl. Forschungen*, vol.24 (Münster, 1972); E. Ennen and M. van Rey, eds, 'Probleme der frühneuzeitlichen Stadt, vor allem der Haupt- und Residenzstädte. Referate und Aussprachen auf der 9. Arbeitstagung des Arbeitskreises für landschaftliche deutsche Städteforschung vom 27-29 März 1973', *Westfäl. Forschungen*, vol.25 (Münster, 1973).

2. M. Bogucka and H. Samsonowicz, *Dzieje miast i mieszczaństwa w Polsce przedrozbiorowej* (*History of towns and town dwellers in Poland before the partitions*) (Wrocław, 1986), p.370 *et seq.*

3. J. Małecki, *Studia nad rynkiem regionalnym Krakowa w XVI W.* (*Research on the regional market of Cracow in the sixteenth century*) (Warsaw, 1963), pp.76-9.

4. M. Bogucka, *Handel zagraniczny Gdańska w pierwszej połowie XVII wieku* (*Gdańsk's foreign trade in the first half of the seventeenth century*) (Wrocław, 1970), p.30 *et seq.*; S. Hoszowski, 'The Polish Baltic Trade in

the 15th-18th Centuries', in *Poland at the XIth International Congress of Historical Sciences in Stockholm* (Warsaw, 1960), p.140 *et seq.*

5. Bogucka, *Handel zagraniczny*, p.69 *et seq.*
6. See M. Bogucka, 'La lettre de change et le crédit dans les échanges entre Gdańsk et Amsterdam dans la première moitié du XVIIe siècle' in H. van der Wee, V.A. Vinogradov and G.G. Kotovsky, eds, *Fifth International Congress of Economic History, Leningrad, 1970* (Moscow, 1975), vol.4, 31-41.
7. M. Bogucka, *Gdańsk jako ośrodek produkcyjny w XIV-XVII wieku (Gdańsk as the centre of production in the fourteenth to seventeenth centuries)* (Warsaw, 1962), pp.165, 300 *et seq.*
8. Bogucka and Samsonowicz, *Dzieje miast*, pp.372, 381.
9. See E. Cieślak, ed., *Historia Gdańska* (Gdańsk, 1982), *passim.*
10. N.S.B. Gras, *The Evolution of the English Corn Market* (Cambridge, 1915), p.95.
11. J. Topolski, 'Sixteenth-century Poland and European Economic Development', in J.K. Fedorowicz, ed., *A Republic of Nobles. Studies in Polish History to 1864* (Cambridge, 1982), p.70 *et seq.*
12. M. Bogucka, 'Warszawa w latach 1526-1720' (Warsaw in the years 1526-1720), in A. Zahorski, ed., *Warszawa w latach 1526-1795 (Warsaw in the years 1526-1795)* (Warsaw, 1984), p.13 *et seq.*
13. See M. Bogucka, 'The Vasa Dynasty in Poland', in *Kungl. Vitterhets Historie och Antikvitets Akademiens* (Årsbok, 1977), pp.176-86; *idem*, 'Warschau als königliche Residenzstadt und Staatszentrum zur Zeit der Renaissance und des Barock', *Zeitschrift für Ostforschung*, vol.33 (1984), 180-95.
14. A. Jarzębski, *Gościniec abo krótkie opisanie Warszawy (A short description of Warsaw)* (Warsaw, 1974), p.180 *et seq.*
15. Bogucka, 'Warszawa w latach 1526-1720', p.20.
16. *Ibid.*, p.187.
17. *Ibid.*, p.48.
18. *Ibid.*
19. *Ibid.*, p.74 *et seq.*
20. *Ibid.*, p.60 *et seq.*
21. *Ibid.*, p.18.
22. *Ibid.*
23. *Ibid.*, p.181 *et seq.*
24. See M. Karpowicz, *Sztuka Warszawy drugiej połowy XVII w. (Art in Warsaw in the second half of the seventeenth century)* (Warsaw, 1975), *passim.*
25. See M. Bogucka, 'Les villes et le développement de la culture sur l'exemple de la Pologne aux XVIe-XVIIIe siècles', in S. Bylina, ed., *La Pologne au XVe Congres International des Sciences Historiques à Bucarest* (Wrocław, 1980), pp.153-69.
26. Bogucka, *Historia Warszawy*, p.197.
27. Bogucka and Samsonowicz, *Dzieje miast*, p.411 *et seq.*
28. Bogucka, *Historia Warszawy*, pp.194-5.
29. *Ibid.*
30. *Ibid.*, p.296 *et seq.*
31. Bogucka and Samsonowicz, *Dzieje miast*, p.381.
32. B. Grochulska, *Warszawa na mapie Polski stanisławowskiej (Warsaw on*

the map of Poland under the rule of King Stanislaus Augustus) (Warsaw, 1980), p.28.

33. *Ibid.*, p.75 *et seq.*
34. J. Michalski, 'Warszawa czyli o antystołecznych nastrojach w czasach Stanisława Augusta' (Warsaw and the anti-capital sentiment in the times of King Stanislaus Augustus), in *Warsaw in the Eighteenth century* (Warsaw, 1972), vol.1.
35. Grochulska, *Warszawa na mapie*, p.75 *et seq.*
36. *Ibid.*, p.161 *et seq.*
37. W. Kula, *Szkice o manufakturach w Polsce XVIII wieku* (*On the history of manufactories in Poland in the eighteenth century*) (Warsaw, 1956), vol.2, 820 *et seq.*
38. Grochulska, *Warszawa na mapie*, p.277 *et seq.*
39. B. Lesnodorski, *Polscy jakobini. Karta z dziejów insurekcji 1794 r.* (*Polish Jacobins. From the History of the Insurrection of 1794*) (Warsaw, 1960), *passim.*
40. *Ibid.*

CHAPTER ELEVEN

Capital Cities and their Hinterlands: Europe and the Colonial Dimension

David R. Ringrose

This chapter explores a unique phase in the urban history of early modern Europe: the emergence in the seventeenth century of major urban centres that were also capital cities. This development placed Europe on the eve of a great transition in its ability to produce and in the efficiency of commercial distribution. Those changes were preceded by a century in which urbanization took place primarily in politically subsidized capital cities. The following pages attempt to characterize the multiplicity of hinterlands created by such cities, and thus to link state building, with its militaristic and aristocratic uses of resources, with the creation of an integrated urban network for Europe. With the help of more specific language, perhaps we can see better how the rise of political capitals coincided with the integration of Europe's urban system.

The role of the city in the organization of the larger society that surrounds it has long fascinated historians. One of the commonplace observations that this has produced is the idea that the larger a city, the wider the range of functions it provides and the more complicated its relations with the larger world. Indeed, capital cities invariably have a variety of cultural, political and social spheres of influence that extend beyond the immediate surroundings and beyond economic constraints. One urban historian has suggested that we define a city's hinterland as the surrounding area that reacts 'in unison' to economic stimuli from the city itself.[1] Such a definition facilitates research on city-region economic relations, but it effectively excludes many forms of urban influence that are not economic in nature but which can have important economic implications. Consequently it is crucial that we do not define the urban hinterland *a priori*. Indeed, a number of areas, including taxation, political influence, urban income and consumption, suggest hinterland relationships that involve differing geographic dimensions. Thus it is useful to approach the problem using concepts such as 'relational spaces' and 'reciprocal relationships' that are only partly economic in nature.[2] The pages that follow first suggest an approach to the study of the factors that created hinterlands and then outline four examples of the network building role of political cities. The approach draws upon the analysis of central places and urban hierarchy, but in this discussion they are treated as implicit in the models drawn from economic geography and anthropology in order to conceptualize urban function.

Continent-wide networks of markets and of cities were important to Europe's accelerating economic growth, but the process that led to integration of a continental urban hierarchy is far from clear. While the merchants of seventeenth century Amsterdam are credited with unifying European markets, they could do so only by exploiting economic opportunities produced by a variety of autonomously driven causes. One such cause was the rapid reorientation of the cultural, political and social life of traditional élites to capital cities during the seventeenth century; another was the addition of new hinterlands to the European urban system.

Chronology of European urbanization

This unsurprising observation becomes more interesting in the context of Jan de Vries' chronology of European urbanization.[3] De Vries shows that each of the three centuries between 1500 and 1800 saw a distinctive pattern of migration to cities. In the sixteenth century new town dwellers were drawn to towns of all sizes, including ten or twelve cities with around 100,000 inhabitants. Each of these larger cities headed a largely self-contained regional urban system, but no continental hierarchy of urban centres was present. The smaller towns, reflecting their surrounding economies, grew vigorously throughout Europe and Anatolia.[4]

Looking ahead two centuries, the situation was quite different. Compared with the sixteenth century, the largest cities of the eighteenth grew slowly and most city-bound migrants were drawn to small and medium-sized centres. By this time, however, all of Europe was connected to a single urban system centred upon London, Paris and Amsterdam. Moreover, the smallest of the three (Amsterdam) had double the population of most of the great sixteenth century cities. These huge cities co-ordinated a single economic and cultural network comprised of rapidly growing smaller centres, even though their own growth was limited by higher urban supply costs and the correspondingly high cost of urban labour.

During the intervening seventeenth century, yet another pattern of urban growth appeared. While large numbers of Europeans still moved to cities, most went to the emerging capital cities, suggesting a change in the market for urban labour.[5] The seventeenth century demand for labour in such towns reflects the rise of sedentary bureaucracies, the growth of Royal Courts and the urbanization of an aristocratic life style. This is evident in the demand for construction, household servants and, by extension, for luxury goods and imported manufactures. This concentration of élite demand was an unplanned side effect of the rise of political capitals which accompanied the politically driven centralization of political resources and decision making.[6] Increasingly the resources that were mobilized in the provinces in the name of a king were transferred to and spent within his capital to support the expanding Royal Court and bureaucracy.

Landed and professional élites were quick to perceive these new opportunities to serve (and exploit) the state and moved their principal residences to the new royal cities. These wealthy migrants invariably brought their own rural incomes into such cities, reinforcing urban growth. This process both concentrated and changed élite consumption. Exposed to a wider range of fashions, and imbued with a value system that linked status and ostentation, courtiers and titled nobles became addicted to consuming goods that acquired status as luxuries, in part because of their exotic origins. Politically sponsored urbanization thus not only coincided with unification of European markets, but augmented the demand for high-value goods that European merchants and manufacturers saw before them.[7]

Hinterlands and 'ports of entry'

This does not mean that every expanding capital city brought prosperity and development to all of the areas with which it interacted. Preindustrial economies grew slowly and, if one sector expanded faster than the average, some of that growth reflected the transfer of resources from other parts of the economy, which suffered accordingly.[8] Thus a capital city could be parasitic within one of its hinterlands while bringing prosperity to others. This is particularly true of the courtly capital cities with which we are concerned because they rarely included export industries. They were economically important because they collected and redistributed wealth, not because they created it.

The attraction of long-distance commerce to political capitals that were centralizing cultural and political resources transformed the metropolitan capital city into a kind of 'port of entry'.[9] The conventional use of this phrase refers to market centres that connect distinct commercial systems. Such ports of entry are often seaports, since maritime and land-based commerce have different characteristics, but they also emerge where trade systems maintained by ethnically distinct trading communities intersect. In the context of a large political capital, the 'port of entry' concept can be adapted to the idea that the capital is the locus of intersection and exchange between distinctive (if spatially overlapping) activities generated by market forces, political coercion or cultural affinities. In this way capital cities transmitted political and social, as well as economic, stimuli between various hinterlands and areas of influence with different spatial limits. Such 'ports of entry' linked, among other things, the coercive political economy of the state and the market-based economy of European commerce.

These multiple hinterlands operated on at least three levels that intersected in the metropolitan centre. The first and most immediate form of hinterland was the field of economic influence that was geographically contiguous to the capital city. Within that region, political control is strong and economic trends in both city and region react quickly to conditions on either side of the exchange. A second level of hinterland is framed by the capital city's links with the principal towns of a contiguous but jurisdictionally defined country, kingdom or principality. Each of those provincial centres has an economic hinterland similar to that of the capital. While the inter-urban connections between provincial city and capital may have a commercial component, the important bonds are social, cultural and political. They are the links that integrate regional oligarchies into the élite that staffs the court and central bureaucracy in the capital city. If it happens that the capital is also a commercial entrepôt, market activity reinforces social and political linkages, but in seventeenth century Europe the commercial links were often secondary to jurisdictional ones in the integration of these intermediate level, 'national' hinterlands. Major capital cities also created a third layer of relations through control of spatially distant but politically dependent centres. The obvious example is that of an empire in which the imperial capital controls several distant colonial capital cities, each of which is in turn a 'port of entry' between its own regional and 'national' hinterlands and also links both to the imperial capital.[10]

Given that colonial networks were primarily political in nature, most colonial capitals actually participated simultaneously (usually illegally) in more than one kind of hinterland/network. Thus a colonial centre like Mexico City was bound to Madrid but also participated in the commercial systems based on London and Amsterdam. Such a stratified perception of multiple hinterlands (regional/economic, 'national' political and colonial), while obviously simplistic, helps us to elaborate upon the significance of new capital cities. As agents of enhanced political power, they multiplied the interconnections within Europe's urban world.

Some theoretical considerations

The remainder of this chapter offers suggestions for conceptualizing this complex relationship and presents four examples. As the setting for political and *rentier* élites with extravagant lifestyles, capital cities are easily perceived as parasites. They appear to have collected and dissipated scarce resources while returning little of value to the countryside. This reflects an assumption derived from development economics that such wealth should have been invested in improving productivity, thus contributing to economic growth. It is a line of reasoning that has led to the use of such categories as 'generative' and 'parasitic' cities.[11] Such teleological assumptions distance us from the choices actually available to people in the past and discount the non-market components of decision-making. By applying modern values to past decisions, we lose the possibility of understanding the logic of past investment choices.

As a way of redefining the issues involved, I am intrigued by two complementary discussions of the interaction between geography, urban function and the state. One depends on geographic and economic determinism and examines the significance for society of constraints imposed by limited transport and communication capabilities. The other focuses on the role of the state and sets out some ideas about urban functions that integrate social and cultural factors into the discussion.[12]

The first model, laid out several years ago by E.W. Fox, envisages a Europe with two overlapping sub-cultures defined by the availability of transport. Towns with cheap water-borne transport could respond to market forces over long distances, allowing them to integrate many localized comparative advantages. Since land transport was expensive, trading cities had less to gain from control of large areas of land and tended to have modest territorial empires and small armies. Consequently they were controlled by commercial oligarchies that governed by committee and consensus. Their most urgent political problems reflected their dependence on distant trading partners and on reciprocal recognition of business practices and contracts.

By contrast, inland states lived with high-cost transport that made it difficult to concentrate bulky food, fuel and raw materials. To sustain a governing élite, inland governments relied on force, corvée labour and arbitrary authority in order to concentrate the necessary resources. This reliance on force pushed inland polities in the direction of authoritarian government, militarization and cultural values that emphasized hierarchy and military skills. While E.W. Fox presents this model in a European context, Eric Wolf makes the same observation about 'inland states' and 'port principalities' in medieval Asia.[13]

The second model, by anthropologist Richard Fox, uses a functional approach to cities and emphasizes the influence of pre-existing states. He arrives at the same dichotomy between commercial and authoritarian societies, but takes us beyond ecological or economic determinism. The relevant parts of his discussion, clearly indebted to Robert Redfield and Milton Singer, define three types of city: the regalian-ritual city, the administrative city and the mercantile city or city-state.[14]

The regalian-ritual city is associated with monarchies that combine the ideal of central authority with poorly integrated segmentary states. In such states, authority is limited by custom, tradition and deference, and the king has little real power to enforce decisions directly. In that context, the capital city was used intermittently for ritual and ceremony that reinforced the legitimacy of royal authority. While such cities had disappeared in Europe by 1600, vestiges of this ceremonial urban function can be seen in the Escorial of Philip II and the Versailles of Louis XIV, and in palace complexes within capital cities, such as Philip IV's Buen Retiro Palace.[15] These examples suggest a persistent use of older forms of ritual legitimization before certain audiences and at great cost, even after the state had more concrete ways of controlling society.

Fox's second type of urban centre is the 'administrative city' or bureaucratic capital. Such cities are associated with strong government but depend upon resources requisitioned from outside the city, making the capital city the collection point for wealth extracted by landed and administrative élites from a large area. This kind of city has a commercial sector, but one that is preoccupied with supplying the élite market. The urban economy is regulated by the bureaucracy, mercantile wealth is regarded with suspicion, and merchants are vulnerable to arbitrary exactions. The dominant values in the bureaucratic capital are those of a state and an élite based on a rural command economy.[16] When such a capital city grows, therefore, it is because the state has been able to erode the segmentary structure of the rural world and channel more resources to the centre.

Fox's third category is the mercantile city, versions of which are seen in Pirenne's medieval city and Weber's occidental city.[17] Mercantile cities obtain their wealth from long-distance commerce combined with export-oriented industry, activities not easily controlled by rudimentary bureaucracies. Mercantile towns suffer when administrative states interfere with their commerce, and thus they thrive best within loosely organized segmentary states or when neighbouring administrative states are losing their coercive capabilities. Examples include Japanese port cities before the Tokugawa period and Renaissance Florence. Urban autonomy encouraged mercantile towns to develop as sovereign polities with self-conscious identities, distinctive legal codes, local militias and self-serving economic policies. The result was the independent city-state or, in European monarchies, the semi-sovereign urban 'state within a state'. These enclaves were marked by greater social mobility and elective mechanisms for filling political offices, in contrast to the patrimonial and ascriptive systems of authoritarian inland states.

The differences between administrative and mercantile cities are more than conceptual, and show up clearly in their physical development. James Vance compares what he calls 'princes' capitals' and 'merchants' towns' and points out that the urban geography of merchants' cities was shaped by land speculation and market forces, while the geography of princes' cities was the product of decisions reflecting 'taste' and ostentation. Vance also suggests that town plans produced by princely élites were economically inefficient. This reasoning evokes the language cited earlier regarding 'parasitic' and 'generative' cities and contains a value judgement that ignores the logic of contemporary investment choices.[18] This is important to reiterate because part of understanding the past is to understand the unplanned economic consequences of decisions that appear illogical in a modern context. Indeed, many such decisions were disguised innovations masked by choices between ostensibly traditional alternatives. The rest of this chapter uses the concepts of urban function, multiple hinterlands and network building as they are illustrated by four capital cities. This will help us link the unpremeditated economic ramifications of capital cities that served traditional élites to the unprecedented growth of European markets, capitalism and industry that began some time in the seventeenth century.

Four examples

Seventeenth-century Lima may seem an unlikely place to start a discussion of European capitals since, as of 1650, Lima had fewer than 30,000 inhabitants. Moreover, the city was many thousands of kilometres and several months of travel from any part of Europe. Yet Lima illustrates graphically how a capital city could create new markets and add new urban hinterlands to the European world. The process entailed reorganization of a pre-existing and independent society so that it could interact with Europe and, to understand the outcome, we must know something of the economic and spatial organization of the Andes under Inca rule.

The capital of the Inca empire and its 7,000,000 people was the Andean city of Cuzco. Cuzco had apparently had well over 100,000 inhabitants in 1530, matching in size the great cities of western Europe. It appears to have been as much a regalian-ritual and ceremonial centre as it was a bureaucratic one and, compared with its European counterparts, had virtually no commercial function. In an adaptation to limited transportation, the Incas used a decentralized system for collecting, storing and redistributing the resources of the state, leaving Cuzco a ceremonial centre for the legitimization of royal authority. Thus the capital contained elaborate palace and temple complexes which absorbed the dominant cults of newly-conquered Andean states. A system of forts, garrisons, storehouses, highways and mobile armies managed the state's resources in regional centres under supervision of administrators from Cuzco. The system was used to co-opt local élites, protect against crop failure, supply passing troops and support the roads, inns and bridges that sustained imperial authority.

Local society and economy was based on strong lineage-based communities that constituted integrated and self-sufficient economic units. In a striking adaptation to their environment, these clans maintained portfolios of land in the numerous ecological niches created by sharp variations in altitude. Highland clans systematically colonized lowland areas in order to create more complementarities within their self-contained economies. While the products of these holdings were exchanged over considerable distances, the transfers remained within the clan economy.[19]

The Inca state was supported from state lands confiscated at the time of conquest. The population paid taxes in the form of labour services that were used to farm state lands, maintain the complex road system and staff the royal storehouses. In addition, men were drafted for the army and women for royal service in Cuzco. Thus most Andean economic life took place outside markets or even regulated trade. The indigenous urban system that resulted extended along the Andean valleys north and south from Cuzco. Other important centres were located along the coast, reflecting the settlement hierarchy of the recently-conquered state of Chimor. Most links between the highland valleys and lowland areas were contained within the state-organized control of labour and clan/family 'vertical economies' or 'economic archipelagos'.

As the Spaniards occupied the Andes, they faced the dual tasks of reorganizing a huge regional economy to fit their needs and of developing and sustaining a large, export-oriented mining industry. They quickly superimposed their own administrative network upon that of the Incas, radically altering exchange patterns and institutions. The Spaniards' first goal was to establish political control and to extract taxes and tribute that could be converted to Spanish forms of wealth. At first this involved confiscation of anything that could profitably be sold in Europe, followed by a scramble to control land and labour. When the magnitude of the Potosí silver lode became apparent, the restructuring of the Andean economy focused on the organization of supply systems for mercury, draft animals, Indian labour, fuel and food. Cuzco had been well located as a capital for the Incas in terms of supply and communications, but the maritime orientation of the Spaniards and the remote location of the Potosí mines dictated the selection of a command centre based on different logistical considerations. While Cuzco remained important within the Spanish Andes, the Spaniards chose to build a new capital city on the Pacific coast.

Lima thus became the administrative and commercial 'port of entry' for transactions between a huge Peruvian hinterland and trade routes that soon reached Spain, Europe and even China. The new capital's physical layout was derived from Spanish practice, and the city quickly acquired a socio-economic profile like that of Spanish port towns.[20] Its internal structure shows that Lima was a projection of European urban life into Peru. Lima came to co-ordinate a network of regional centres, each with its own economic hinterland. This Limeño 'relational hinterland' was structured by bureaucratic and ecclesiastical hierarchies centred in Lima and by interlocking systems of economic exchange that were regulated in Lima and designed to support Spanish objectives.

If Lima was Peru's 'port of entry', the new viceroyalty's second centre of gravity was the silver-mining district of Potosí. This shift of attention from Cuzco to Potosí restructured the Andean urban system that had emerged under Inca authority. Charcas, La Paz and La Plata were founded as relay centres for commerce between the central highlands and Potosí, mobilizing labour and supplies for the mines. In this changing urban system Cuzco remained important, but its functions changed dramatically. Once a centre for imperial authority, religious ceremonial and élite consumption, Cuzco became the subordinate administrative and episcopal centre for the southern half of the new viceroyalty. It also functioned as the economic centre that co-ordinated the flow of food, fuel, labour and livestock from central Peru to the silver mines. While the Andean urban system was thus being transformed, Lima itself generated a new coastal urban system that reached from Santiago in Chile to Acapulco in Mexico and exchanged wheat, corn, cacao, coca, wine, sugar, silver, Chinese silks and porcelain, American cloth and European trade goods.[21]

The revised Andean urban system in the highlands and the new network along the Pacific coast were connected by transverse routes that channelled all traffic into and out of the viceroyalty through Lima. One road linked the mercury mines at Huancavelica with the port of Chincha. There, mercury was transhipped south to Arica where a second route took it inland to Potosí. A third route connected the coastal district of Arequipa with the interior highway that ran between Cuzco and Potosí. Coastal vineyards provided large quantities of wine, for shipment to the interior in return for silver from Potosí and coca from Cuzco and Charcas.[22] Yet another land route linked Lima directly with Cuzco.

The overall outcome was a radical reorganization of the indigenous economy in which the native urban system was redefined and supplemented. The result was both a political domain and a series of regional economic networks, all subservient to Lima. Lima was thus a metropolitan city in its own right: a 'port of entry' that monitored exchanges between a number of overlapping Andean hinterlands and trade networks that extended as far as Europe, Mexico and, by way of Manila, the rich trade network of Canton and the South China Sea.

This transformation had a complex and interactive social component that can be glimpsed by citing one example. Lima's position was achieved in part by a brutal reconfiguration of the structures that had maintained the Inca transportation system. The Spaniards began by commandeering the system of communally-maintained transporters, roads and inns. As native transporters fled or died of European diseases, and the roads deteriorated, the Spaniards tried various ways to coerce or induce the local populations to maintain the roads and provide transport. Initially the native communities resisted with a combination of sabotage and flight, but they quickly learned to use Spanish legal institutions to their own advantage, taking control of a vital component of the colonial mining economy. By 1600 Indian leaders had combined their own community organizations, recognized by the crown, with Spanish legal practices and market institutions to seize control of overland transport through a large part of the highlands. Since this included the crucial inland transport links that brought the silver from Potosí to Lima, these indigenous communities had captured a powerful position in the viceroyalty. This autonomous niche limited their vulnerability to exploitation by political authority and is one of many interdependent relationships between provincial society and royal government.[23] Such compromises were crucial to sustaining the links that redistributed incomes between Peru, Lima and Madrid, but are often left out of analyses based on economic models.

What does this have to do with the integration of European markets? The 30,000 people of Lima look like a small addition to the urban network of Europe, but the European population of Lima's Peruvian hinterlands was considerably larger and was highly urbanized. By 1650 the urban system subordinate to Lima contained another 60,000 people, who considered themselves Europeans and lived in a market economy. Moreover, the colonial government systematically forced the indigenous population to buy European products, while the Spanish population probably had more disposable income per person than most European markets of similar size.

Thus, while Lima at first glance was a modest European capital by the standards of the seventeenth century, its port of entry function greatly enhanced its importance. Lima itself was new to the urban system and functioned as a gateway between Europe and a new urban hierarchy. As a political and social centre, Lima had restructured an entire empire. It was a new capital city that added both its own immediate hinterland and the 'national' hinterland/urban network of Peru to the European world. Lima itself became both a colonial capital and the metropolis for a new kingdom as large as many in Europe. It is true that the population and gross regional product of Peru fell dramatically below those of the Inca period, and that Andean society paid a brutal price for its integration into the European world. In the process, however, Peru provided not only silver but an important addition to the markets available to European commerce. The quantitative weight of this is hard to measure, but the eagerness of the French, for example, to penetrate the Peruvian market around 1700 is striking.[24]

Mexico City had a similar experience, but one that included some distinctive social and ecological adjustments. Aztec Tenochtitlan, with 300,000 people, was easily twice the size of any western European city of 1500 except Paris. It was also the capital of an empire shaped by transport limitations more severe than any known in Europe.[25] Away from the coastal areas around the lakes in the Valley of Mexico, transport depended entirely on human porters. Such limited transport technology produced an economic landscape of small, well-defined, city-oriented economic regions. Each was roughly 20 kilometres in radius, a distance determined by the economics of transport by human porters.[26] Tenochtitlan reached its large size because it could draw upon a hinterland that included the coastal plains around a lake system 25km wide and 50km long. Supplemented by an elaborate road system in the lake shore regions, water transport thus gave the capital a supply zone several times larger than that of any other city in Mexico.[27] Within that region, plentiful water and cheap labour allowed five and six crops a year on some land.

Outside the economic zone created by the lake system, the Aztecs maintained control with force, political intermarriage, imperial taxation and regulations that channelled trade in luxury goods and ritual items to the capital city.[28] High-value goods thus came to the capital as tribute or as part of a regulated commerce. While many of these products were consumed in Tenochtitlan, some were sold in distant cities or distributed by the Aztec government to reward local allies and armies. Thus the commerce of the capital was controlled as a way of reinforcing political power.[29] Tenochtitlan obtained most of its basic foodstuffs within the zone of cheap transport around the lakes, where the labour-intensive and year-round nature of agriculture left little labour and few resources for rural industry or the production of high-value raw materials that otherwise came as tribute or which could bear the cost of expensive transport. Thus the Aztec capital was a politically created 'port of entry', linking networks of local and long-distance trade in an economic context defined by the sharp difference between the cost of water-borne transport and human porterage. Only goods that could sustain the cost of expensive transport reached the capital from distant sources in significant quantities. Basic staples came largely from the hinterland around the lakes in the Valley of Mexico via freight-carrying canoes, while that same lake-shore economy remained unconnected with long-distance commerce except in the capital itself.

Pack animals and carts are perceived as inefficient modes of transport in European economic history, but they represented a transport revolution in Mexico and contributed to the reorganization of a Mexican economy dependent on human porters. A professional carrier transported 22 kilograms about 20 kilometres a day. A muleteer and mule carried 115 kilograms the same distance, while a large wagon could move 900 to 1400 kilograms 15 to 18 kilometres each day.[30] The new technology required more fixed capital in the form of animals, carts and roads than did a system of professional human carriers, but the reduction in the cost of land transport haulage was nevertheless considerable, especially in the context of a rapidly declining population and labour supply.

Indeed, the Spaniards had to adjust to two unplanned changes in Mexico that were precipitated by the conquest. The collapse of the Mexican population reduced the supply of labour both for transport and for the intensive agriculture of the Valley of Mexico. Simultaneously, grazing, deforestation and declining maintenance of hillside terraces changed the watershed in the valley. This reduced the level of the lakes around the capital city and disrupted the water transport that had supplied the Aztec capital.

Consequently, the introduction of a new transport technology induced a dramatic inversion of the pattern of hinterlands around the capital city. The intensively-farmed land near the city slipped into disuse or grazing. A logical response to declining manpower, this also reflected improved overland transport. In a major shift of its supply hinterland, the Mexican capital now obtained its wheat and corn from valleys around Puebla, Toluca, Michoacán and the Bajío, 100–200 kilometres from the city.[31] This shift became more pronounced with the emergence of the mining economy, but was well under way before the first big silver discoveries in 1546.

This interaction of urban markets, transport technology and labour supply is only one aspect of the creation of several hinterlands linked to Mexico City. As in Peru, the conquest brought the founding of several Spanish towns, usually on pre-existing urban sites, and the creation of Spanish administrative, judicial and episcopal hierarchies dependent upon the capital. After the silver discoveries, however, the dominant feature of the process was the emergence of a huge silver mining industry and concomitant regional specializations that were a response to the markets presented by the mining centres.

By about 1550, the royal highway running north from Mexico City had just reached Querétaro, only 200 kilometres to the north. The discovery of silver at Zacatecas, Guanajuato, Culiacán and elsewhere induced massive investments in pacification and road building. Within ten years, heavy wagons could travel the 700 kilometres from Mexico City to Zacatecas. Not long thereafter, Zacatecas itself was a way station on the route to distant mining locations much farther to the north and west.[32]

As the mining industry and road network grew, parts of Michoacán and the Bajío, within 100–200 kilometres of the capital city, were soon sending food 500 kilometres to Zacatecas. By 1600, foodstuffs reached there from Puebla, 900 kilometres south west of Zacatecas, passing through Mexico City on the way.[33] More valuable goods reached the mining areas via Mexico City from Guatemala, Venezuela, Puebla and the Pacific coast.[34] The result was a supply network that crossed the entire Mexican interior. It was centred upon and organized in Mexico City, and thus complemented the supply system of the city itself.

The central role of the capital city was reinforced by its resident merchant community. By 1598 the city had 252 wholesale merchants and a major Consulado controlled by a smaller, wealthy core.[35] The capital paid three times as much in *alcabalas* (sales taxes) as the next largest city in the viceroyalty.[36] Cotton, sugar, rice, tobacco, leather, cacao, cochineal, indigo, cloth, wool, silk, porcelains, citrus and wine came from Europe, China and all over Mexico by way of roads that met in the capital.[37] The role of the capital city in the physical distribution of goods was reinforced by control of capital and credit by Mexico City merchants. These merchants increasingly channelled imports to retailers in regional markets, who depended on the capital city for capital, credit and merchandise.[38] The mining industry itself depended on such merchants and, in the words of Louisa Hoberman, 'Mining, the provision of credit, and the money supply were all knit together through the activities of Mexico City's merchant élite.'[39] The same was true of the sugar and cochineal industries.[40]

The significance of the preceding for seventeenth century Europe is heightened by recent research. New work on mine output, silver arrivals in Europe and European trade with the Caribbean all suggest that Mexico's seventeenth century depression never happened. There may have been a mild contraction corresponding with the Thirty Years' War, but the population decline seems not to have curtailed mining. Moreover, the last great Mexican epidemics took place in the 1590s and, by 1650, Mexico's population as well as its economic activity clearly were on the rise.[41]

The political decision to use Tenochtitlan as the capital of Spanish Mexico thus had three ramifications. Initially the Spaniards linked an indigenous system that combined trade and tribute to the economy of Europe, reorganizing the pre-existing urban hinterlands and inter-urban links around the capital. Subsequently, the silver industry vastly expanded the scope of the enterprise and encouraged new interregional exchanges. Finally, this dynamic economy attracted European capital and immigrants and created a new colonial market for Europe. While the reconstructed Mexico City had less than half the population of Aztec Tenochtitlan, and, as in Peru, the Spanish population in Mexico seems small, its *per capita* income was very high by early modern standards and it represented a new net addition to the European world. The markets available to Europe through this Europeanized port of entry slipped partially from Spanish control, but Mexico City, even more than Lima, remained an important part of the network of political centres dependent on Madrid, as well as part of the European commercial economy.

Lima and Mexico City are examples of the politically-driven construction of hinterlands that extended the European urban system. In the first case, a totally new city was created to impose political authority, a mining economy and a fiscal system upon an alien society. In the process, Lima became a new outpost for the pattern of consumption that marked Europe's early modern élites. Mexico City differed in that the pre-existing regional network and capital were simply reconstructed. Indigenous elements, new transport technology and the integration of agriculture, mining and urban capital, created a series of hinterlands focused on Mexico City. As a consequence, Europe's commerce with Mexico became the largest single part of its trade with seventeenth-century America. Both cities are examples of metropolitan centres and royal capitals that were also colonial dependencies.

Madrid combines elements of the preceding cases, but also included them within its own colonial hinterland. The Habsburg capital represents the most spectacular rise to metropolitan status of sixteenth- and seventeenth-century Europe. A town with barely 10,000 inhabitants in

1500, by 1630 Madrid may have had 175,000 people and controlled political and commercial networks that reached from Naples and Brussels to Mexico, Lima, Manila and Goa. The rise of Madrid created or reorganized hinterlands at regional, national and imperial levels. This was undeniably a political process that produced new economic configurations. Following the city's designation as capital in 1561, Madrid developed a regional hinterland that redefined the urban system of Castile. She also became the metropolitan centre for the cities of peninsular Spain, attracting courtiers, officials and merchants from other cities and, simultaneously, the political metropolis for colonial capitals like Lima and Mexico City, linking Spain with the huge hinterlands being constructed by her colonial 'ports of entry'.[42]

As in Mexico and Peru, the construction of a new capital city produced important dislocations in the pre-existing urban system of the surrounding area, and the economy of the Castilian interior paid dearly. While Madrid became the Habsburg centre for élite consumption, the urban support systems of the older Castilian cities were disrupted, prompting the people who had provided commercial and professional services in those towns to follow their clients to the capital.

In a very real sense, therefore, the Habsburg Empire subordinated the Castilian hinterland of Madrid to its need for a capital city just as it used Lima and Mexico City to impose itself on the Inca and Aztec Empires. The awareness of a 'conquest' is less obvious, but the results were similar. As in Mexico and Peru, the subordination of interior Castile to a new capital city is associated with declines in population and gross regional product. Not only was the Castilian interior de-urbanized outside Madrid, but Old and New Castile lost a quarter of their population between 1600 and 1650.[43] The decline was not as dramatic as in Mexico or Peru, but was remarkable in a European context that did not involve deadly new diseases. As did Lima and Mexico City, Madrid facilitated the upward redistribution and geographic concentration of élite income in a process that also encouraged a shift from local to European suppliers.[44]

Thus, while the Habsburg Empire was creating metropolitan cities in Mexico and Peru, it created an even bigger one in Madrid, and with similar effects. The presence of crown, Court, bureaucracy and higher nobility linked Madrid to a worldwide network of administrative control and fiscal manipulation, but at the cost of exposing the Spanish interior to new and damaging economic pressures. Madrid's aggregate wealth attracted professional, commercial and financial personnel from the secondary cities of the interior. Meanwhile, the crown used its authority to reorient the regional market to the capital, disrupting the supply systems of other cities in the region and reinforcing the concentration of

urban life in Madrid. By the mid-seventeenth century rural Castile had
become poorer, but Madrid had attracted a large wealthy élite. That
urban milieu encouraged consumption in which uniqueness and foreign
origin became essential markers in the elaborate rituals of display,
protocol and precedence that established one's status at Court. Much of
Spain's élite market was thus shifted from local to long-distance
suppliers.

The rapid rise of Madrid thus produced the three kinds of hinterland
suggested at the beginning. Madrid emerged as the centre of an
economic hinterland that encompassed much of Old and New Castile,
depressing the other cities in the region. She was also the political centre
of a 'national' jurisdictional hinterland that encompassed all of Spanish
Iberia. Finally, Madrid controlled a series of vice-regal capitals, including Mexico City and Lima in America, which functioned as political and
fiscal 'ports of entry' through which Spanish political agents gained
access to the political systems of distant regions.

As a final example, we can examine the case of Paris, where the city's
role as a capital was well established by the start of the sixteenth
century, but was substantially augmented in the seventeenth century. In
particular, this illustrates some of the interplay between the immediate
economic hinterland of a capital city and the jurisdictional hinterland
created by the government housed in that city. The largest city in
western Europe, Paris already held 300,000 people by 1560. During the
next 40 years the population fluctuated greatly, reaching 350,000 in
1588, dropping dramatically to some 200,000 in the siege of 1590, then
returning to perhaps 300,000 by 1600.[45] As of 1637, the population had
exceeded 400,000, reaching perhaps 550,000 by the end of the seventeenth century.[46] With over half a million inhabitants, Paris was the
second largest city in eighteenth-century Europe. While the Royal Court
moved frequently and seldom stayed long in sixteenth-century Paris,
numerous royal agencies settled there permanently. As a result, a large
part of the royal bureaucracy, representing an even bigger share of the
value of royal offices, gravitated to the capital. Because the city had long
been the capital of the French monarchy, it had for some time been one
of Europe's major cities. Already well established as a capital in the
preceding century, the politically driven expansion of seventeenth-
century Paris seems less dramatic than the cases cited earlier.[47]

The conjunction of political crisis and rapid fluctuation in the size of
the Parisian population, at a time when most other European cities were
expanding, helps to verify the premise that the fortunes of the French
state had a crucial role in the Parisian economy. This perception of the
urban economy is implicit in an observation made after the Court had
settled in Paris that the king 'possessed the largest, strongest and finest

palaces and châteaux, received more guests, held a finer Court, had more prayers said for him and bought more than anyone else in the city'.[48]

If we focus on the period after the Religious Wars, and examine the subsequent renewed growth of Paris, the story is very like those of Lima, Mexico City and Madrid. In the course of the seventeenth century, Paris almost doubled its population, a change that reflects the growing strength of the French state rather than the condition of the French economy. Beginning in the reign of Henry IV, the city experienced a wave of land speculation and construction of public facilities, city walls, palaces and aristocratic *hôtels*.[49] This reflects the renewed ability of the French state to extract fiscal resources from the kingdom, a conscious decision to refurbish Paris as capital city, and the transfer of private *rentier* income from the provinces to the capital as the nobility took up residence there. Massive construction coincided with and was inspired by the fact that, from 1594 to after 1660, the king and his Court were normally in residence in Paris.[50] The expansion of the state under Henry IV, Louis XIII and Louis XIV, combined with the domestication of the aristocracy, offers a better explanation for the growth of the city than do rural economic conditions. The city was conforming to the model of an administrative capital in other ways as well. Under Henry IV the crown began to extend its control over police, criminal courts, the press, welfare and urban planning and development. At the same time, the merchant community was drawn by the crown's fiscal activities into the bureaucratic and *fermier* élite that managed the state's financial affairs.[51] Thus the fit with R. Fox's model of the administrative city is good.

This massive capital city strongly influenced an economic hinterland that extended at least 100 kilometres out from Paris in every direction. On the edges of that zone were a few cities with an urban dynamic of their own but, by the end of the seventeenth century, none exceeded one tenth the size of Paris. Furthermore, as the city grew, the smaller towns within that region tended to decline as the region was ever more tightly subordinated to the needs of the capital.[52] The parallel with the much more sudden and dramatic impact of Madrid within Castile is quite clear.

Reflecting the one-sided nature of the economies of many capital cities, Paris' rise as a residential and political centre was accompanied by economic limits upon its ability to develop industries beyond the manufacturing that serviced the city's internal markets. Food and raw materials were confronted by too many entry and exit duties for the city to compete as an entrepôt or exporter of finished goods. At the same time, the costs of supplying a city the size of Paris meant food prices and minimum subsistence wages inside the city were higher in monetary terms than in the provinces. In an age when manufacturing was labour intensive and transportation was expensive, there were few incentives to bring goods to Paris for processing and re-export.[53]

Meanwhile, as part of the process by which the growing scale and complexity of tax farming and royal borrowing strengthened the Paris-based administrative network that defined the kingdom, the state also arrived at a new working arrangement between the crown and provincial élites. William Beik shows how, after failing to coerce funds from the notables of Languedoc in the first part of the century, the crown found a mutually satisfactory compromise that provided important new income to the central government. By providing royal guarantees for loans borrowed by provincial authorities, the crown enabled provincial élites to expand substantially the volume of loans they could float in order to satisfy their obligations to the state. About 60 per cent of these funds passed to the crown as a way of raising cash without taxes; the rest lined the pockets of the local notables who processed the loans. At the same time, investors in those loans obtained annuities that were attractive because of the security of royal guarantees. Thus an ever more complex and interdependent network of public finance, clientage, patronage and office holding linked Paris and other French cities as the state tapped local capital and integrated local élites into the social and political network of the central government.[54] This elaboration of economic and social interdependence between Paris and its 'national' hinterland in fact replicates in general form the bonds created between Madrid and the regional élites of Spain, between Mexico and its viceroyalty, and between Lima and Peru. Thus the story of Paris highlights the role of the French state in the rise of its capital city and the growing importance of Paris as a 'port of entry', joining the immediate economic hinterland of the city, the jurisdictional hinterland of the crown and social and financial groups at the social and spatial centre of France.

The growing bond between state and provincial élites, illustrated in the case of Languedoc, is confirmed by the appearance around the capital of a network of communications and élite travel that reached all parts of France and Europe. In fact, Paris presents a paradox in that, while it was impossible to move goods efficiently inside the city, it acquired a system of stagecoaches and mail service that linked it with the entire European world.[55] Such a development was one aspect of the increasing interdependence between the capital city and its various hinterlands. Obviously these are only a few examples of the networks that evolved around Paris, and they say nothing about migration flows, investments by city dwellers in the surrounding rural economy and many other issues. These developments were part of a fundamental change in the French urban system. From a world of regionally autonomous *bonnes villes*, by the eighteenth century France was clearly evolving an urban system defined in part by economic development and in part by the power and influence of the state.[56]

As in the other cities cited, the rapid expansion of Paris as a political capital brought a corresponding concentration and elaboration of élite demand. The size of the Parisian market itself, and the political and financial networks of the crown, placed Paris near the pinnacle of Europe's evolving urban system and helped to draw large parts of Europe into that system. This is the source of Colbert's preoccupation with the French balance of payments and his attempts to create import substitution industries for products such as porcelain, silks, mirrors and tapestries.

Implications and observations

Seventeenth-century Europe was on the eve of a great transition in the technology of production and in the efficiency of commercial distribution. As the preceding examples show, that transition was preceded by a century in which urbanization took place in politically-subsidized capital cities. Despite the efficiency of Dutch shipping, long-distance trade still depended heavily on élite demand. To quote the anthropologist Bruce Trigger: 'Because of the high cost of transport in non-industrial societies, long-distance trade is restricted mainly to goods and materials that are of great value or can be produced in limited areas. Otherwise local copies would drive the more expensive imported items off the market.'[57]

Lima, Mexico City, Madrid and Paris represent in different ways the rise of a host of 'political cities' at a time when the rest of the European urban world was stagnant. In some cases, capital cities organized new urban hinterlands and functioned as 'ports of entry' between those hinterlands and the European economy. In other cases, they reorganized old hinterlands and redistributed the resources of an expanding state, both concentrating and increasing the disposable income of their traditional élites. In the process, capital cities helped to build and fuel the great 'engine of trade' of the eighteenth century. Such generalizations were made as early as the sixteenth century by Giovanni Botero.[58]

As G. William Skinner and Charles Tilly suggest,[59] the evolution of a large urban network involves two complementary processes. In one, urban hierarchies develop from the bottom up in response to local and regional needs. The other process is the construction and interconnection from above of multiple urban hinterlands, sometimes in a search for markets, but often to extend or strengthen political and fiscal control. In contrast to the China presented by Skinner, the integration of really large urban systems in Europe had for centuries been restricted by political disunity. The centralizing monarchies of seventeenth-century Europe helped to change this pattern. In the tension between regionally oriented, market-based urbanization and politically-sponsored urban hierarchies that bridged across urban hinterlands of differing geographic scope, seventeenth century Europe saw the emphasis shift notably to the political side.

This shift entailed creation or strengthening of regional, national and colonial urban hinterlands, all linked to Europe. Capital cities then operated as ports of entry between these distinctive, politically-generated hinterlands. This fostered the growth and geographic concentration of luxury markets in a way that suggests an extension of Richard Goldthwaite's thesis on Renaissance Italy.[60] Goldthwaite suggests that the focusing of Eurasian luxury trade and bullion flows upon medieval Italy not only allowed Florence to serve as an entrepôt, but stimulated development of an industrial base that produced luxury goods for export, making Florence a classic example of the commercial city as defined by R. Fox. By extension, the rise of capital cities, and their enhanced role as multi-faceted ports of entry, suggests an expansion of luxury consumption in the seventeenth century that needs to be evaluated alongside explanations that emphasize the Dutch grain trade or the Atlantic trade in plantation commodities. Only then can we see clearly the links between state building, the emergence of capital cities and the increasingly intense demand that prompted, not just the *First Industrial Revolution* as presented by Phyllis Deane, but also the more prolonged and diffuse *Age of Manufactures* of Maxine Berg and Myron Guttman.[61]

Metropolitan capitals generated economic change because they shaped economy and society in specific ways. They strengthened the efficacy of the state and its clients in their extraction of wealth from rural society. This involved both coercion and compromises between the state and local communities, whether the Indian transporters of Peru or the *parlementaire* élite of Languedoc. Often at the cost of economic dislocation and declining regional income, capital cities redistributed income so as to increase élite purchasing power while centralizing such élites in capital cities. They thus promoted élite habits of conspicuous consumption that stimulated long-distance trade. The existence of more elaborate luxury trades made lower value trade easier to organize. This was because such commercial infrastructures often suffered from excess capacity. With infrastructure subsidized by valuable commodities of modest bulk, less valuable goods could then enter the mix if they covered direct costs of handling and made even a modest contribution to the cost of the commercial system.

Thus capital cities are not parasites in any simple sense. They do not come into existence because they are logical places to produce or distribute goods and services, although that may be a factor. Nor do capital cities necessarily increase the collective well-being of the societies that they help to govern. Nevertheless, in seventeenth-century Europe, such cities created or restructured urban hinterlands and added important new markets in an economy characterized by expensive transport and an emphasis on high-value trade goods. Although they embodied values and social structures that conflicted with an open market environment, political capitals created administrative networks and trade that bridged the gaps between the market-inspired regional urban hierarchies of the sixteenth century.

New capital cities thus altered international demand at a critical moment in the process of European market integration. In effect, they transmuted very traditional values, social patterns and political objectives into entrepreneurial opportunities. This augmented the range of opportunities that Dutch and English merchants were able to exploit as they unified the European urban system and established the central role of Amsterdam and London within a continent-wide urban system.

Notes

1. B. Lepetit, 'Les capitales et leurs arrière-pays. Quelques propositions d'étude', comment on E. Aerts and P. Clark, eds, *Metropolitan Cities and their Hinterlands in Early Modern Europe* (Leuven, 1990), p.9 of type script.
2. Lepetit, 'Les capitales', pp.4–6.
3. J. de Vries, *European Urbanization, 1500–1800* (London, 1984), pp.98–101, 136–42, 167, 257–8; see also P.M. Hohenberg and L.H. Lees, *The Making of Urban Europe, 1000–1950* (Cambridge, Mass., 1985), pp.226–38.
4. P. Bairoch, *Cities and Economic Development from the Dawn of History to the Present* (Chicago, 1988), pp.3–18 (first published as *De Jerico à Mexico: villes et économie dans l'histoire* (Paris, 1985). See also L.T. Erder and S. Faroqhi, 'The development of the Anatolian urban network during the sixteenth century', *Journal of the Economic and Social History of the Orient*, vol.23 (1980), 265–303.
5. De Vries, *European Urbanization*, pp.139–42.
6. C. Tilly, *Coercion, Capital and European States, AD 990–1990* (Oxford, 1990), pp.17–24.
7. R. Davis, *The Rise of the Atlantic Economies* (Ithaca, N.Y., 1973), pp.86–107, 231–6; P. Deane, *The First Industrial Revolution* (Cambridge, 1982), pp.53–60.
8. Lepetit, 'Les capitales', p.2.
9. *Ibid.*, p.9.
10. While this essay uses the example of Madrid and the Spanish Empire, Amsterdam, London, Lisbon and possibly Stockholm held similar

positions.

11. B.F. Hoselitz, 'Generative and parasitic cities', *Economic Development and Cultural Change*, vol.3 (1954-5), 278-9; Hohenberg and Lees, *Urbanization of Europe*, pp.117-8, 165.

12. E.W. Fox, *History in Geographical Perspective* (New York, 1971); R. Fox, *Urban Anthropology: Cities in their Cultural Settings* (Englewood Cliffs, N.J., 1977).

13. E. Wolf, *Europe and the People Without History* (Berkeley, 1982), p.57.

14. Fox, *Urban Anthropology*; R. Redfield and M.B. Singer, 'The cultural role of cities', *Economic Development and Cultural Change*, vol.3 (1954-5), 53-73. Fox also identifies what he labels colonial cities and industrial cities, but both are associated with the nineteenth century and after in his typology.

15. J. Brown and J.H. Elliott, *A Palace for a King: The Buen Retiro and the Court of Philip V* (New Haven, 1980).

16. Fox, *Urban Anthropology*, p.62.

17. H. Pirenne, *Medieval Cities: Their Origins and the Revival of Trade* (Princeton, 1925, 1970), p.56; M. Weber, *The City* (Glencoe, Ill., 1958), pp.54-5; Fox, *Urban Anthropology*, p.94.

18. J.E. Vance, Jr., *The Continuing City: Urban Morphology in Western Civilization* (Baltimore, 1990), pp.232-5.

19. Summarized in J. Murra, 'High altitude Andean societies and their Economies', in E. Genovese and L. Hochberg, eds, *Geographic Perspectives in History* (Oxford, 1989), pp.205-14. A more extensive discussion, possibly overemphasizing certain religious factors, is found in G.W. Conrad and A.A. Demarest, *Religion and Empire: The Dynamics of Aztec and Inca Expansionism* (Cambridge, 1984), pp.96-110.

20. Vance, *Continuing City*, pp.212-18; J. Lockhart, *Spanish Peru, 1532-1560: A Colonial Society* (Madison, 1968), *passim*, esp. pp.221-36.

21. L.A. Clayton, 'Trade and Navigation in the seventeenth-century vice-royalty of Peru', in P. Bakewell, J. Johnson and M. Dodge, eds, *Readings in Latin American History*, vol.1, *The Formative Centuries* (Durham, N.C., 1985), pp.175-88; C.S. Assadourian, *El sistema de la economía colonial. Mercado interno, regiones y espacio económico* (Lima, 1982), *passim*.

22. L.M. Glave, *Trajinantes: Caminos indígenas en la sociedad colonial. Siglos XVI-XVII* (Lima, 1989), pp.37-40.

23. Glave, *Trajinantes*, *passim*.

24. C.D. Malamud, 'España, Francia y el "commercio directo" con el espacio peruano (1695-1730): Cádiz y Saint Malo', in J. Fontana, ed., *La economía española a final del Antiguo Régimen*, vol.3, *Comercio y Colonias* (Madrid, 1982), pp.67-73.

25. R. Hassig, *Trade, Tribute and Transportation: The Sixteenth-Century Political Economy of the Valley of Mexico* (Norman, Okla., 1985).

26. W. Bray, 'Land-use, settlement patterns and politics in prehispanic Middle America: a review', in P.J. Ucko, R. Tringham and G.W. Dimbleby, eds, *Man, Settlement and Urbanism* (London, 1972), pp.919-20.

27. R.S. Santley, 'The structure of the Aztec transport network', in C.D. Trombold, ed., *Ancient Road Networks and Settlement Hierarchies in the New World* (Cambridge, 1991), pp.198-210.

28. A compact general description of Aztec society and political organization is in Conrad and Demarest, *Religion and Empire*, pp.20-30. Also see E.E.

Calnek, 'The city-state in the Basin of Mexico: late pre-Hispanic period', in R.P. Schaedel, J.E. Hardoy and N. Scott Kinzer, eds, *Urbanization in the Americas from its Beginnings to the Present* (The Hague, 1978), pp.463-70.

29. Bray, 'Land-use', pp.921-2.

30. D.R. Ringrose, *Transportation and Economic Stagnation in Spain, 1750-1850* (Durham, N.C., 1970), pp.44, 47; *idem*, 'Carting in the Hispanic World: an example of divergent development', in Bakewell, Johnson and Dodge, *Readings in Latin American History*, vol.1.

31. D.A. Brading, *Miners and Merchants in Bourbon Mexico, 1768-1810* (Cambridge, 1971), pp.60-1.

32. *Ibid.*, pp.14-32.

33. *Ibid.*, p.64.

34. *Ibid.*, p.74.

35. L. Schell Hoberman, *Mexico's Urban Elite, 1590-1660: Silver, State and Society* (Durham, N.C., 1991), pp.20-1.

36. *Ibid.*, p.22.

37. *Ibid.*, pp.24-32.

38. *Ibid.*, pp.78-80; J. Kisza, 'Business and society in late colonial Mexico City' (Ph.D. thesis, University of California, Los Angeles, 1980), pp.72, 101-21, 252-60; B. Kapp, 'Les relations économiques extérieurs du Mexique (1821-1911) d'après les sources françaises', in *Ville et Commerce: Deux essais d'histoire hispano-americaine* (Paris, 1974), p.22.

39. Hoberman, *Mexico's Merchant Elite*, pp.82-92. The quotation is from p.92.

40. *Ibid.*, pp.96-8, 118; Kisza, 'Business and Society', pp.64-6, 83-90.

41. Hoberman, *Mexico's Merchant Elite*, pp.2-3, 6-9, 12-17; M. Morineau, *Incroyables gazettes et fabuleux metaux: Les retours des trésors americains d'après les gazettes hollandaises (XVI-XVIII siècles)* (London, 1985), pp.42-119, 218-350.

42. The list of such cities in 1630 also includes Lisbon, Naples, Milan and Brussels.

43. Bartolomé Yun Casalilla, *Sobre la transición al capitalismo en Castilla: Economía y sociedad en Tierra de Campos (1500-1830)* (Salamanca, 1987), pp.397-454.

44. D.R. Ringrose, *Madrid and the Spanish Economy, 1560-1850* (Berkeley, 1983); *idem*, 'Towns, Transport and Crown: Geography and the Decline of Spain', in Genovese and Hochberg, eds, *Geographic Perspectives in History*, pp.57-80.

45. J. Jacquart, *Paris et l'Ile-de-France au temps des paysans (XVIe-XVIIe siècles)* (Paris, 1990), pp.227-36; J.-P. Babelon, *Nouvelle histoire de Paris: Paris au XVIe siècle* (Paris, 1986), pp.159-66.

46. Jacquart, *ibid.*; René Pillorget, *Nouvelle histoire de Paris: Paris sous les premiers Bourbons, 1595-1661* (Paris, 1988), pp.97-8.

47. L. Bernard, *The Emerging City: Paris in the Age of Louis XIV* (Durham, N.C., 1970), pp.5-6.

48. O. Ranum, *Paris in the Age of Absolutism: an Essay* (New York, 1968), p.5; Fox, *Urban Anthropology*, p.76.

49. Pillorget, *Nouvelle histoire de Paris*, pp.273-337, offers a truly impressive catalogue of construction projects and urban design initiatives.

50. The presence of the Court involved over 9000 palace attendants and royal

       guards in addition to the aristocratic household and government agencies associated with it. Pillorget, *Nouvelle histoire de Paris*, pp.40-59.

51.   *Ibid.*, pp.122-34.
52.   See above, p.108.
53.   S. Kaplan, *Provisioning Paris: Merchants and Millers in the Grain and Flour Trade During the Eighteenth Century* (Ithaca, N.Y., 1984), pp.80-7.
54.   W. Beik, *Absolutism and Society in Seventeenth-Century France: State Power and Provincial Aristocracy in Languedoc* (Cambridge, 1988), pp.10-13, 246-78.
55.   Vance, *Continuing City*, pp.221-4; Fox, *Urban Anthropology*, pp.76-9; Bernard, *Emerging City*, pp.29-82.
56.   B. Lepetit, *Les villes dans la France moderne (1740-1840)* (Paris, 1988), pp.121-2.
57.   B. Trigger, 'Determinants of urban growth in pre-industrial societies', in Ucko, Tringham and Dimbleby, eds, *Settlement and Urbanism*, pp.585-6.
58.   G. Botero, *The Magnificence and Greatness of Cities* (trans. R. Peterson, London, 1979, facsimile of 1606 edn), pp.55-93.
59.   G.W. Skinner, 'Cities and the hierarchy of local systems', in *idem*, ed., *The City in Late Imperial China* (Stanford, 1977), pp.275-351; C. Tilly, 'The geography of European statemaking and capitalism since 1500', in Genovese and Hochberg, eds, *Geographic Perspectives in History*, pp.158-82.
60.   R.A. Goldthwaite, 'The Renaissance economy: the preconditions for luxury consumption', in *Aspetti della vita economica medievale: Atti del Convegno de Studi nel X Anniversario della morte di Federigo Melia* (Florence, 1984), pp.658-75; *idem*, *The Building of Renaissance Florence: an Economic and Social History* (Baltimore, 1980), pp.29-114.
61.   Deane, *The First Industrial Revolution;* M. Berg, *The Age of Manufactures, 1700-1820* (London, 1985); M. Guttman, *Toward the Modern Economy: Early Industry in Europe, 1500-1800* (New York, 1988).

Index